STELLAR

CREATED BY ROBERT KIRKMAN & MARC SILVESTRI

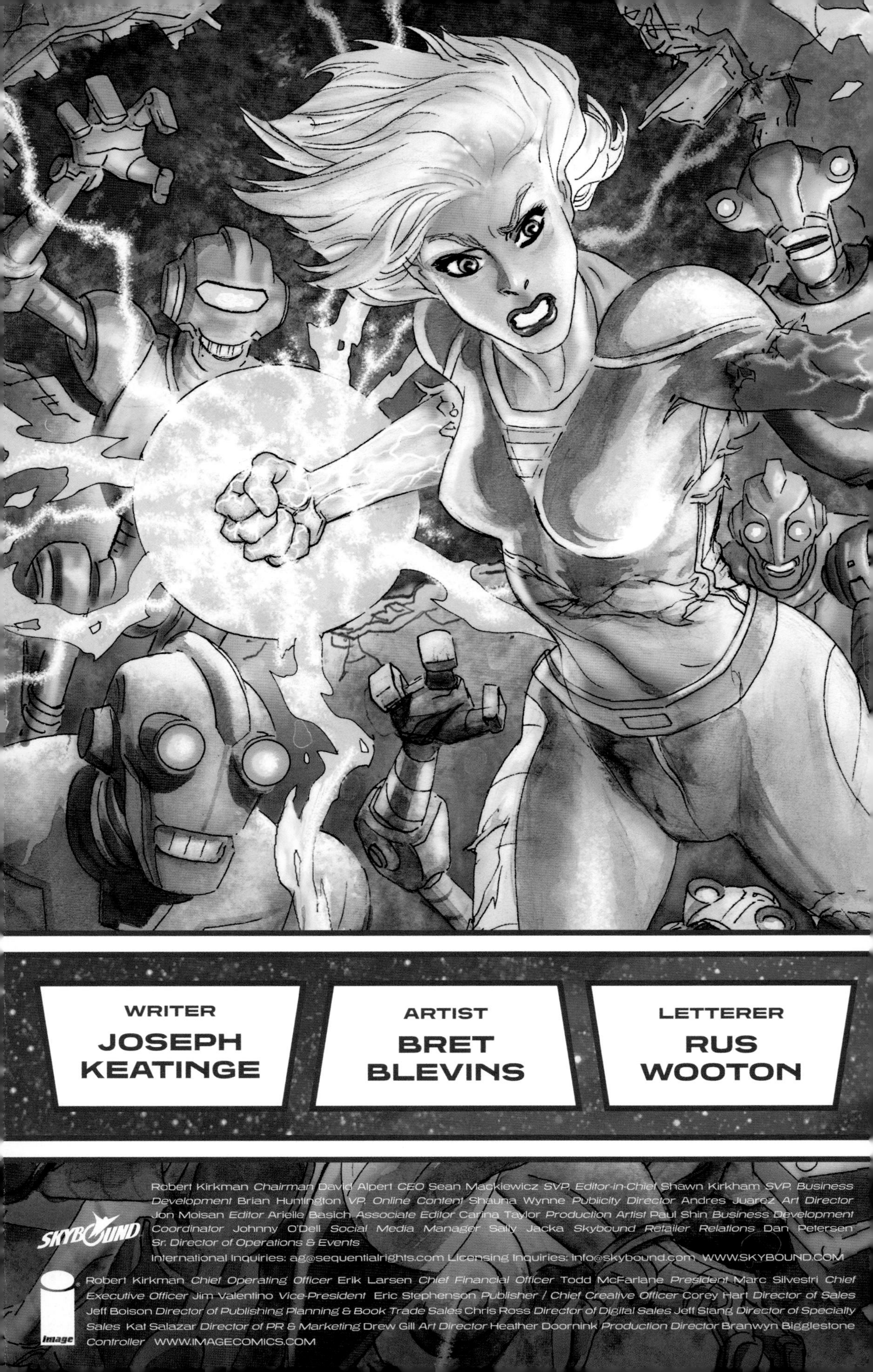

WRITER
JOSEPH KEATINGE

ARTIST
BRET BLEVINS

LETTERER
RUS WOOTON

Robert Kirkman *Chairman* David Alpert *CEO* Sean Mackiewicz *SVP, Editor-in-Chief* Shawn Kirkham *SVP, Business Development* Brian Huntington *VP, Online Content* Shauna Wynne *Publicity Director* Andres Juarez *Art Director* Jon Moisan *Editor* Arielle Basich *Associate Editor* Carina Taylor *Production Artist* Paul Shin *Business Development Coordinator* Johnny O'Dell *Social Media Manager* Sally Jacka *Skybound Retailer Relations* Dan Petersen *Sr. Director of Operations & Events*

International Inquiries: ag@sequentialrights.com Licensing Inquiries: info@skybound.com WWW.SKYBOUND.COM

Robert Kirkman *Chief Operating Officer* Erik Larsen *Chief Financial Officer* Todd McFarlane *President* Marc Silvestri *Chief Executive Officer* Jim Valentino *Vice-President* Eric Stephenson *Publisher / Chief Creative Officer* Corey Hart *Director of Sales* Jeff Boison *Director of Publishing Planning & Book Trade Sales* Chris Ross *Director of Digital Sales* Jeff Stang *Director of Specialty Sales* Kat Salazar *Director of PR & Marketing* Drew Gill *Art Director* Heather Doornink *Production Director* Branwyn Bigglestone *Controller* WWW.IMAGECOMICS.COM

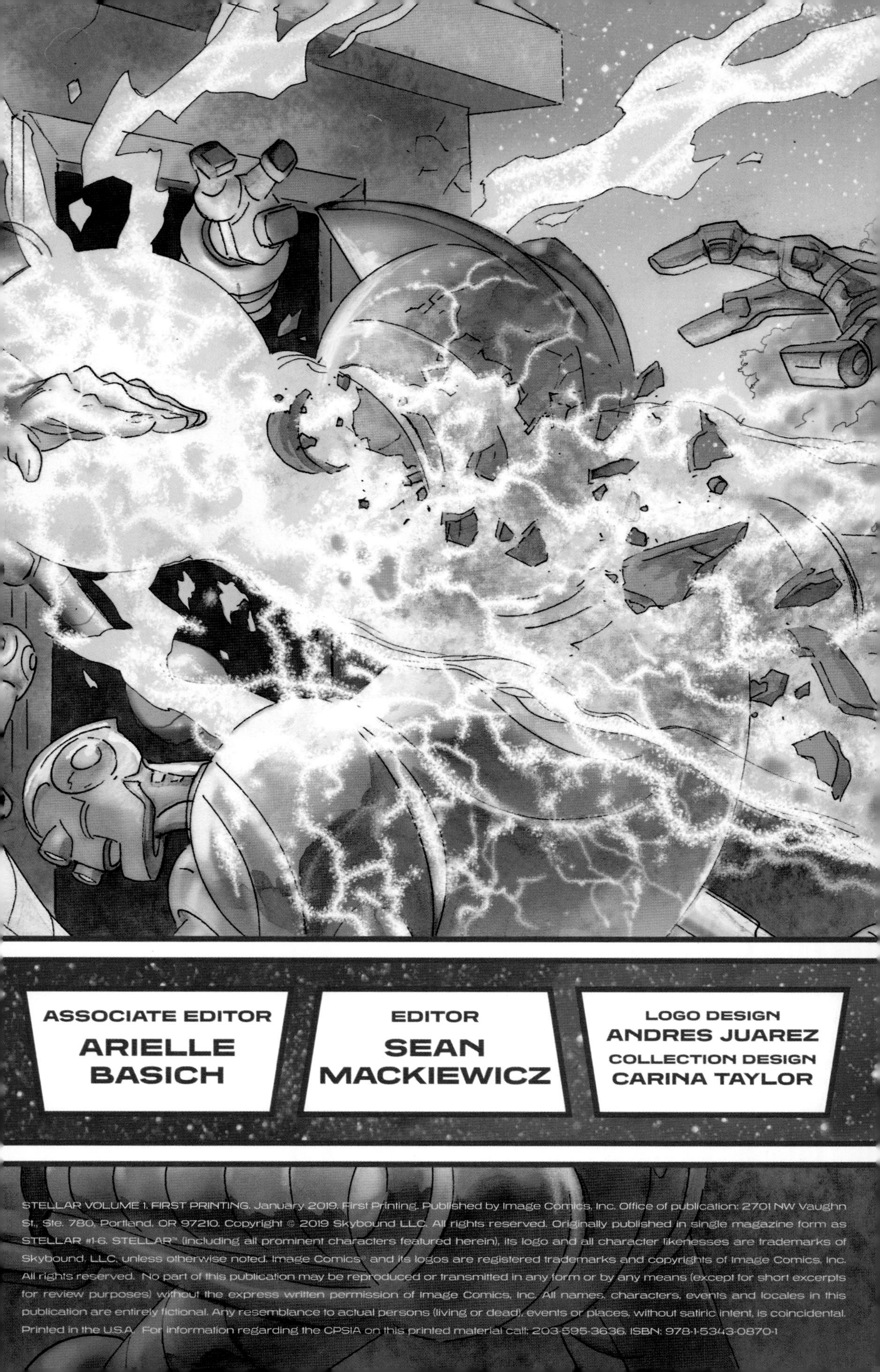

ASSOCIATE EDITOR
ARIELLE BASICH

EDITOR
SEAN MACKIEWICZ

LOGO DESIGN
ANDRES JUAREZ

COLLECTION DESIGN
CARINA TAYLOR

STELLAR VOLUME 1. FIRST PRINTING. January 2019. First Printing. Published by Image Comics, Inc. Office of publication: 2701 NW Vaughn St., Ste. 780, Portland, OR 97210. Printed in the U.S.A. For information regarding the CPSIA on this printed material call: 203-595-3636. ISBN: 978-1-5343-0870-1

SHE
OWES THEM
A BETTER
WORLD

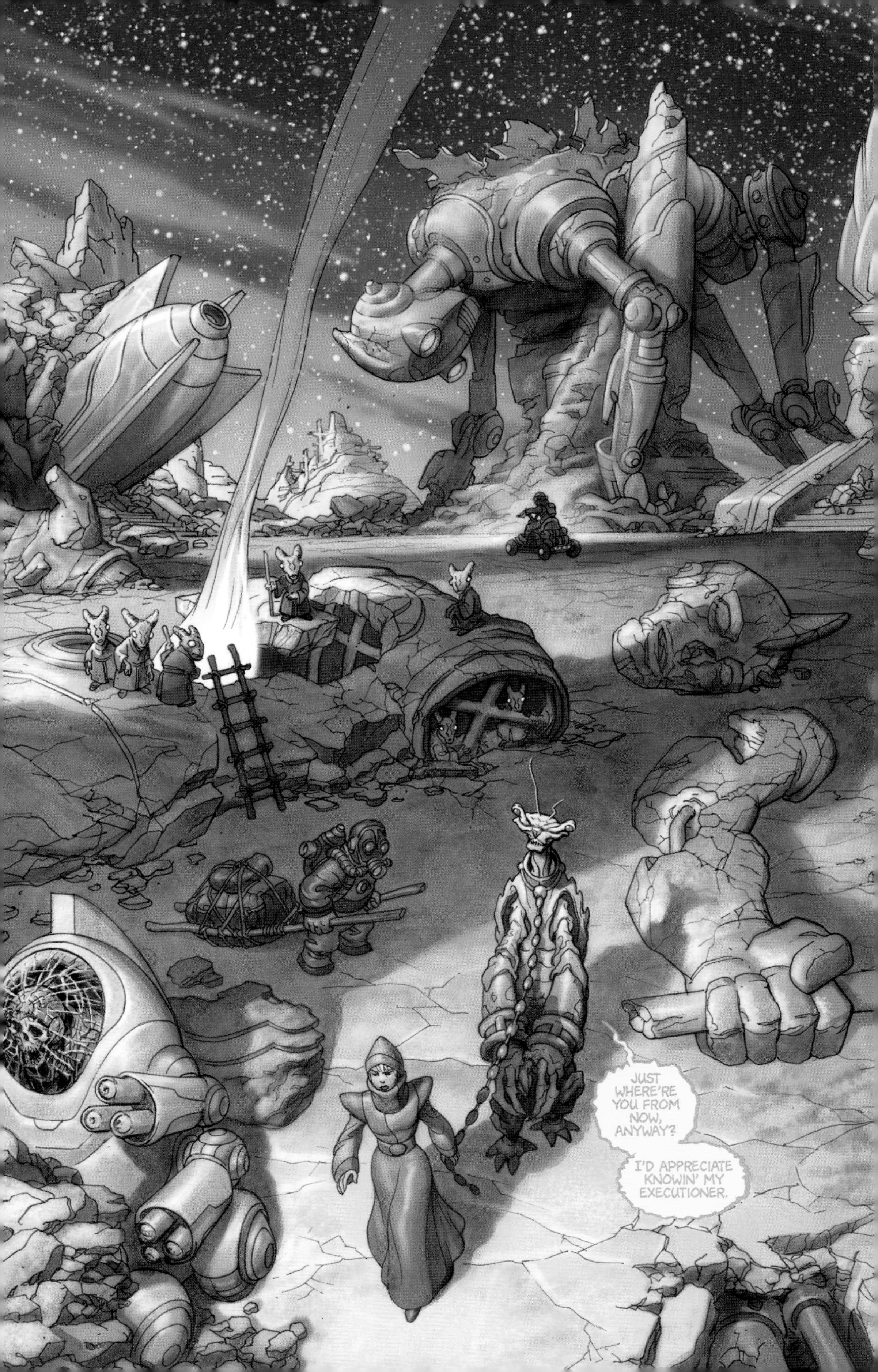
JUST WHERE'RE YOU FROM NOW, ANYWAY?
I'D APPRECIATE KNOWIN' MY EXECUTIONER.

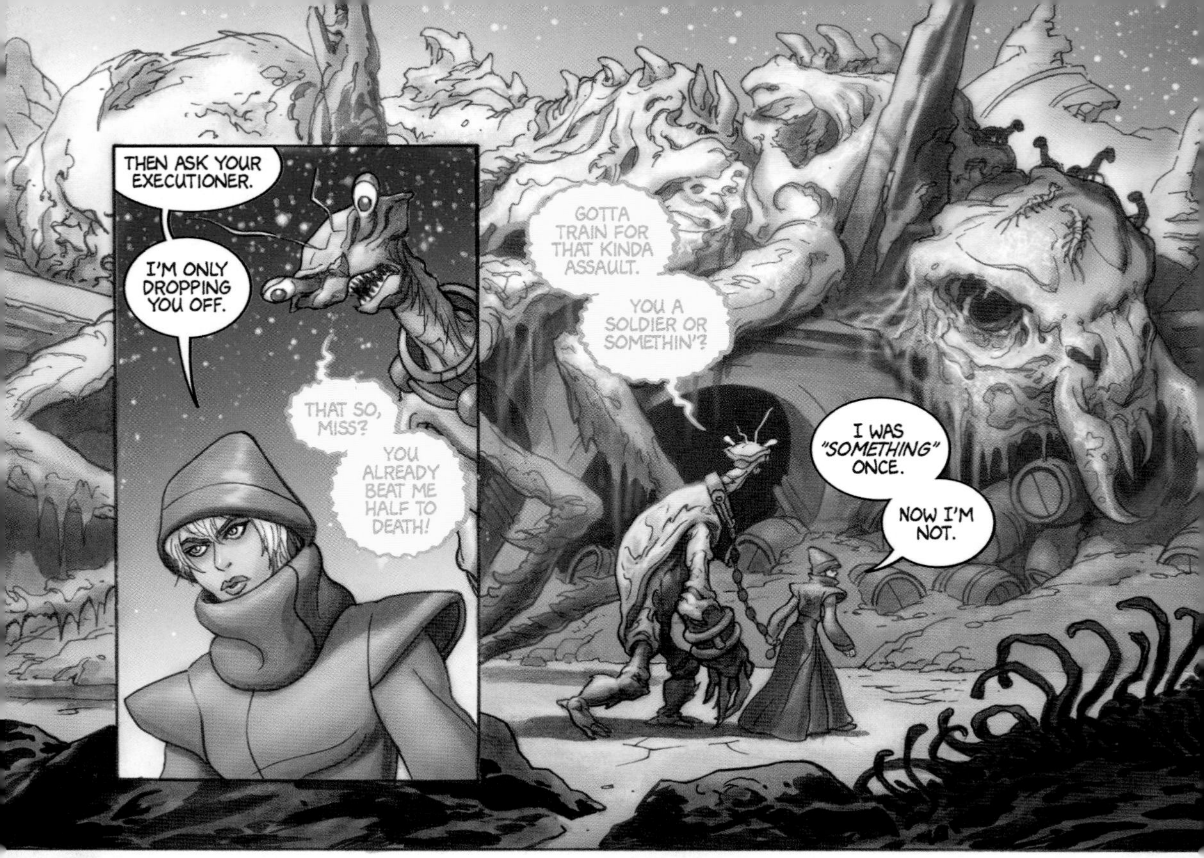
THEN ASK YOUR EXECUTIONER.
I'M ONLY DROPPING YOU OFF.
THAT SO, MISS?
YOU ALREADY BEAT ME HALF TO DEATH!
GOTTA TRAIN FOR THAT KINDA ASSAULT.
YOU A SOLDIER OR SOMETHIN'?
I WAS "SOMETHING" ONCE.
NOW I'M NOT.

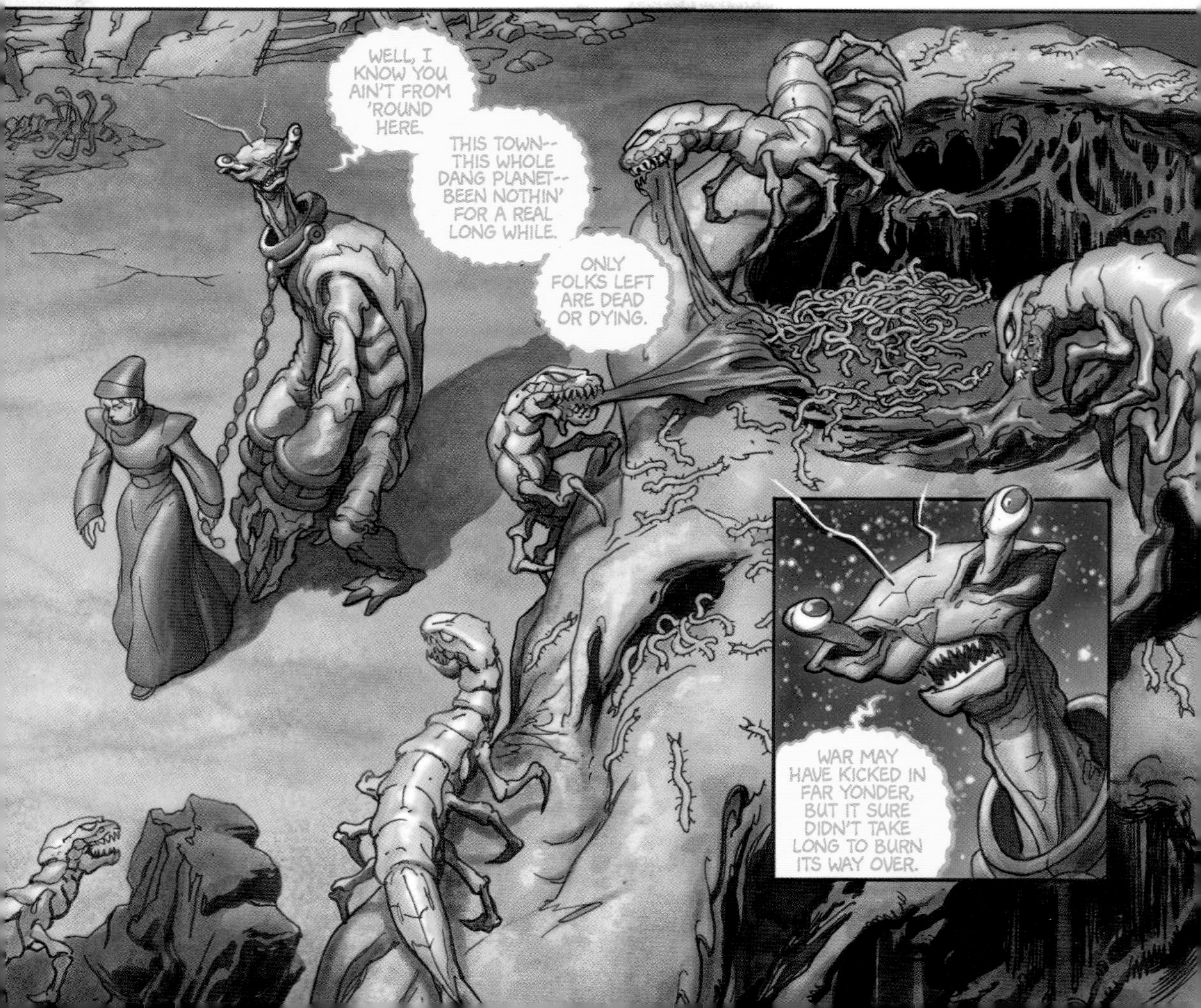
WELL, I KNOW YOU AIN'T FROM 'ROUND HERE.
THIS TOWN-- THIS WHOLE DANG PLANET-- BEEN NOTHIN' FOR A REAL LONG WHILE.
ONLY FOLKS LEFT ARE DEAD OR DYING.
WAR MAY HAVE KICKED IN FAR YONDER, BUT IT SURE DIDN'T TAKE LONG TO BURN ITS WAY OVER.

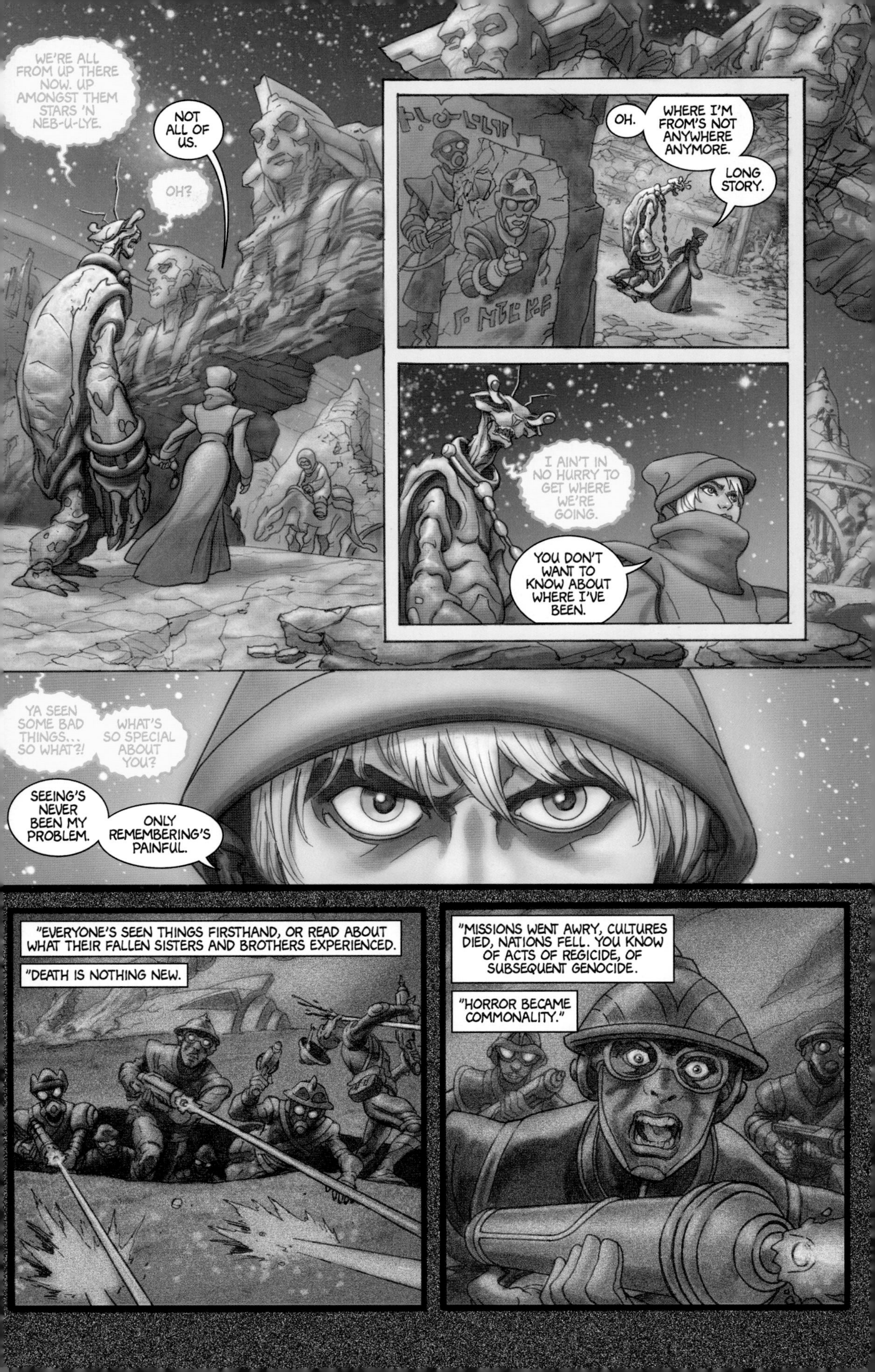
WE'RE ALL FROM UP THERE NOW. UP AMONGST THEM STARS 'N NEB-U-LYE.
NOT ALL OF US.
OH?
OH.
WHERE I'M FROM'S NOT ANYWHERE ANYMORE.
LONG STORY.
I AIN'T IN NO HURRY TO GET WHERE WE'RE GOING.
YOU DON'T WANT TO KNOW ABOUT WHERE I'VE BEEN.
YA SEEN SOME BAD THINGS... SO WHAT?!
WHAT'S SO SPECIAL ABOUT YOU?
SEEING'S NEVER BEEN MY PROBLEM.
ONLY REMEMBERING'S PAINFUL.
"EVERYONE'S SEEN THINGS FIRSTHAND, OR READ ABOUT WHAT THEIR FALLEN SISTERS AND BROTHERS EXPERIENCED.
"DEATH IS NOTHING NEW.
"MISSIONS WENT AWRY, CULTURES DIED, NATIONS FELL. YOU KNOW OF ACTS OF REGICIDE, OF SUBSEQUENT GENOCIDE.
"HORROR BECAME COMMONALITY."

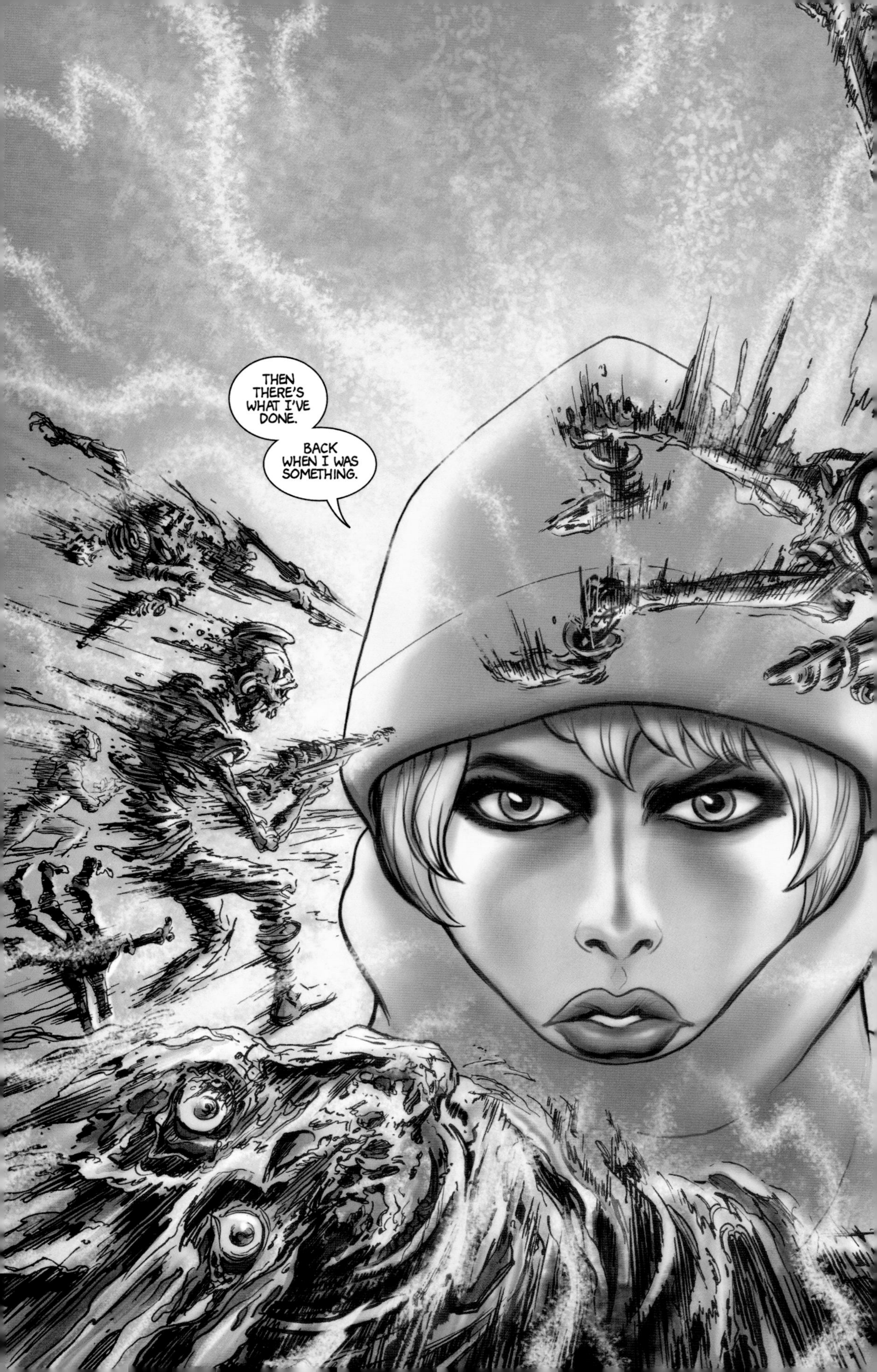
THEN THERE'S WHAT I'VE DONE.
BACK WHEN I WAS SOMETHING.

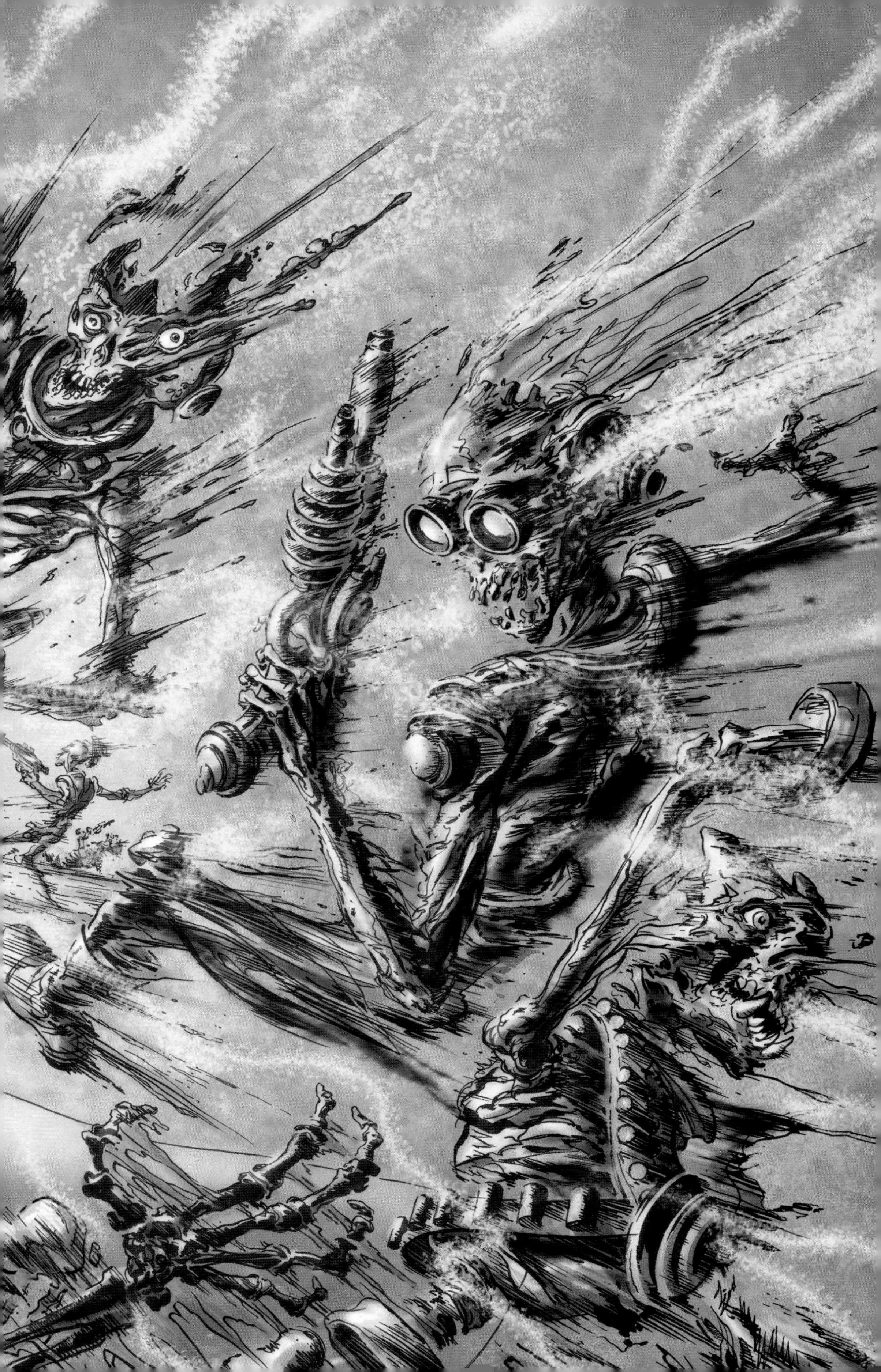

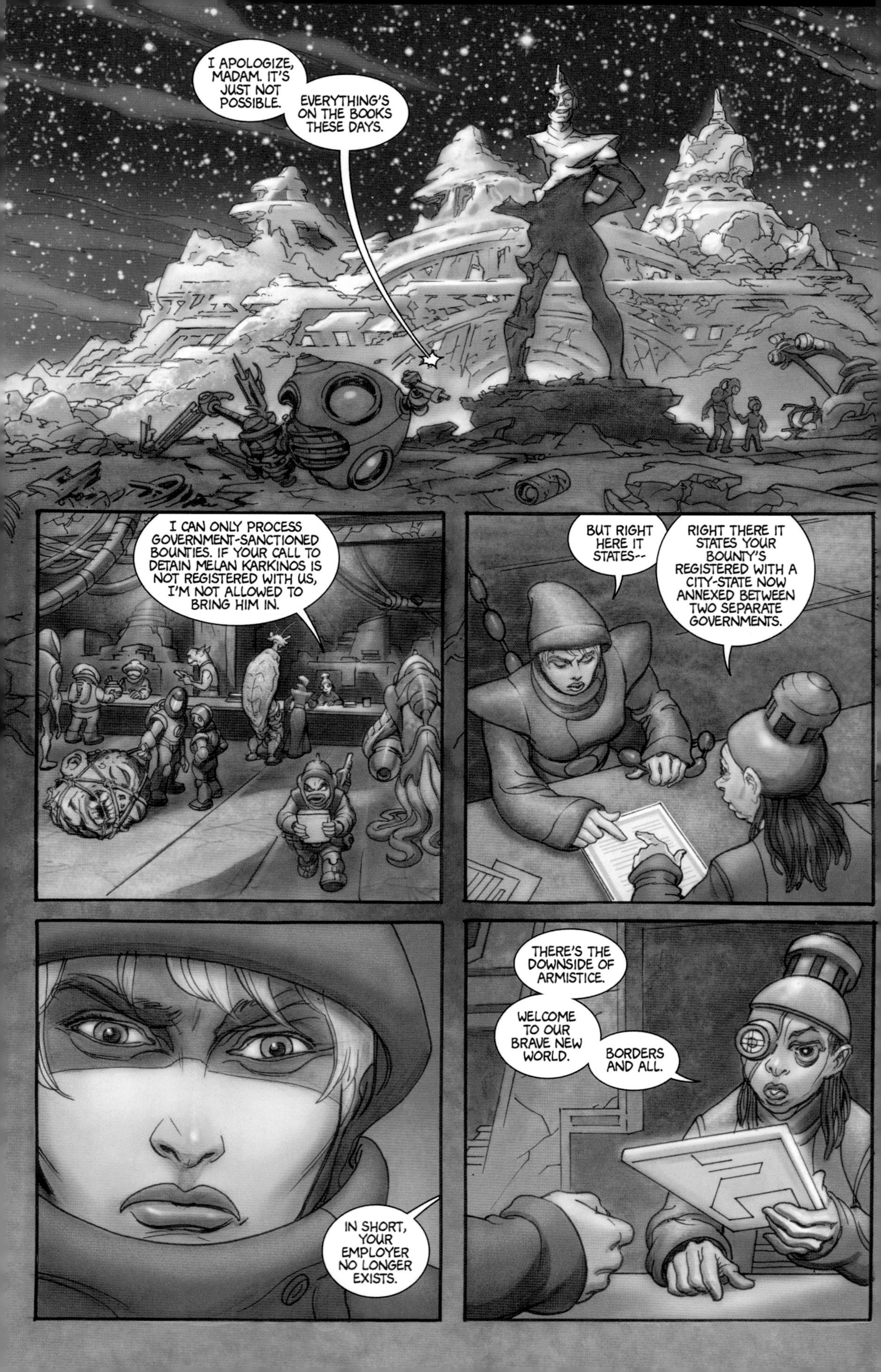
I APOLOGIZE, MADAM. IT'S JUST NOT POSSIBLE.
EVERYTHING'S ON THE BOOKS THESE DAYS.
I CAN ONLY PROCESS GOVERNMENT-SANCTIONED BOUNTIES. IF YOUR CALL TO DETAIN MELAN KARKINOS IS NOT REGISTERED WITH US, I'M NOT ALLOWED TO BRING HIM IN.
BUT RIGHT HERE IT STATES--
RIGHT THERE IT STATES YOUR BOUNTY'S REGISTERED WITH A CITY-STATE NOW ANNEXED BETWEEN TWO SEPARATE GOVERNMENTS.
IN SHORT, YOUR EMPLOYER NO LONGER EXISTS.
THERE'S THE DOWNSIDE OF ARMISTICE.
WELCOME TO OUR BRAVE NEW WORLD.
BORDERS AND ALL.

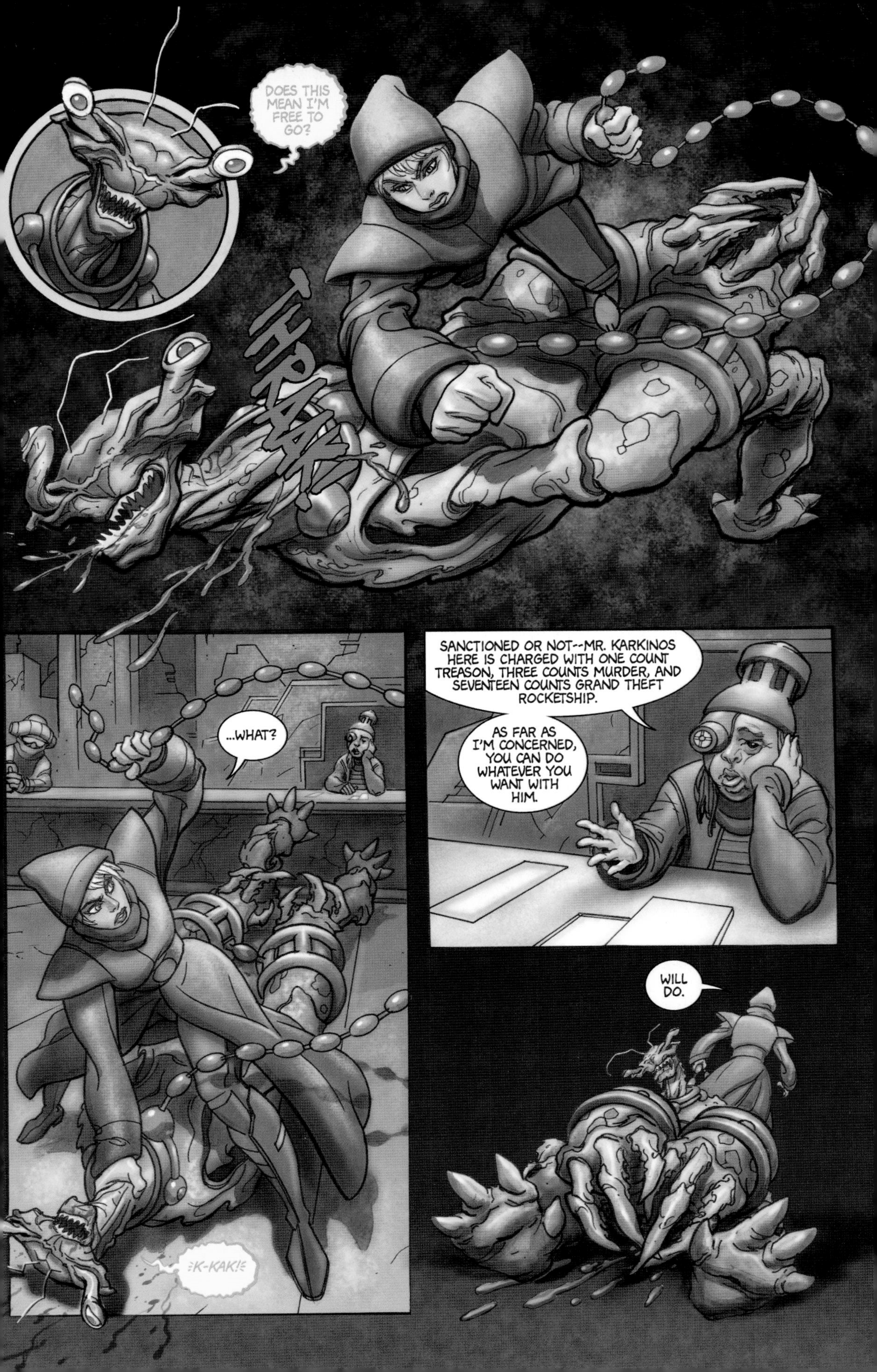
DOES THIS MEAN I'M FREE TO GO?
THRAK!
...WHAT?
SANCTIONED OR NOT--MR. KARKINOS HERE IS CHARGED WITH ONE COUNT TREASON, THREE COUNTS MURDER, AND SEVENTEEN COUNTS GRAND THEFT ROCKETSHIP.
AS FAR AS I'M CONCERNED, YOU CAN DO WHATEVER YOU WANT WITH HIM.
K-KAK!
WILL DO.

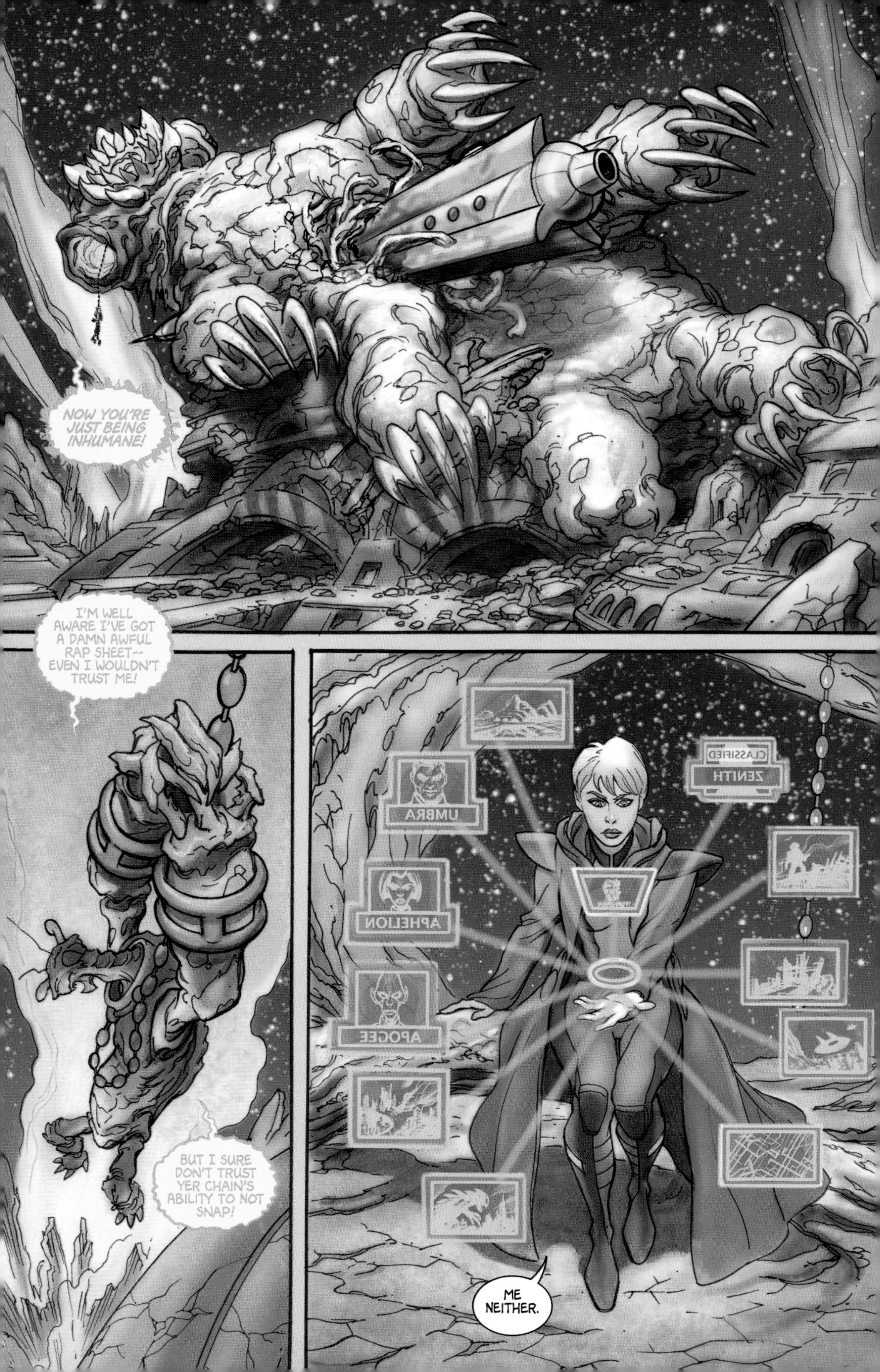
NOW YOU'RE JUST BEING INHUMANE!
I'M WELL AWARE I'VE GOT A DAMN AWFUL RAP SHEET-- EVEN I WOULDN'T TRUST ME!
BUT I SURE DON'T TRUST YER CHAIN'S ABILITY TO NOT SNAP!
UMBRA
CLASSIFIED
ZENITH
APHELION
APOGEE
ME NEITHER.

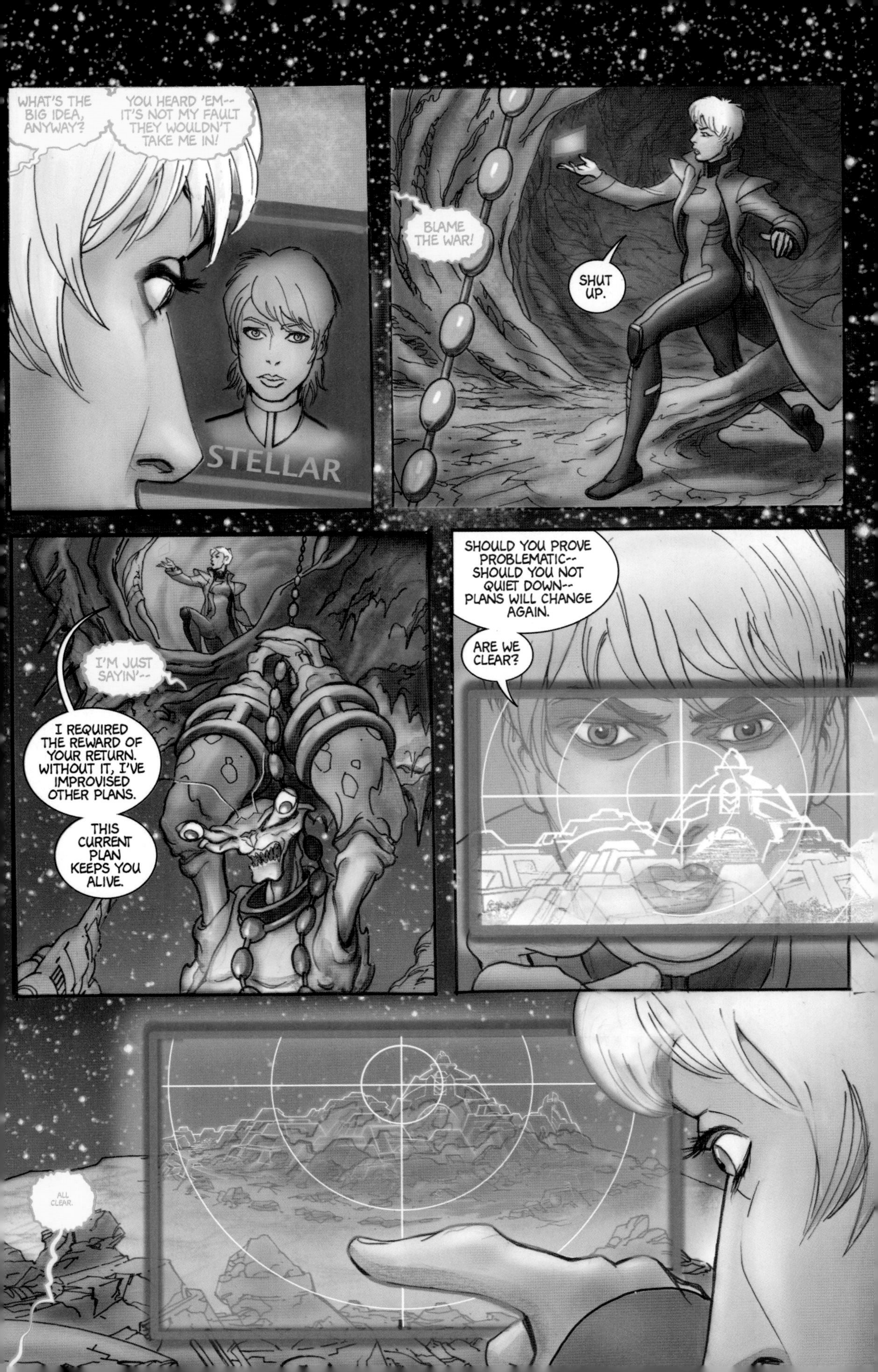
WHAT'S THE BIG IDEA, ANYWAY?
YOU HEARD 'EM-- IT'S NOT MY FAULT THEY WOULDN'T TAKE ME IN!
STELLAR
BLAME THE WAR!
SHUT UP.
I'M JUST SAYIN'--
I REQUIRED THE REWARD OF YOUR RETURN. WITHOUT IT, I'VE IMPROVISED OTHER PLANS.
THIS CURRENT PLAN KEEPS YOU ALIVE.
SHOULD YOU PROVE PROBLEMATIC-- SHOULD YOU NOT QUIET DOWN-- PLANS WILL CHANGE AGAIN.
ARE WE CLEAR?
ALL CLEAR.

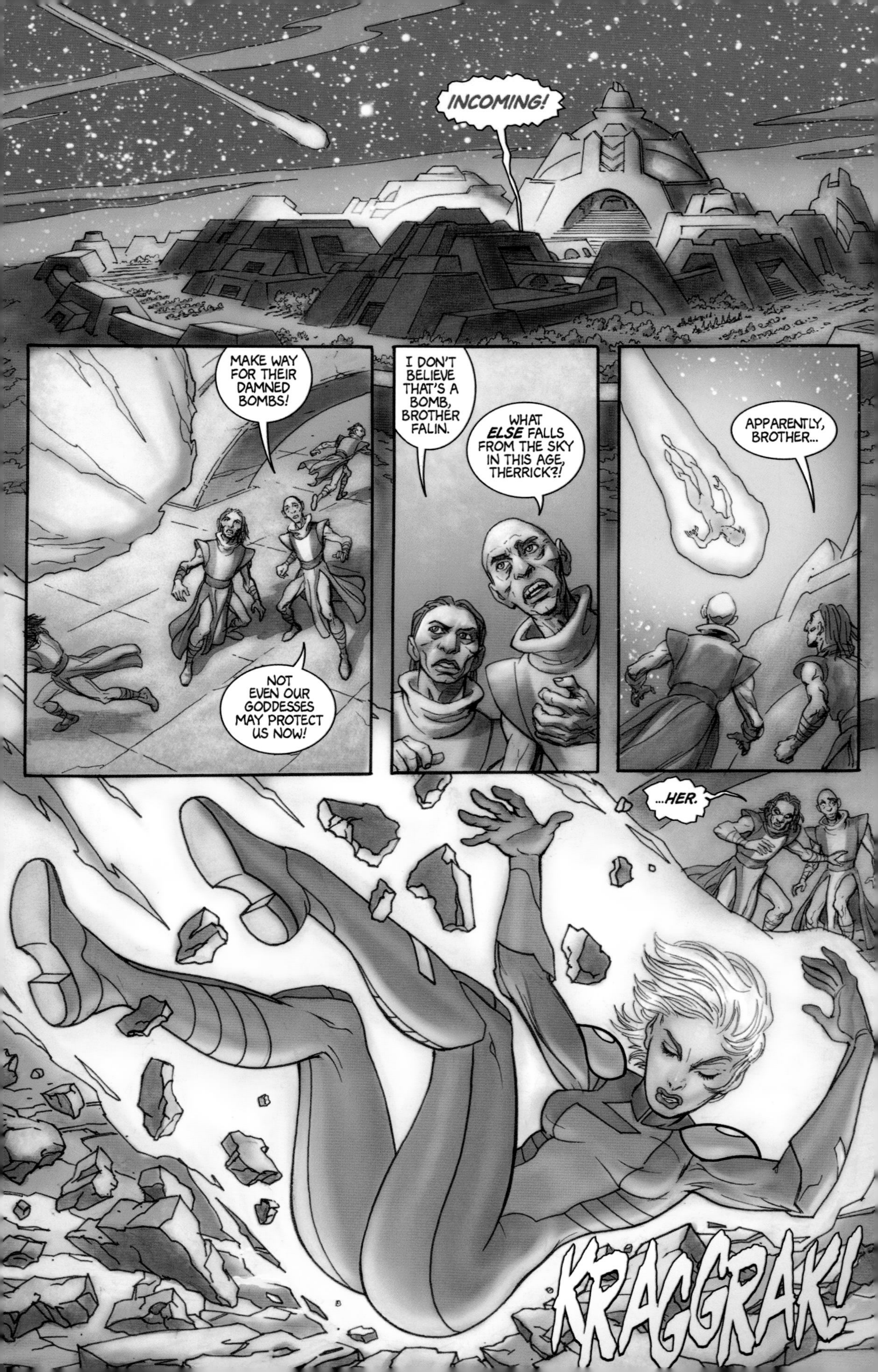
INCOMING!
MAKE WAY FOR THEIR DAMNED BOMBS!
NOT EVEN OUR GODDESSES MAY PROTECT US NOW!
I DON'T BELIEVE THAT'S A BOMB, BROTHER FALIN.
WHAT ELSE FALLS FROM THE SKY IN THIS AGE, THERRICK?!
APPARENTLY, BROTHER...
...HER.
KRAGGRAK!

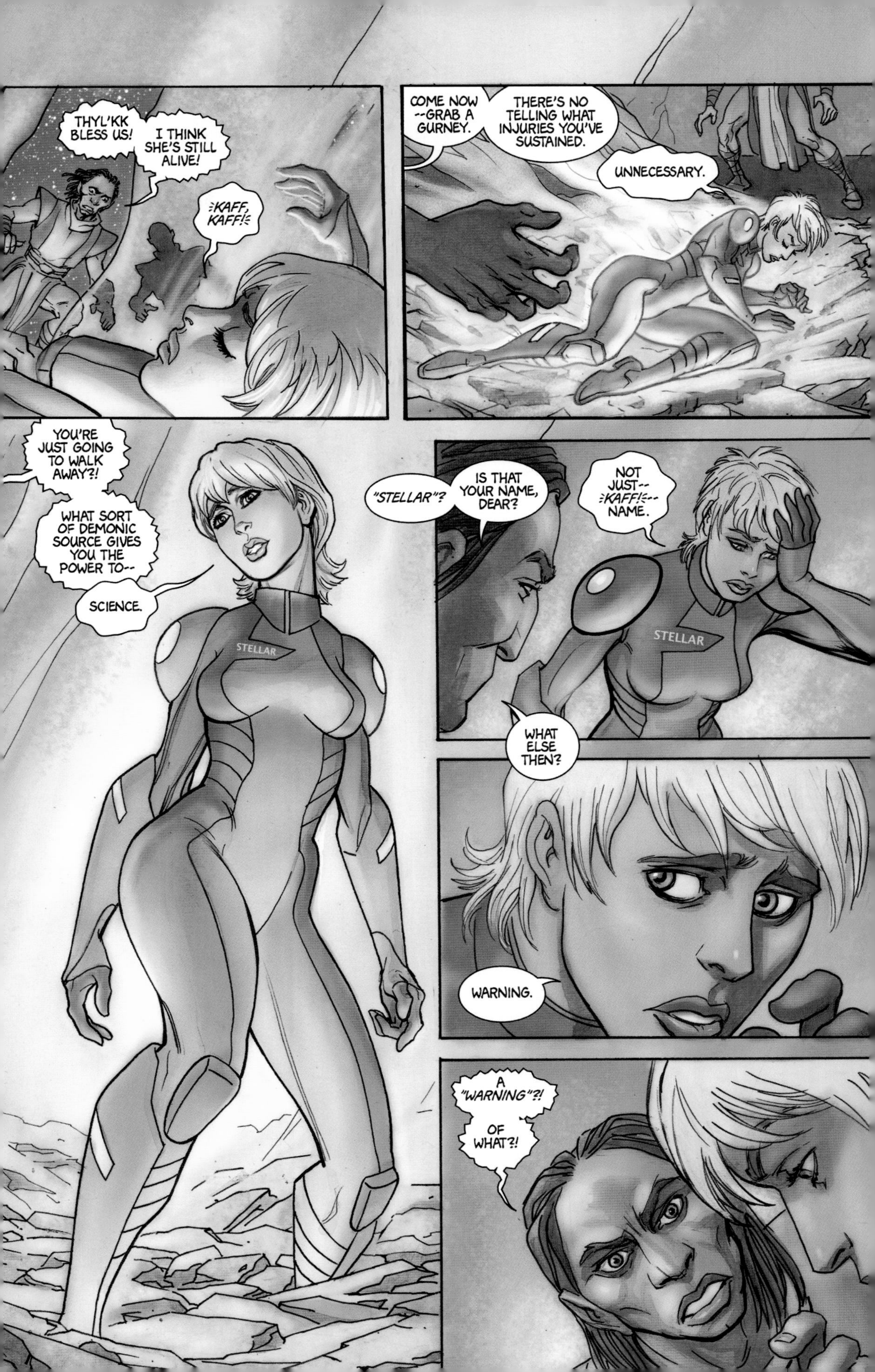
THYL'KK BLESS US!
I THINK SHE'S STILL ALIVE!
KAFF, KAFF!
COME NOW --GRAB A GURNEY.
THERE'S NO TELLING WHAT INJURIES YOU'VE SUSTAINED.
UNNECESSARY.
YOU'RE JUST GOING TO WALK AWAY?!
WHAT SORT OF DEMONIC SOURCE GIVES YOU THE POWER TO--
SCIENCE.
STELLAR
"STELLAR"?
IS THAT YOUR NAME, DEAR?
NOT JUST-- KAFF!-- NAME.
STELLAR
WHAT ELSE THEN?
WARNING.
A "WARNING"?!
OF WHAT?!

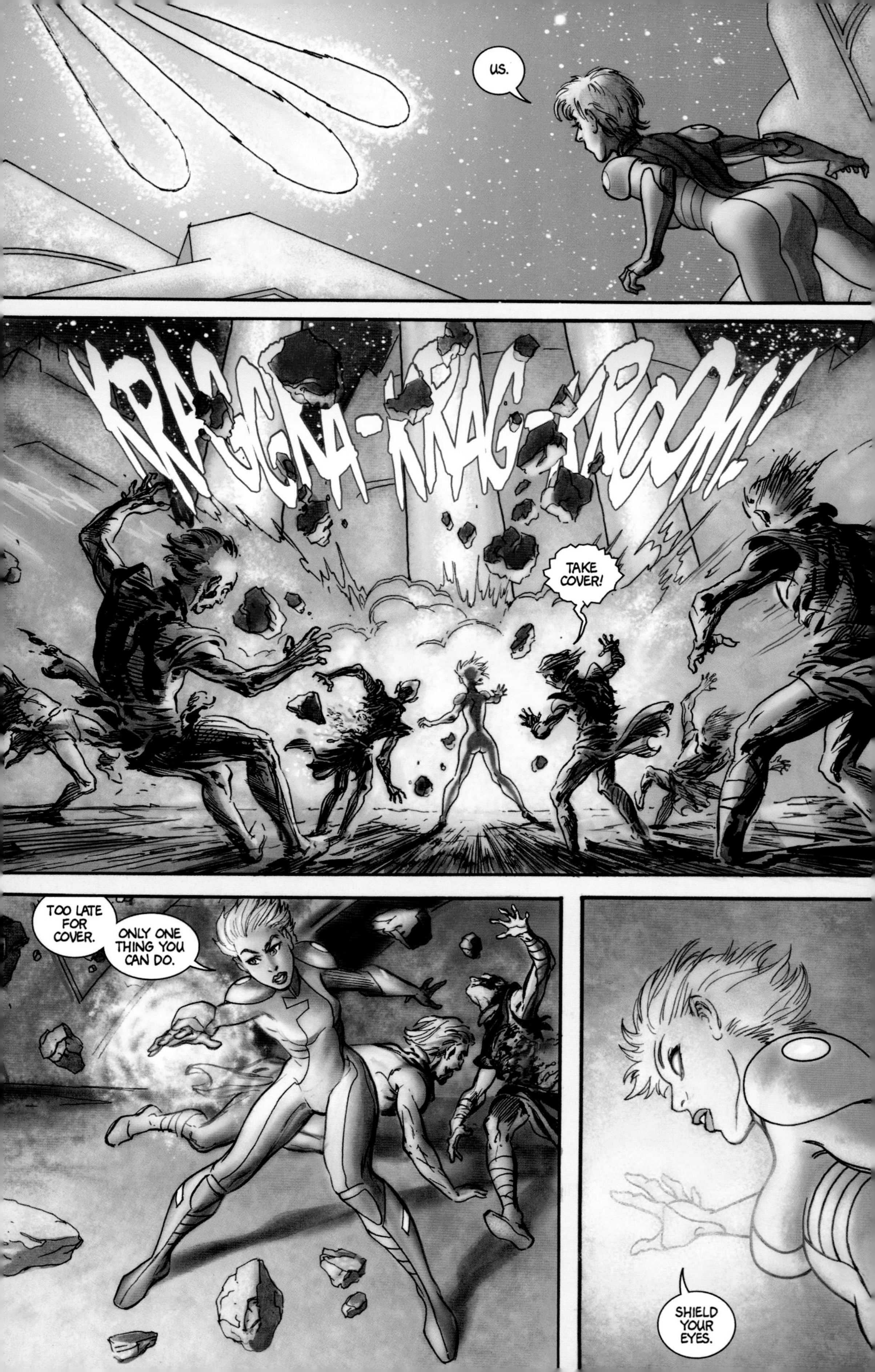

US.
KRAGGRA-KRAG-KROOM!
TAKE COVER!
TOO LATE FOR COVER.
ONLY ONE THING YOU CAN DO.
SHIELD YOUR EYES.

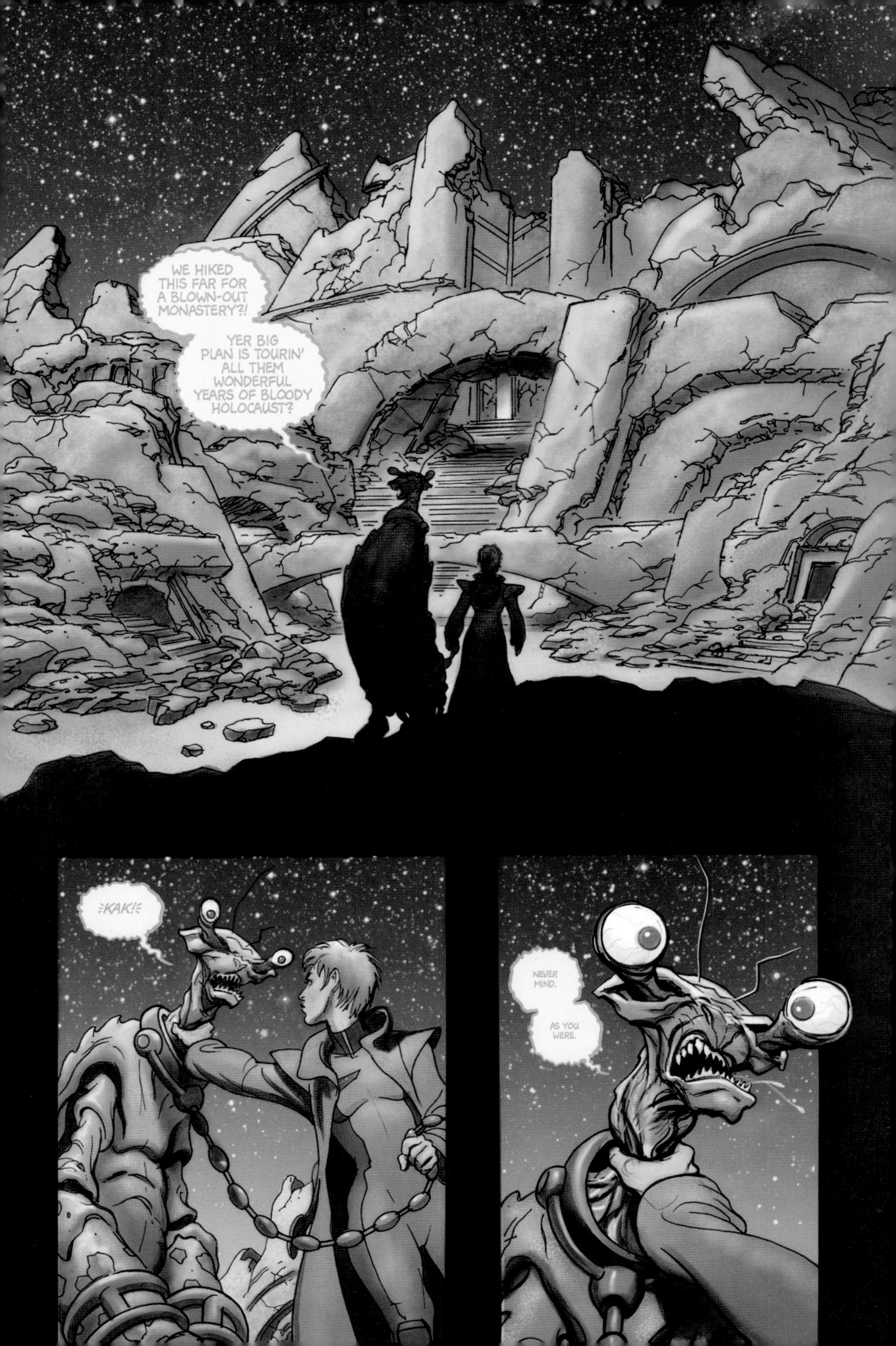
WE HIKED THIS FAR FOR A BLOWN-OUT MONASTERY?!
YER BIG PLAN IS TOURIN' ALL THEM WONDERFUL YEARS OF BLOODY HOLOCAUST?
KAK!
NEVER MIND.
AS YOU WERE.

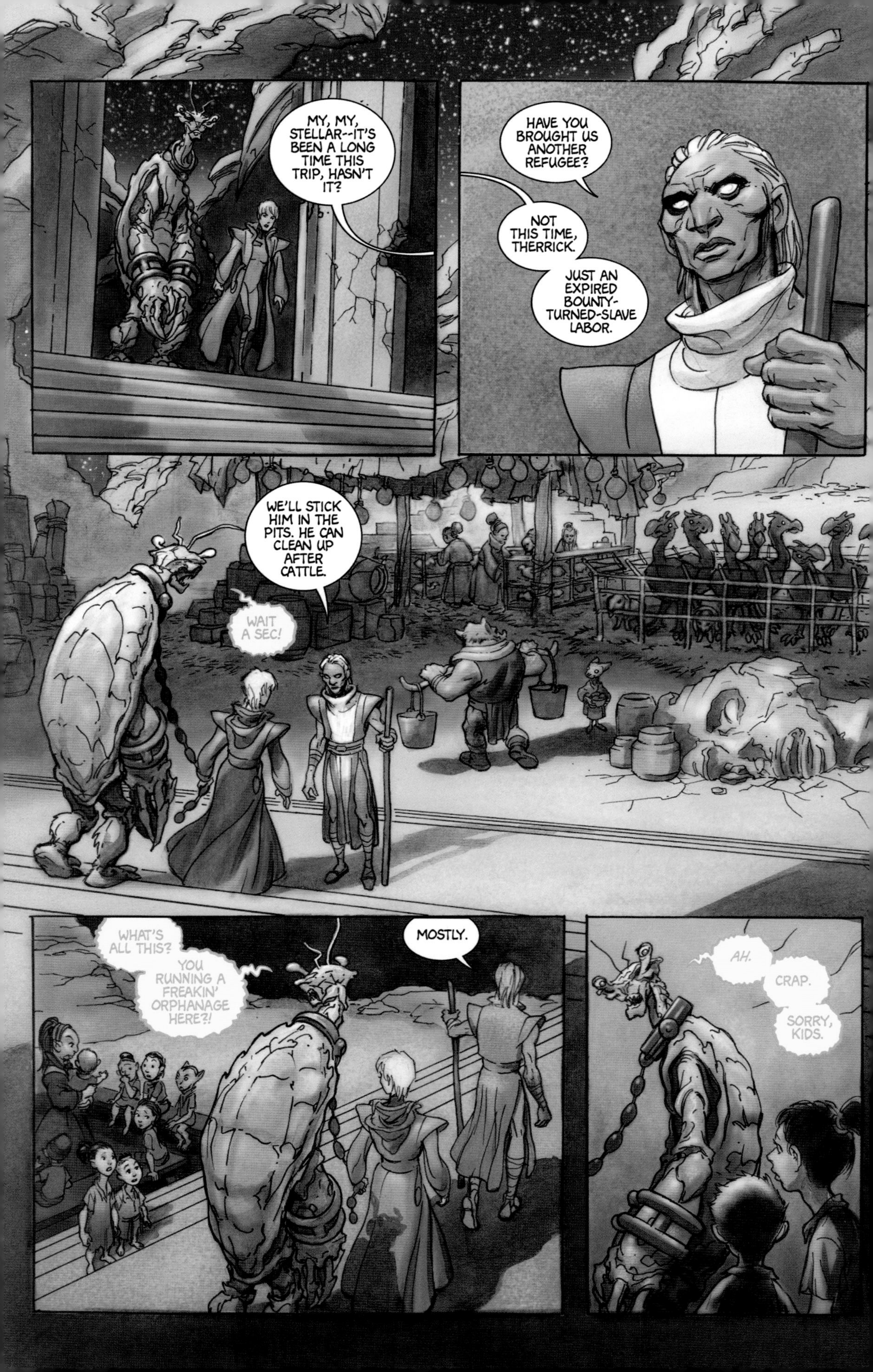
MY, MY, STELLAR--IT'S BEEN A LONG TIME THIS TRIP, HASN'T IT?
HAVE YOU BROUGHT US ANOTHER REFUGEE?
NOT THIS TIME, THERRICK.
JUST AN EXPIRED BOUNTY-TURNED-SLAVE LABOR.
WE'LL STICK HIM IN THE PITS. HE CAN CLEAN UP AFTER CATTLE.
WAIT A SEC!
WHAT'S ALL THIS?
YOU RUNNING A FREAKIN' ORPHANAGE HERE?!
MOSTLY.
AH.
CRAP.
SORRY, KIDS.

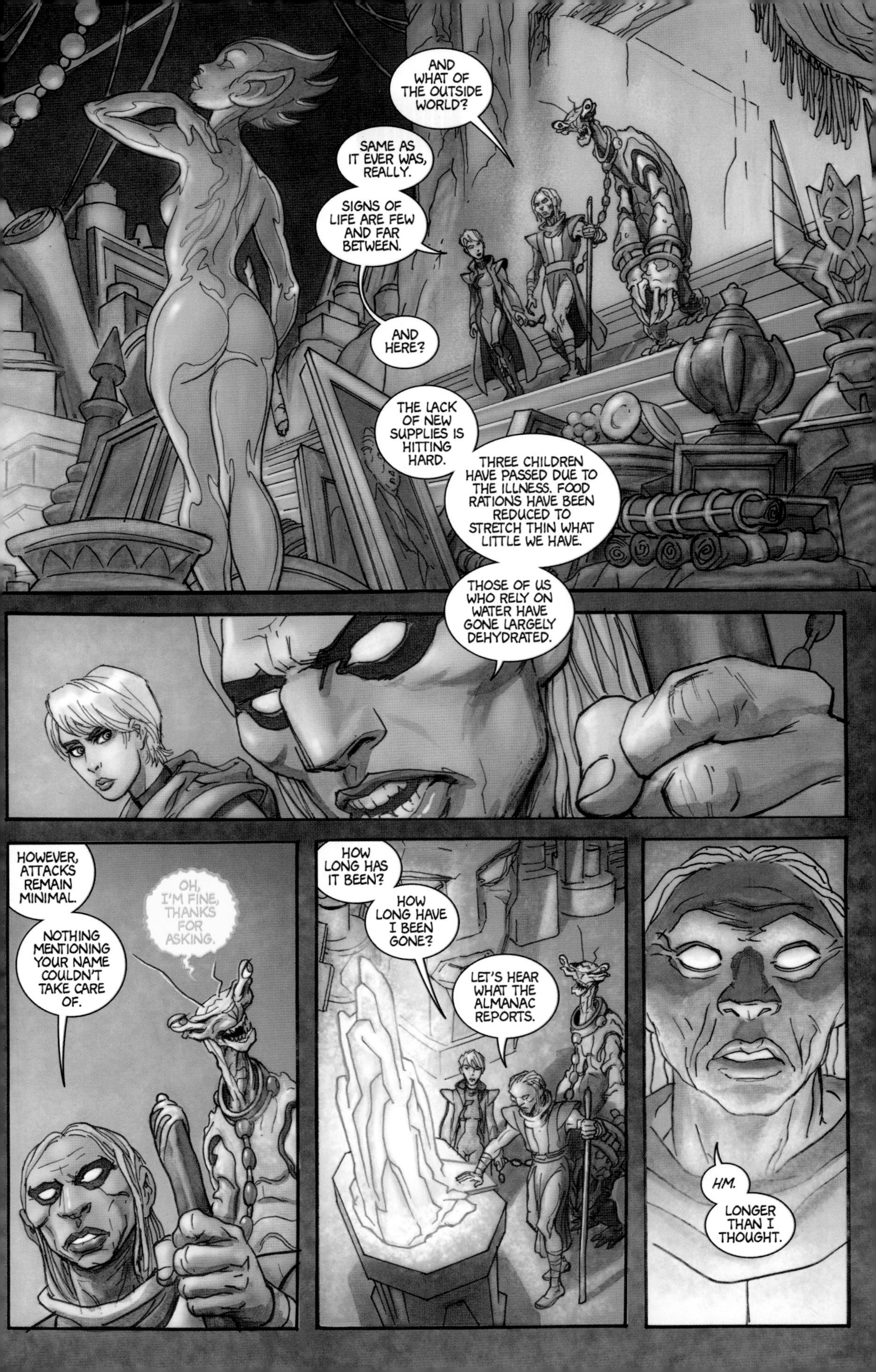
AND WHAT OF THE OUTSIDE WORLD?
SAME AS IT EVER WAS, REALLY.
SIGNS OF LIFE ARE FEW AND FAR BETWEEN.
AND HERE?
THE LACK OF NEW SUPPLIES IS HITTING HARD.
THREE CHILDREN HAVE PASSED DUE TO THE ILLNESS. FOOD RATIONS HAVE BEEN REDUCED TO STRETCH THIN WHAT LITTLE WE HAVE.
THOSE OF US WHO RELY ON WATER HAVE GONE LARGELY DEHYDRATED.
HOWEVER, ATTACKS REMAIN MINIMAL.
NOTHING MENTIONING YOUR NAME COULDN'T TAKE CARE OF.
OH, I'M FINE, THANKS FOR ASKING.
HOW LONG HAS IT BEEN?
HOW LONG HAVE I BEEN GONE?
LET'S HEAR WHAT THE ALMANAC REPORTS.
HM.
LONGER THAN I THOUGHT.

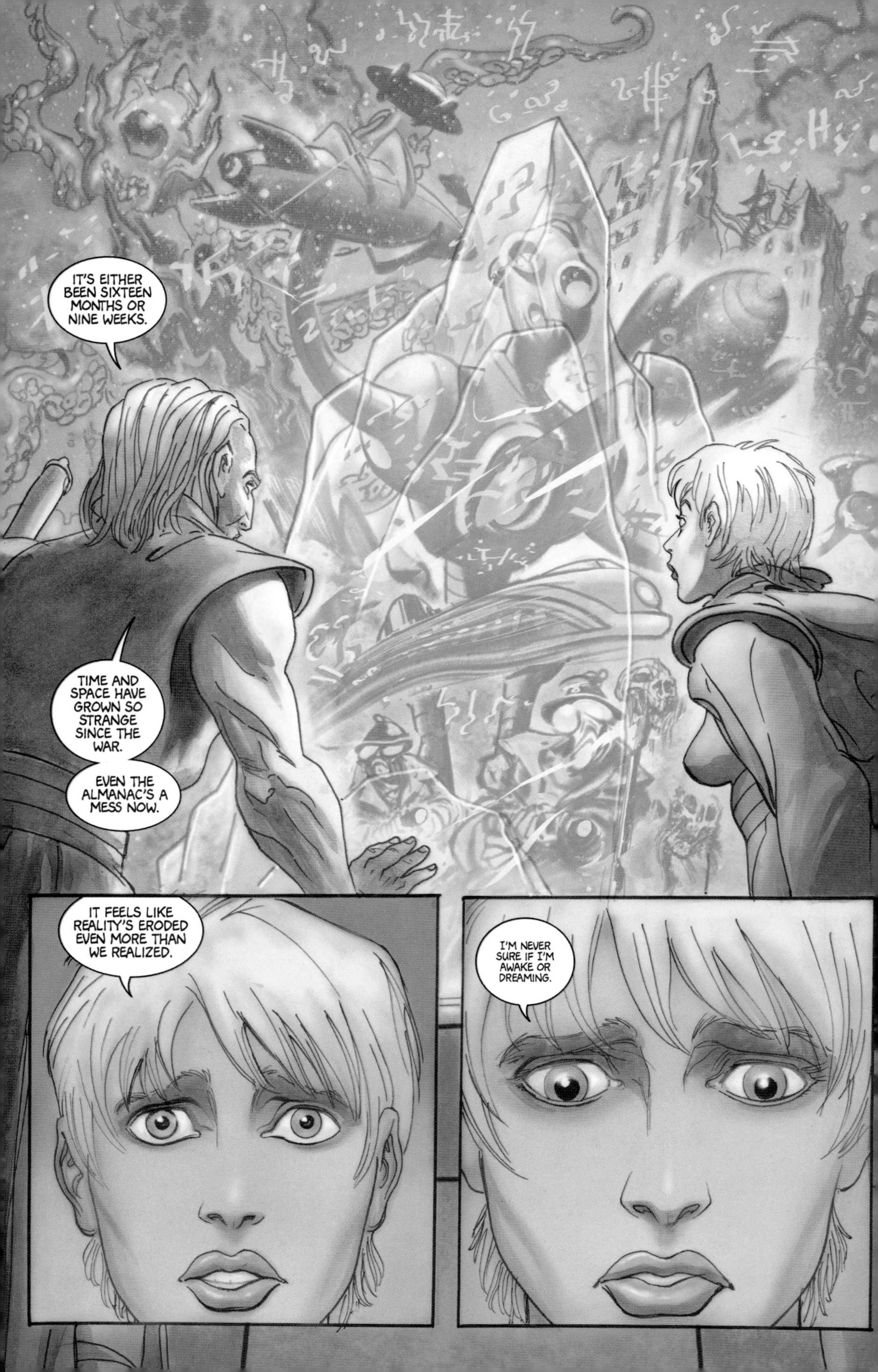
IT'S EITHER BEEN SIXTEEN MONTHS OR NINE WEEKS.
TIME AND SPACE HAVE GROWN SO STRANGE SINCE THE WAR.
EVEN THE ALMANAC'S A MESS NOW.
IT FEELS LIKE REALITY'S ERODED EVEN MORE THAN WE REALIZED.
I'M NEVER SURE IF I'M AWAKE OR DREAMING.

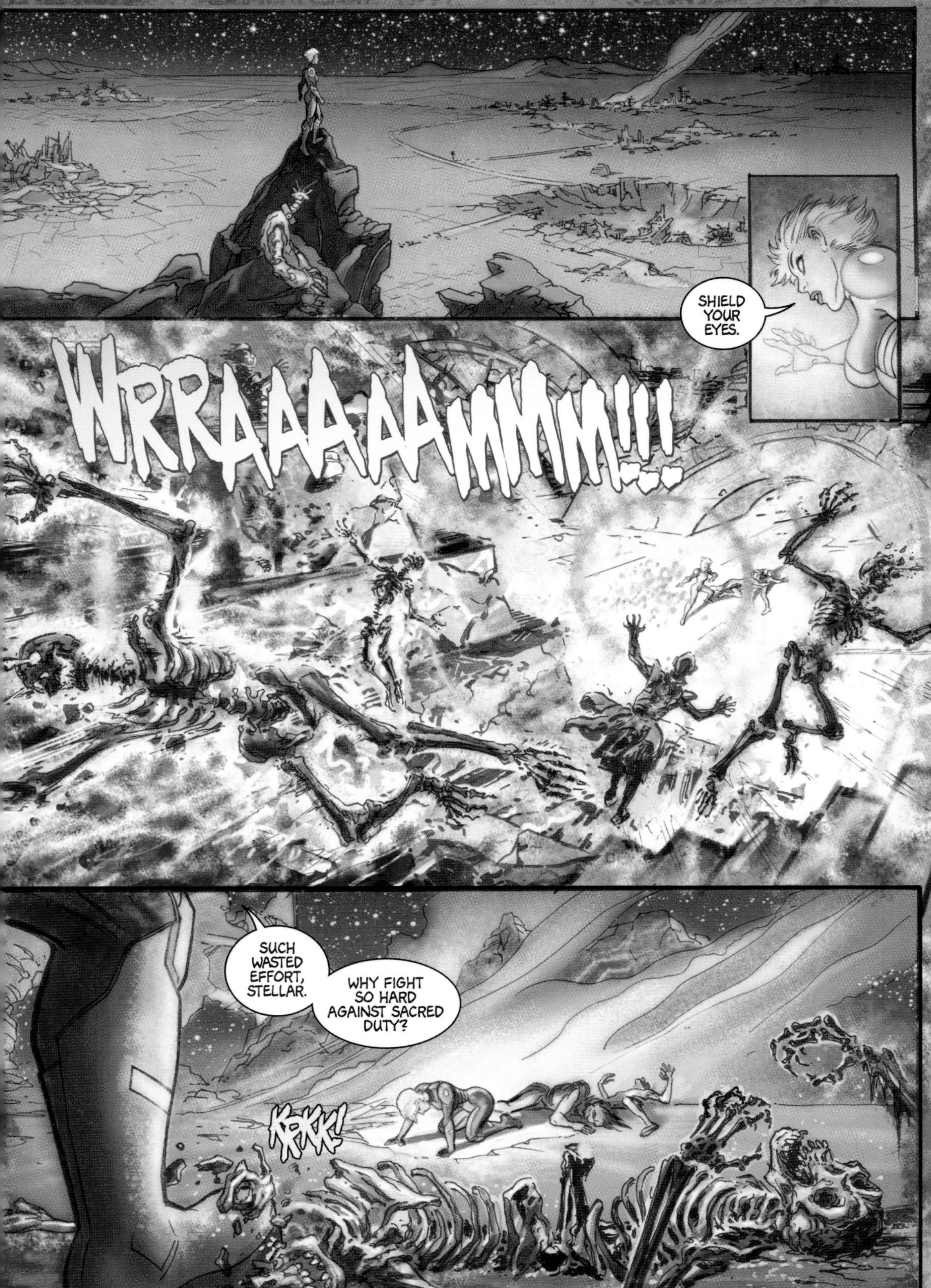
SHIELD YOUR EYES.
WRRAAAAAMMMM!!!
SUCH WASTED EFFORT, STELLAR.
WHY FIGHT SO HARD AGAINST SACRED DUTY?
KRKK!

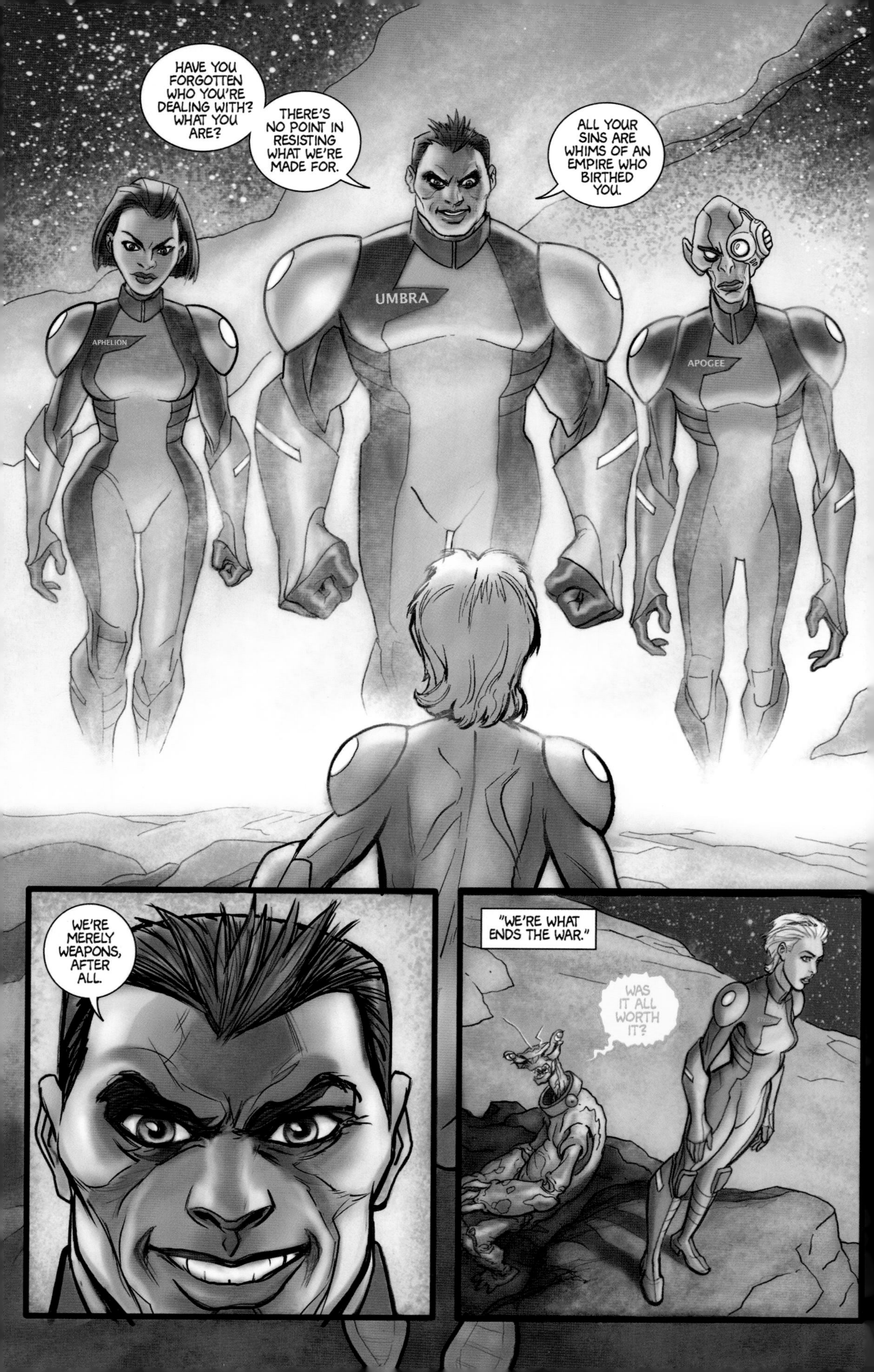
HAVE YOU FORGOTTEN WHO YOU'RE DEALING WITH? WHAT YOU ARE?
THERE'S NO POINT IN RESISTING WHAT WE'RE MADE FOR.
ALL YOUR SINS ARE WHIMS OF AN EMPIRE WHO BIRTHED YOU.
APHELION
UMBRA
APOGEE
WE'RE MERELY WEAPONS, AFTER ALL.
"WE'RE WHAT ENDS THE WAR."
WAS IT ALL WORTH IT?

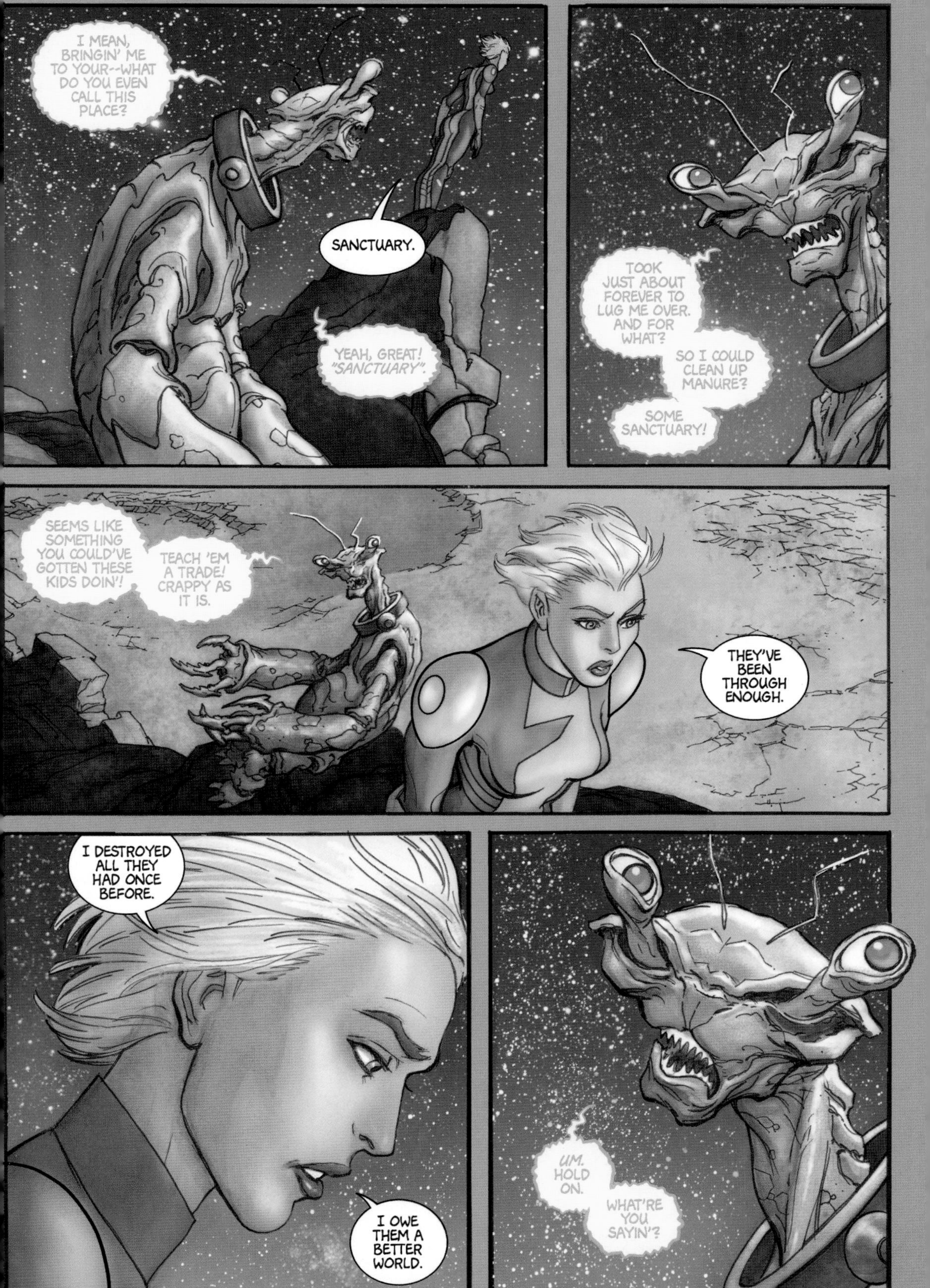
I MEAN, BRINGIN' ME TO YOUR--WHAT DO YOU EVEN CALL THIS PLACE?
SANCTUARY.
YEAH, GREAT! "SANCTUARY".
TOOK JUST ABOUT FOREVER TO LUG ME OVER. AND FOR WHAT?
SO I COULD CLEAN UP MANURE?
SOME SANCTUARY!
SEEMS LIKE SOMETHING YOU COULD'VE GOTTEN THESE KIDS DOIN'!
TEACH 'EM A TRADE! CRAPPY AS IT IS.
THEY'VE BEEN THROUGH ENOUGH.
I DESTROYED ALL THEY HAD ONCE BEFORE.
I OWE THEM A BETTER WORLD.
UM. HOLD ON.
WHAT'RE YOU SAYIN'?

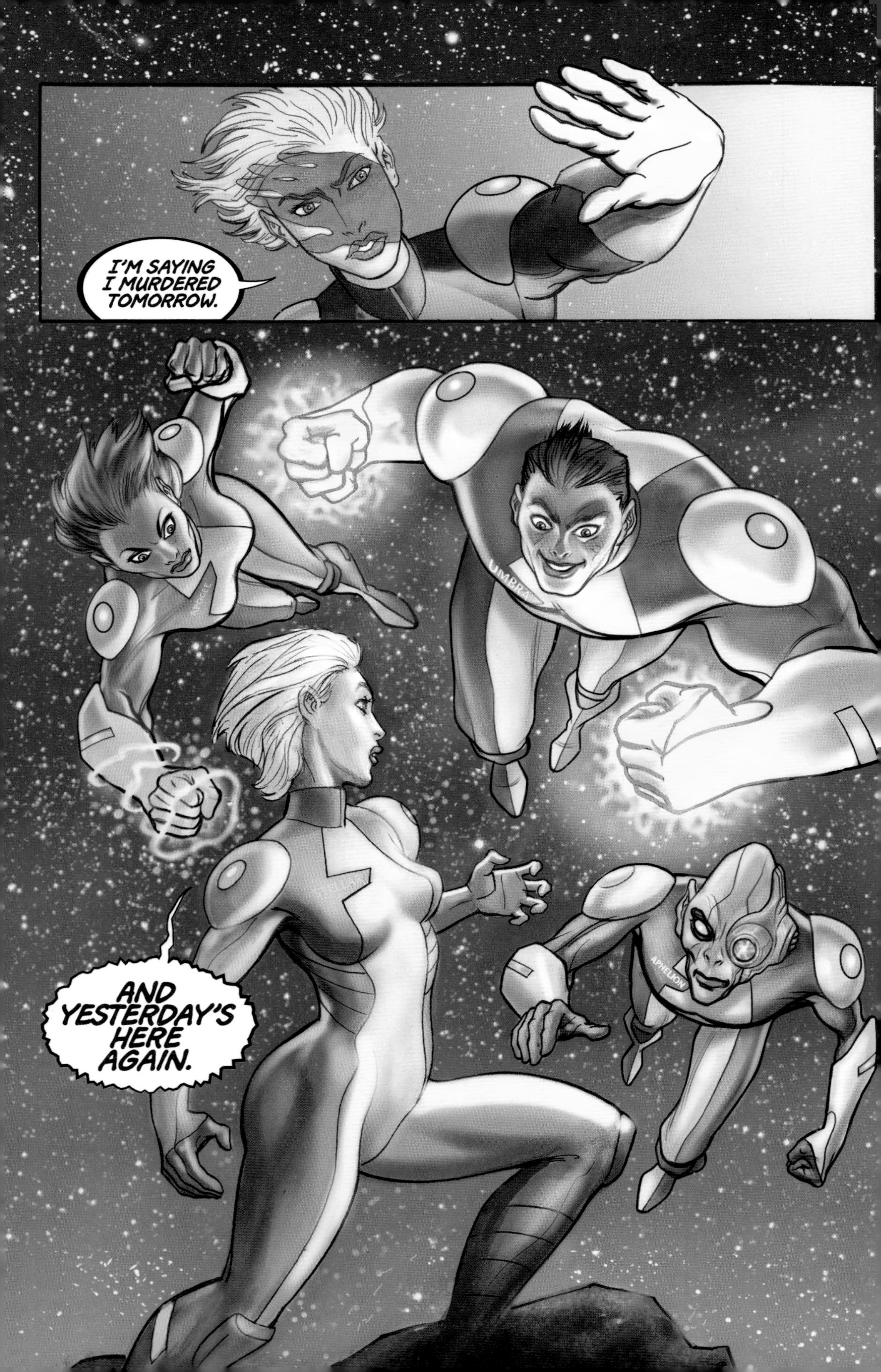
I'M SAYING I MURDERED TOMORROW.
APOGEE
UMBRA
STELLAR
APHELION
AND YESTERDAY'S HERE AGAIN.

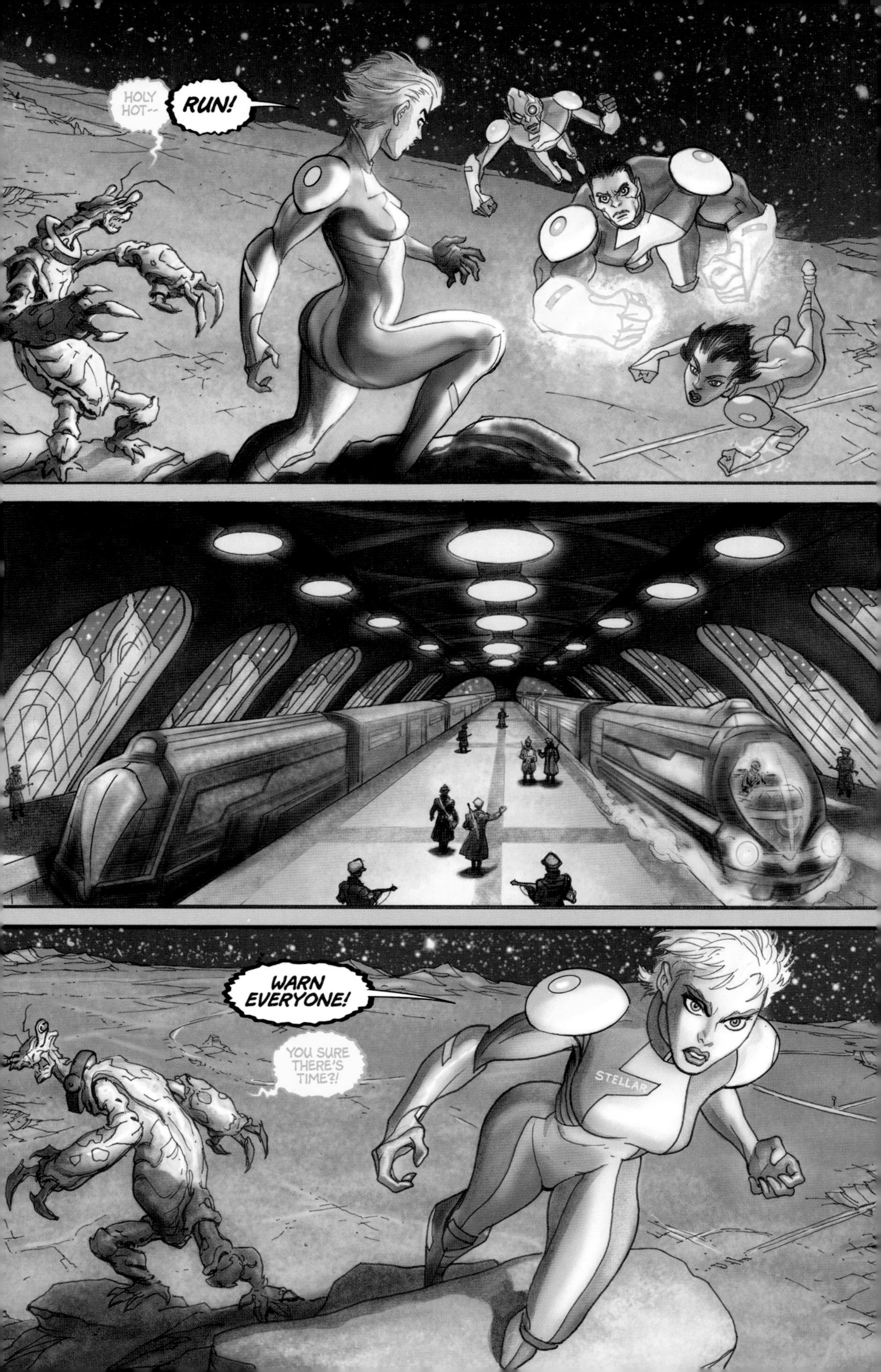
HOLY HOT--
RUN!
WARN EVERYONE!
YOU SURE THERE'S TIME?!
STELLAR

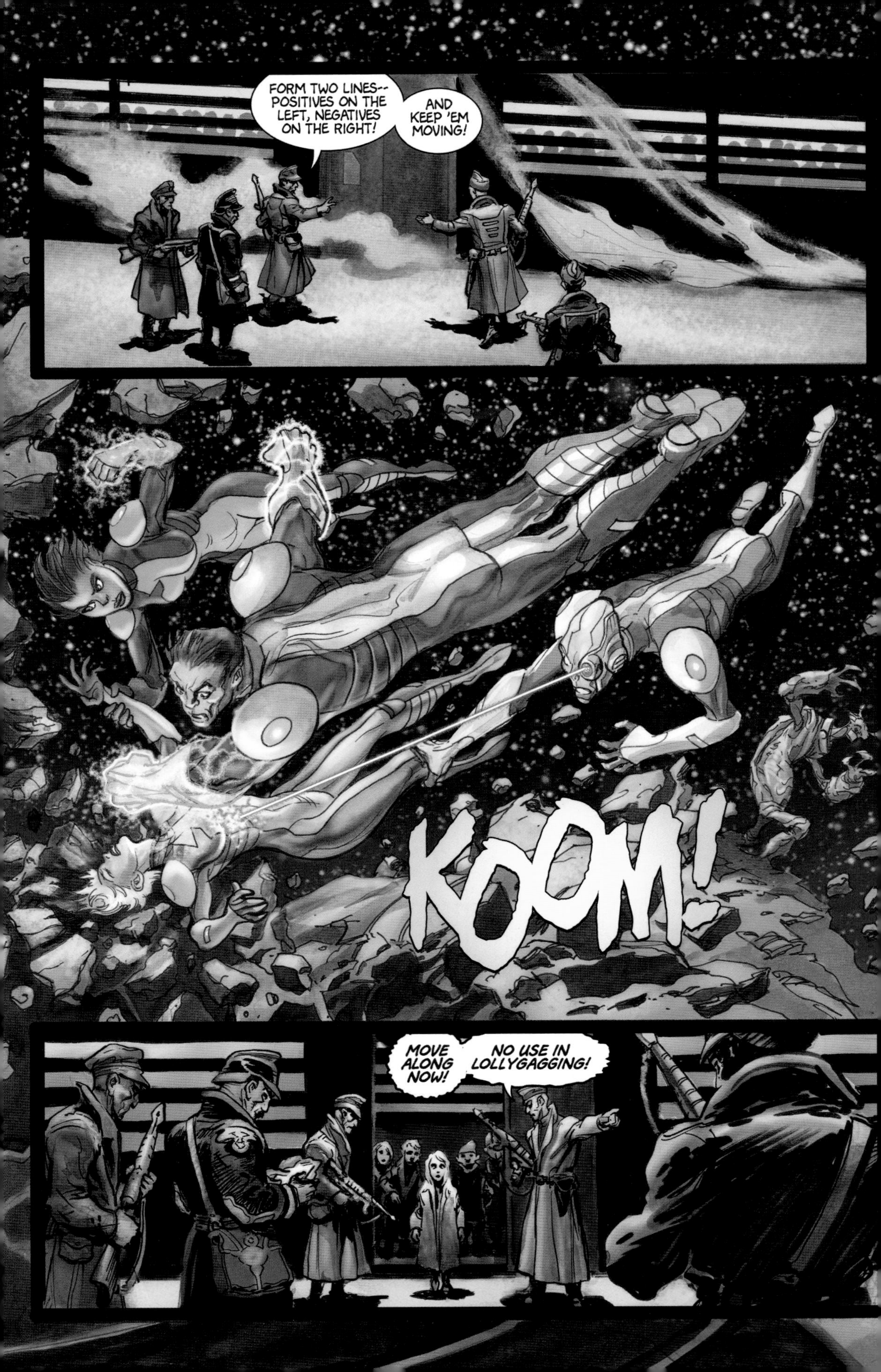
FORM TWO LINES--POSITIVES ON THE LEFT, NEGATIVES ON THE RIGHT!
AND KEEP 'EM MOVING!
KOOM!
MOVE ALONG NOW!
NO USE IN LOLLYGAGGING!

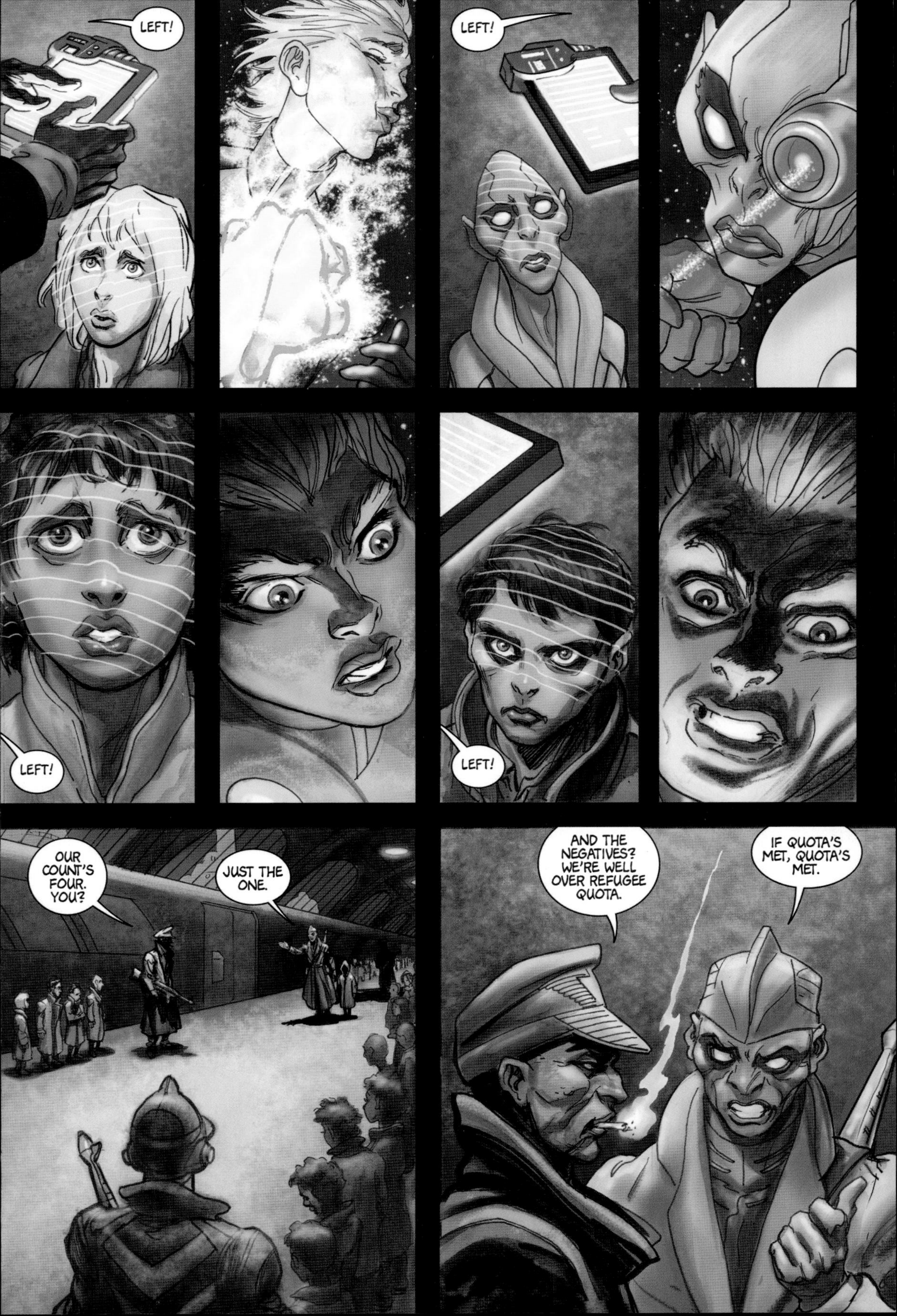
LEFT!
LEFT!
LEFT!
LEFT!
OUR COUNT'S FOUR. YOU?
JUST THE ONE.
AND THE NEGATIVES? WE'RE WELL OVER REFUGEE QUOTA.
IF QUOTA'S MET, QUOTA'S MET.

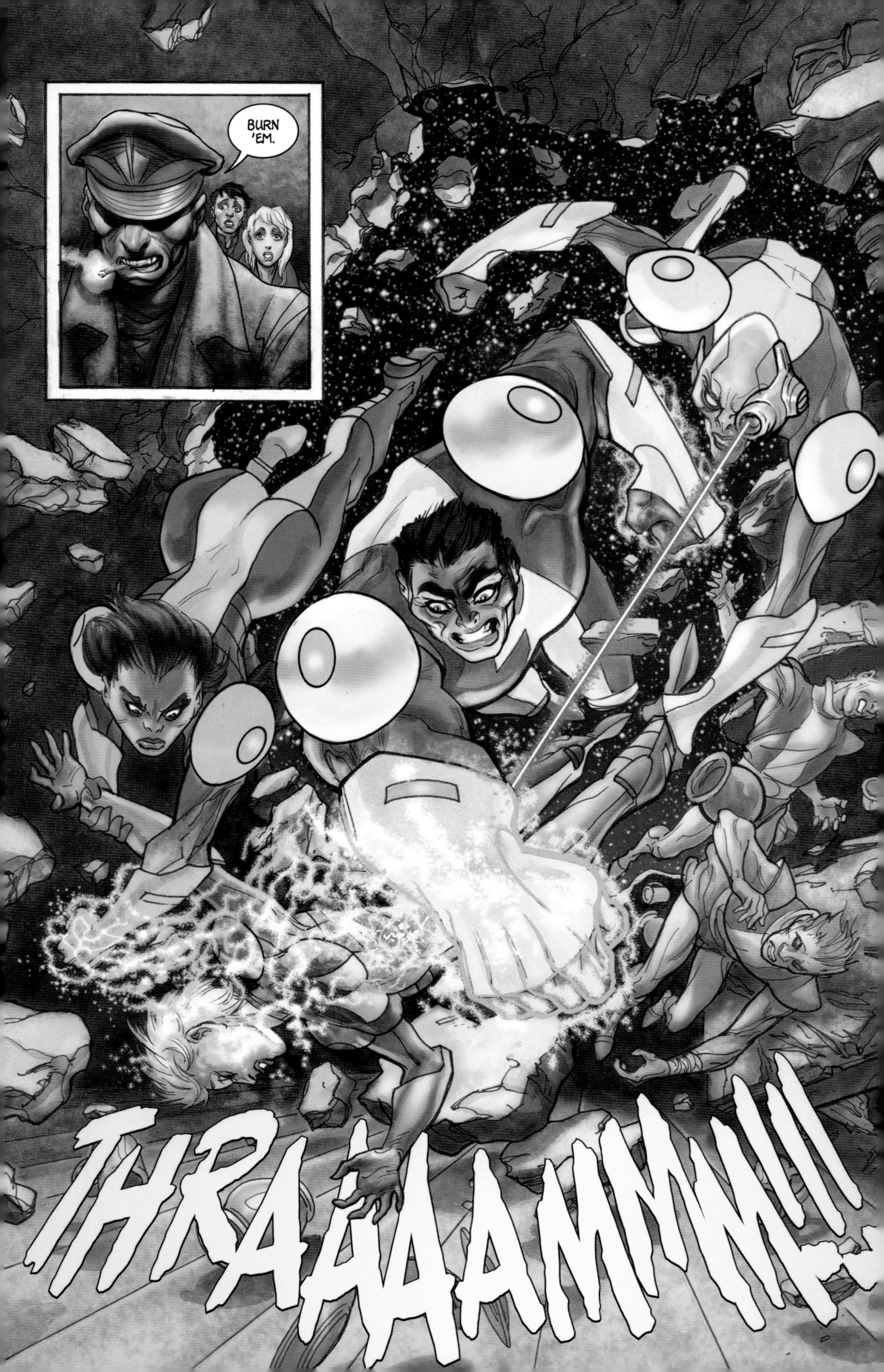
BURN 'EM.
THRAAAAMMM!!

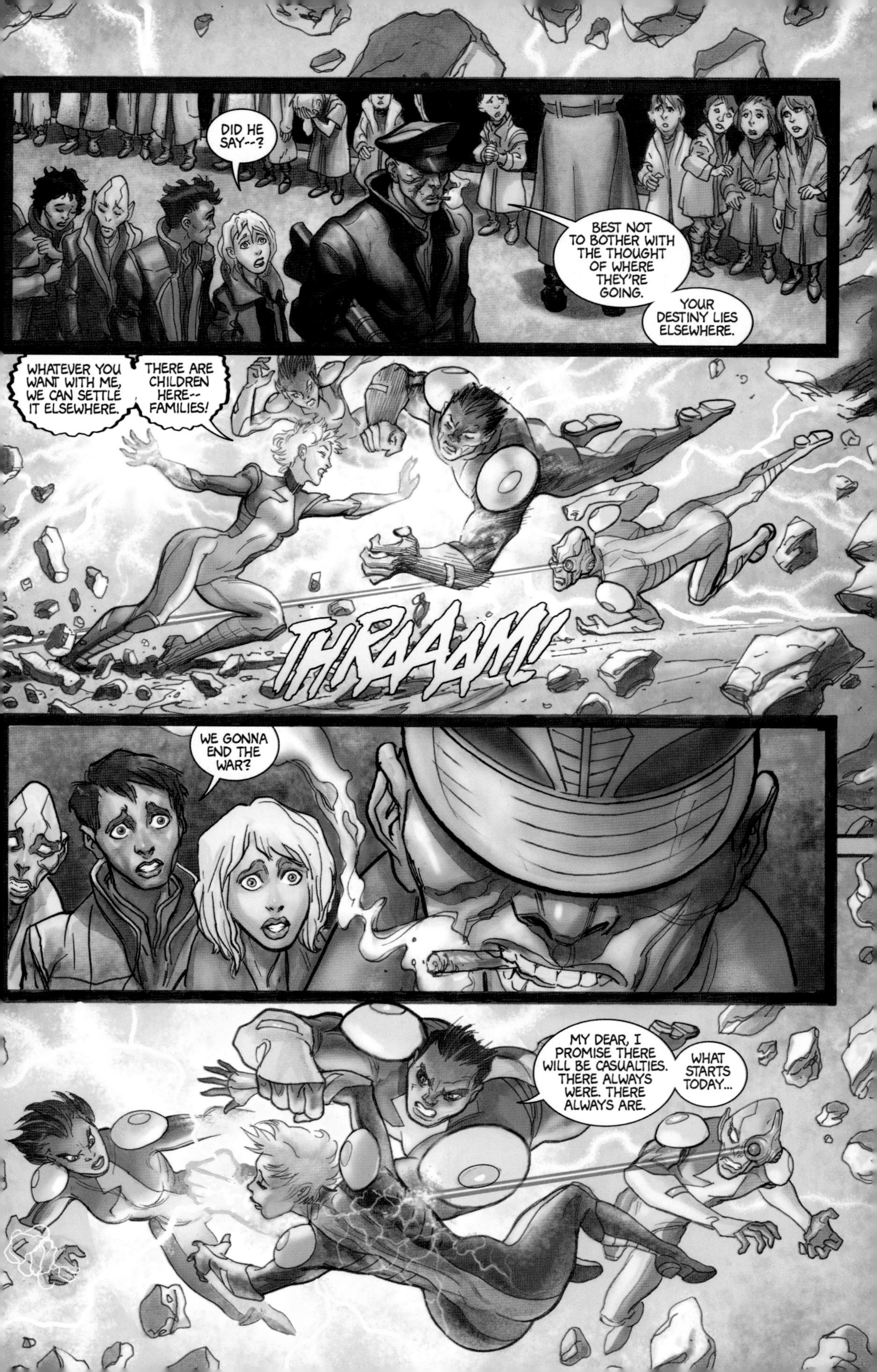
DID HE SAY--?
BEST NOT TO BOTHER WITH THE THOUGHT OF WHERE THEY'RE GOING.
YOUR DESTINY LIES ELSEWHERE.
WHATEVER YOU WANT WITH ME, WE CAN SETTLE IT ELSEWHERE.
THERE ARE CHILDREN HERE--FAMILIES!
THRAAAM!
WE GONNA END THE WAR?
MY DEAR, I PROMISE THERE WILL BE CASUALTIES. THERE ALWAYS WERE. THERE ALWAYS ARE.
WHAT STARTS TODAY...

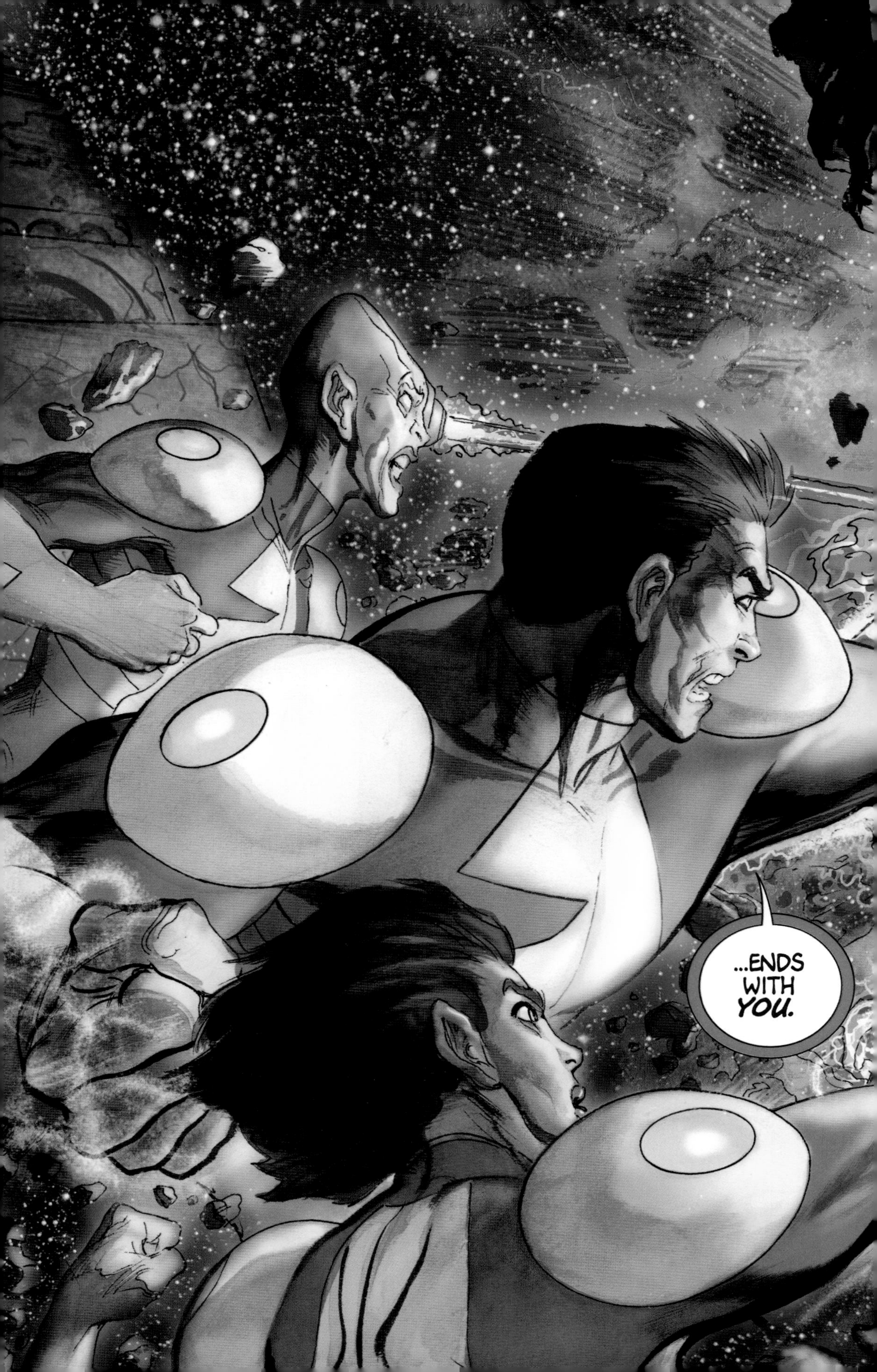
...ENDS WITH YOU.

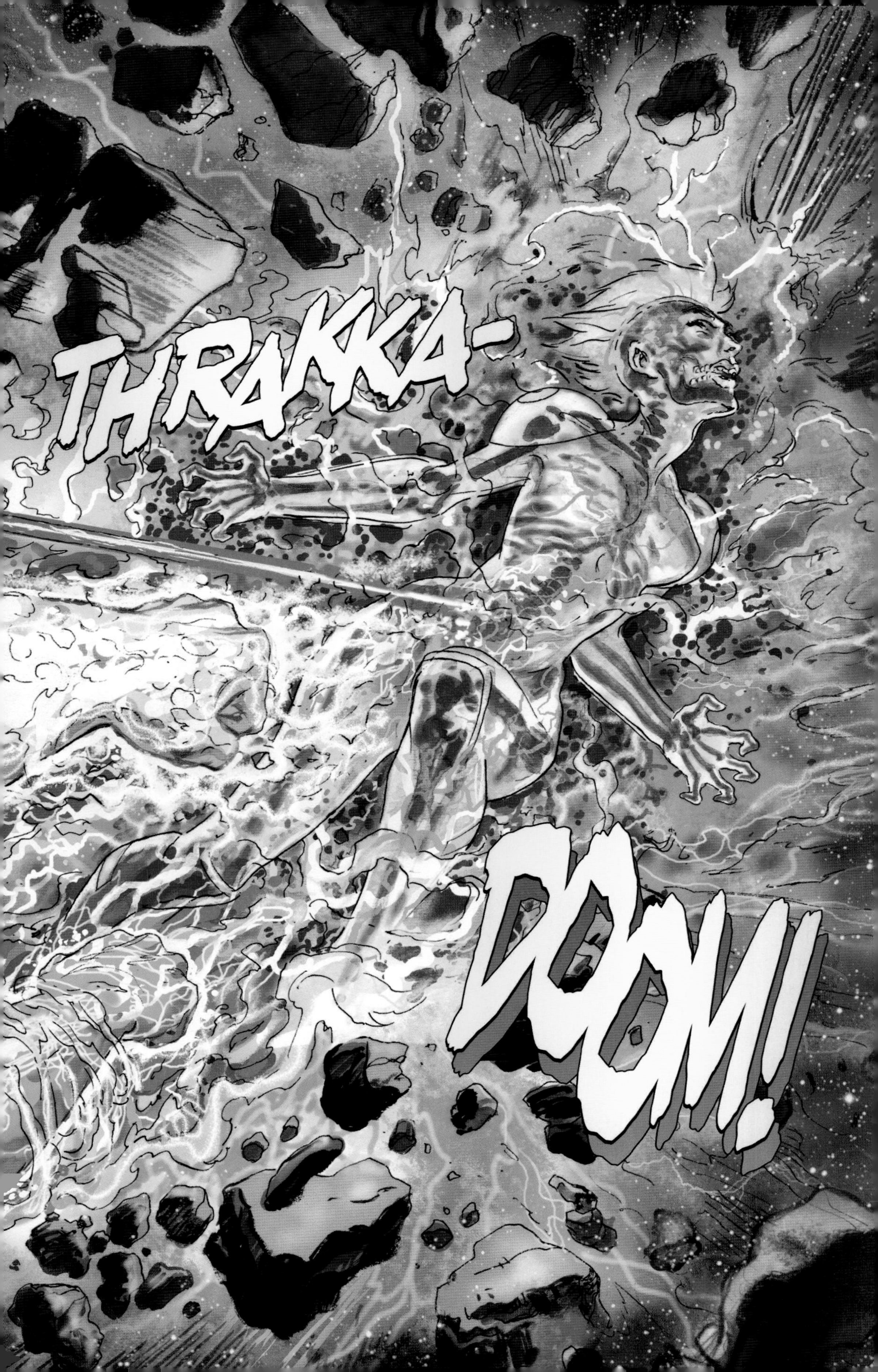
THRAKKA-
DOOM!

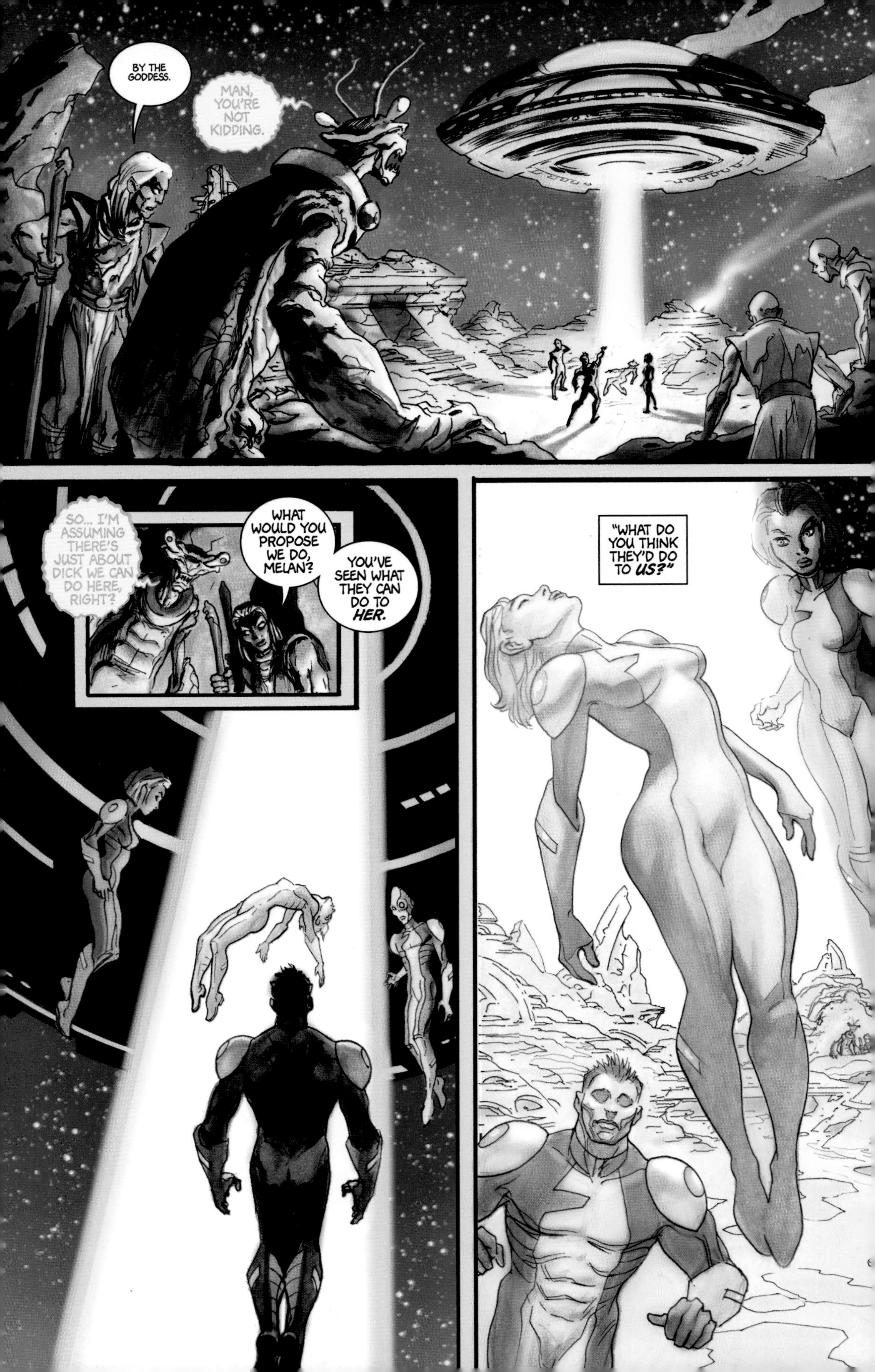
BY THE GODDESS.
MAN, YOU'RE NOT KIDDING.
SO... I'M ASSUMING THERE'S JUST ABOUT DICK WE CAN DO HERE, RIGHT?
WHAT WOULD YOU PROPOSE WE DO, MELAN?
YOU'VE SEEN WHAT THEY CAN DO TO HER.
"WHAT DO YOU THINK THEY'D DO TO US?"

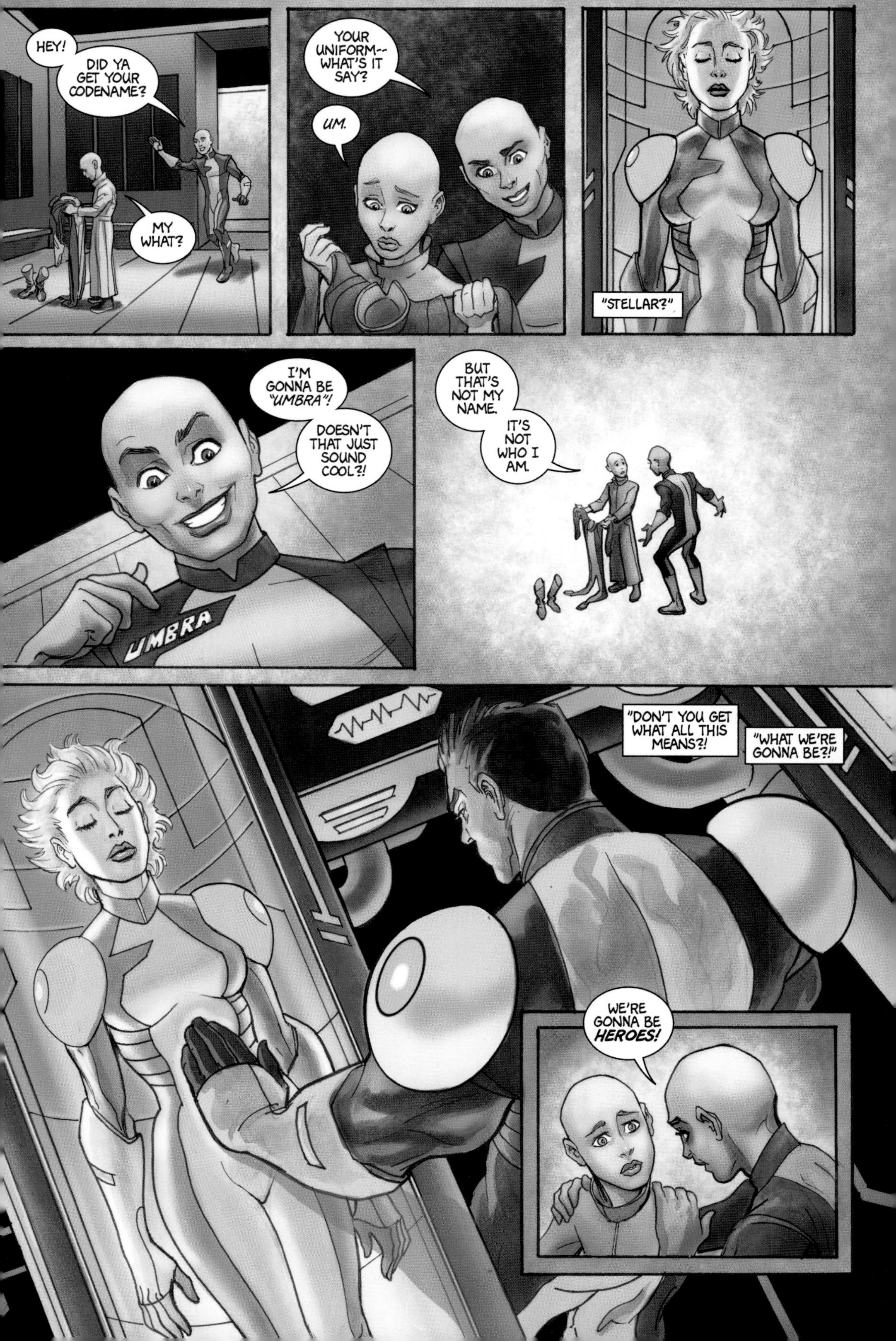
HEY!
DID YA GET YOUR CODENAME?
MY WHAT?
YOUR UNIFORM-- WHAT'S IT SAY?
UM.
"STELLAR?"
I'M GONNA BE "UMBRA"!
DOESN'T THAT JUST SOUND COOL?!
UMBRA
BUT THAT'S NOT MY NAME.
IT'S NOT WHO I AM.
"DON'T YOU GET WHAT ALL THIS MEANS?!
"WHAT WE'RE GONNA BE?!"
WE'RE GONNA BE HEROES!

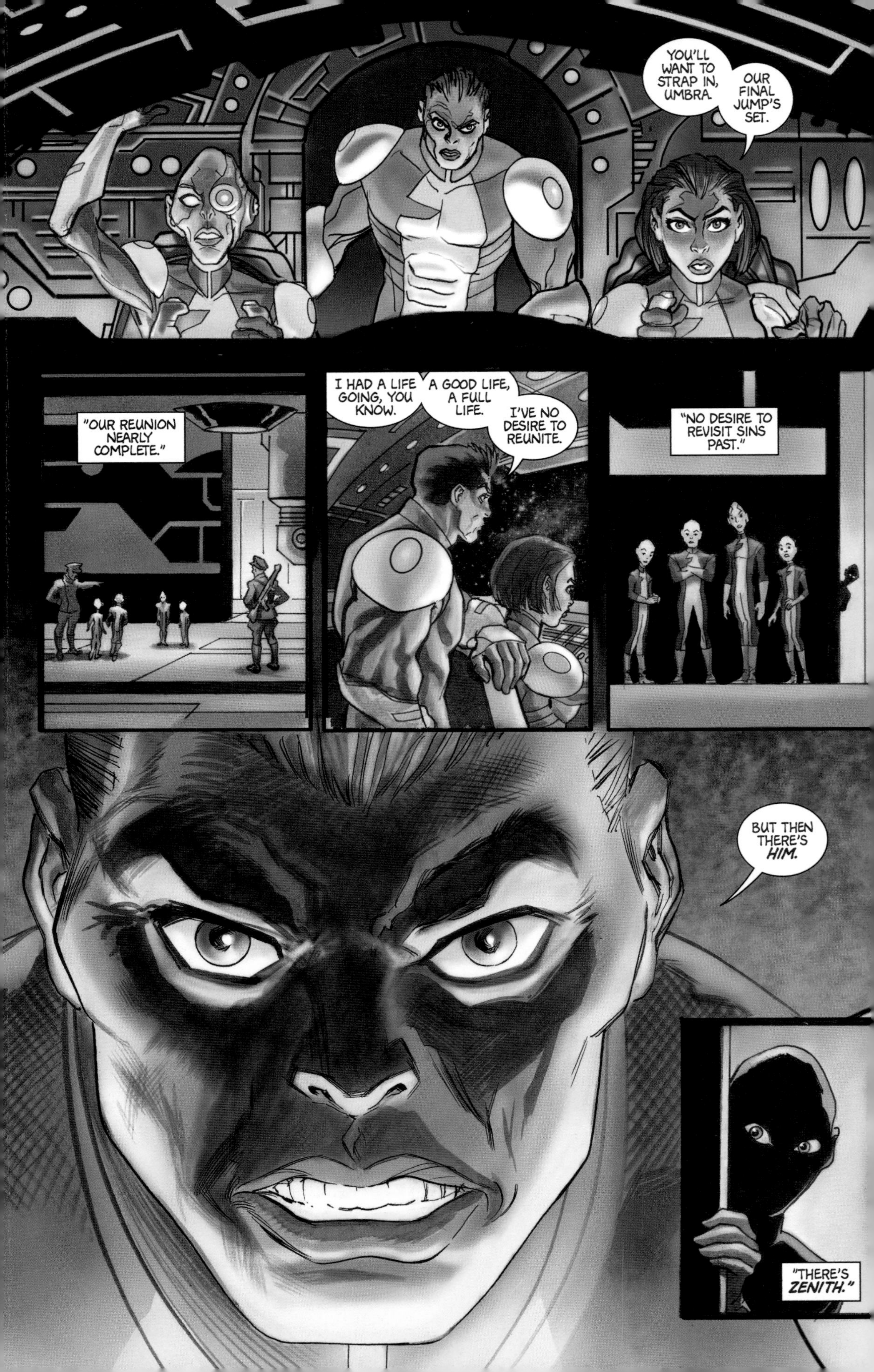
YOU'LL WANT TO STRAP IN, UMBRA.
OUR FINAL JUMP'S SET.
"OUR REUNION NEARLY COMPLETE."
I HAD A LIFE GOING, YOU KNOW.
A GOOD LIFE, A FULL LIFE.
I'VE NO DESIRE TO REUNITE.
"NO DESIRE TO REVISIT SINS PAST."
BUT THEN THERE'S *HIM.*
"THERE'S *ZENITH.*"

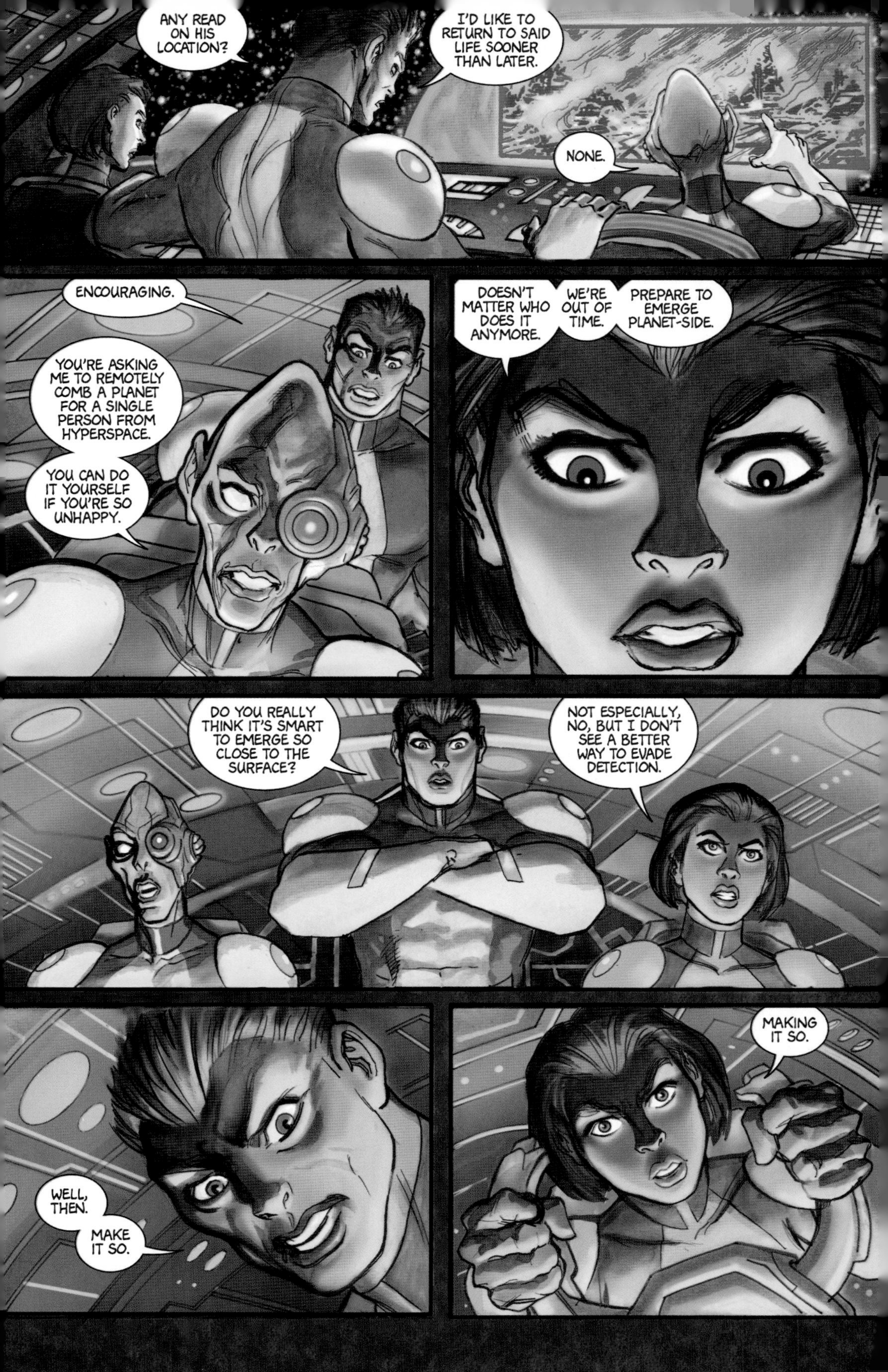
ANY READ ON HIS LOCATION?
I'D LIKE TO RETURN TO SAID LIFE SOONER THAN LATER.
NONE.
ENCOURAGING.
YOU'RE ASKING ME TO REMOTELY COMB A PLANET FOR A SINGLE PERSON FROM HYPERSPACE.
YOU CAN DO IT YOURSELF IF YOU'RE SO UNHAPPY.
DOESN'T MATTER WHO DOES IT ANYMORE.
WE'RE OUT OF TIME.
PREPARE TO EMERGE PLANET-SIDE.
DO YOU REALLY THINK IT'S SMART TO EMERGE SO CLOSE TO THE SURFACE?
NOT ESPECIALLY, NO, BUT I DON'T SEE A BETTER WAY TO EVADE DETECTION.
WELL, THEN.
MAKE IT SO.
MAKING IT SO.

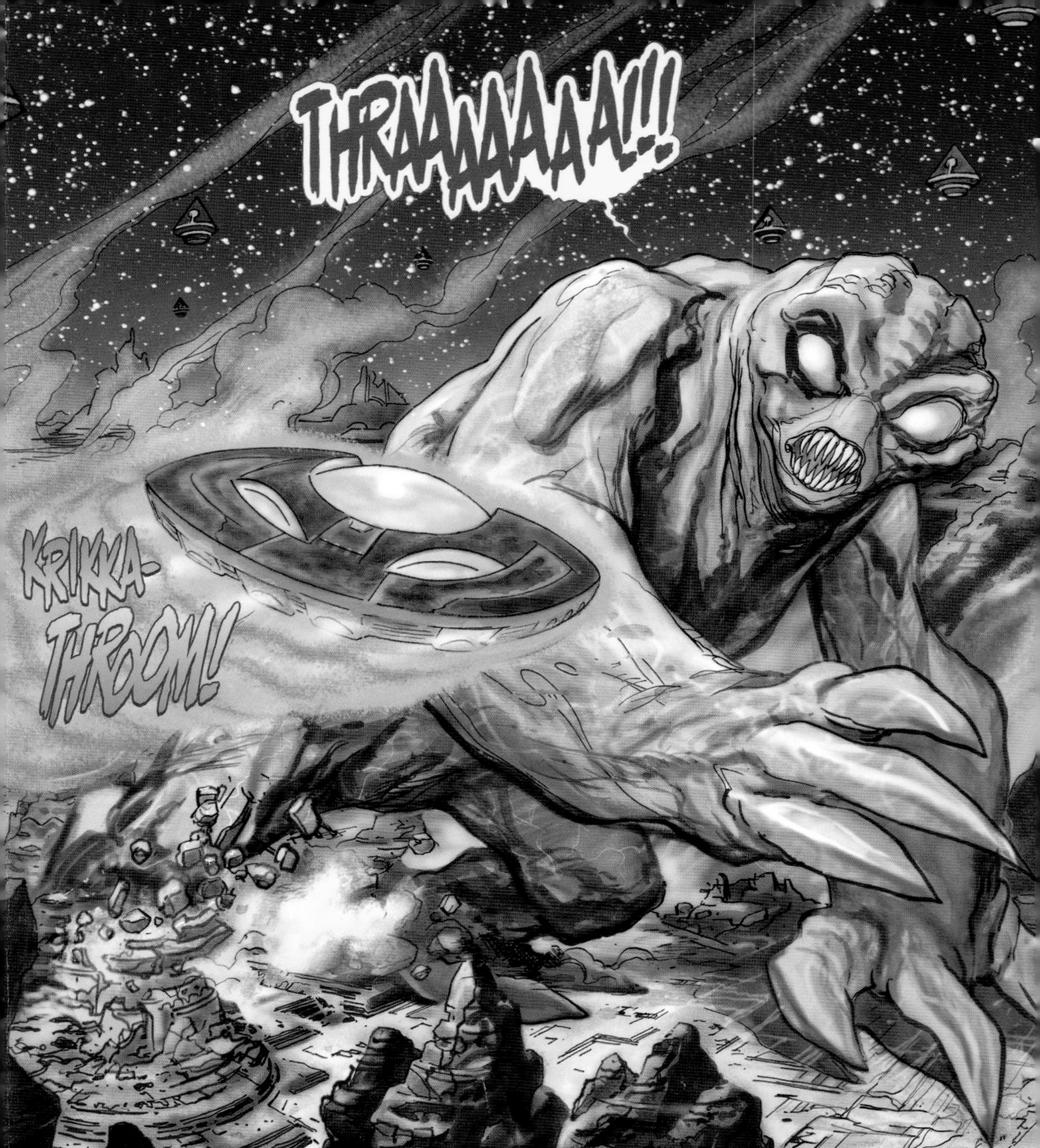
THRAAAAAAA!!!
KRIKKA-
THROOM!
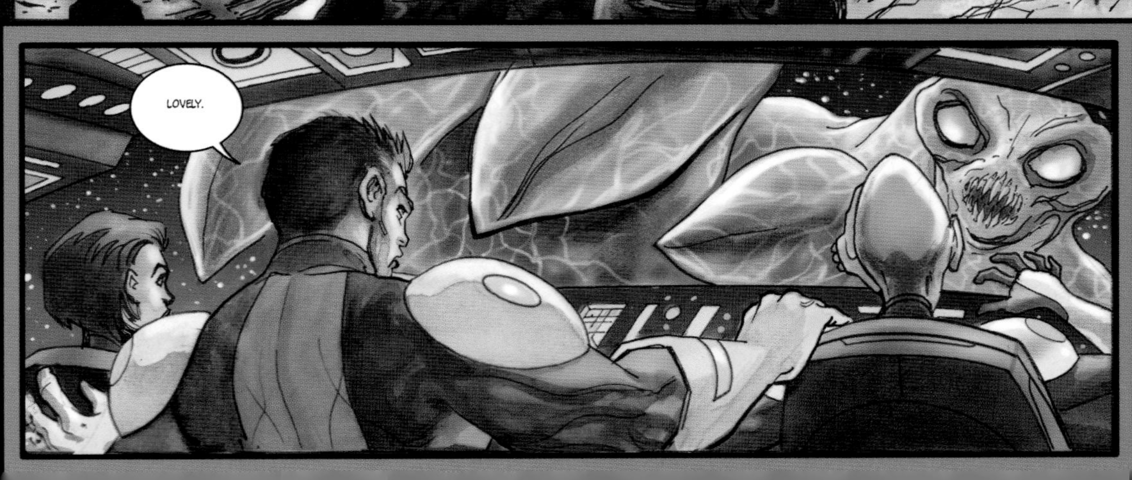
LOVELY.

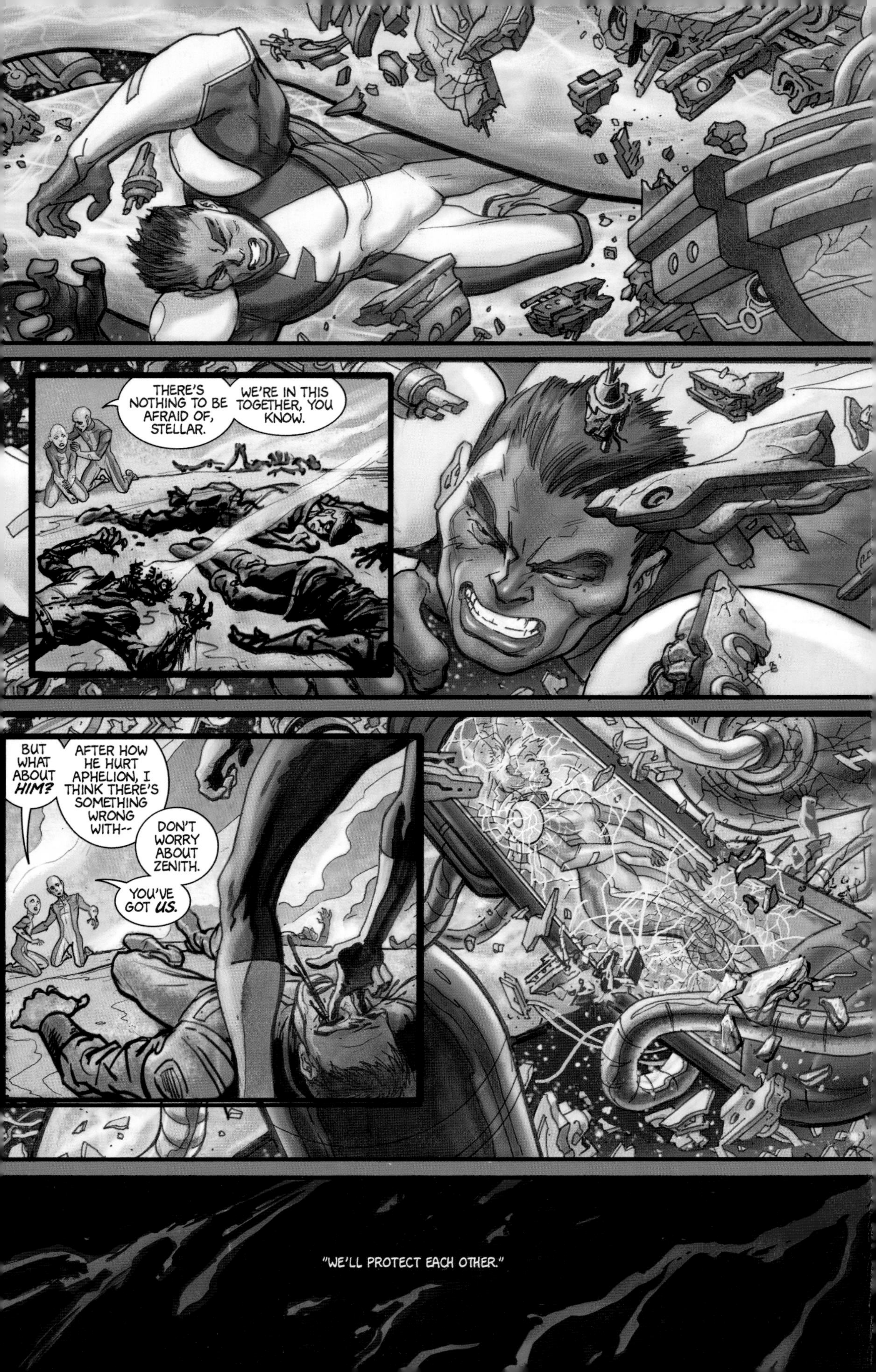
THERE'S NOTHING TO BE AFRAID OF, STELLAR.
WE'RE IN THIS TOGETHER, YOU KNOW.
BUT WHAT ABOUT HIM?
AFTER HOW HE HURT APHELION, I THINK THERE'S SOMETHING WRONG WITH--
DON'T WORRY ABOUT ZENITH.
YOU'VE GOT US.
"WE'LL PROTECT EACH OTHER."

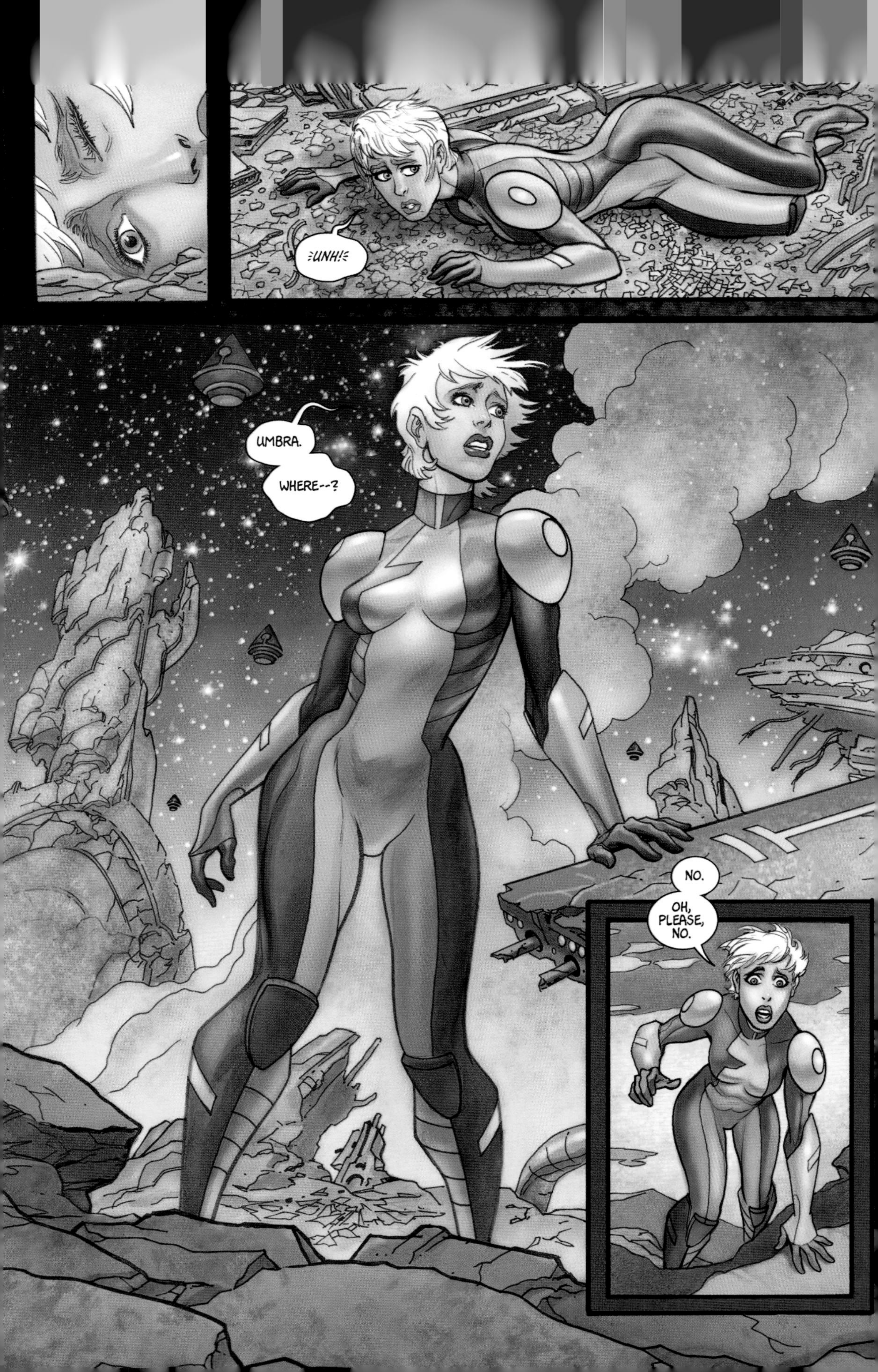
UNH!
UMBRA.
WHERE--?
NO.
OH, PLEASE, NO.

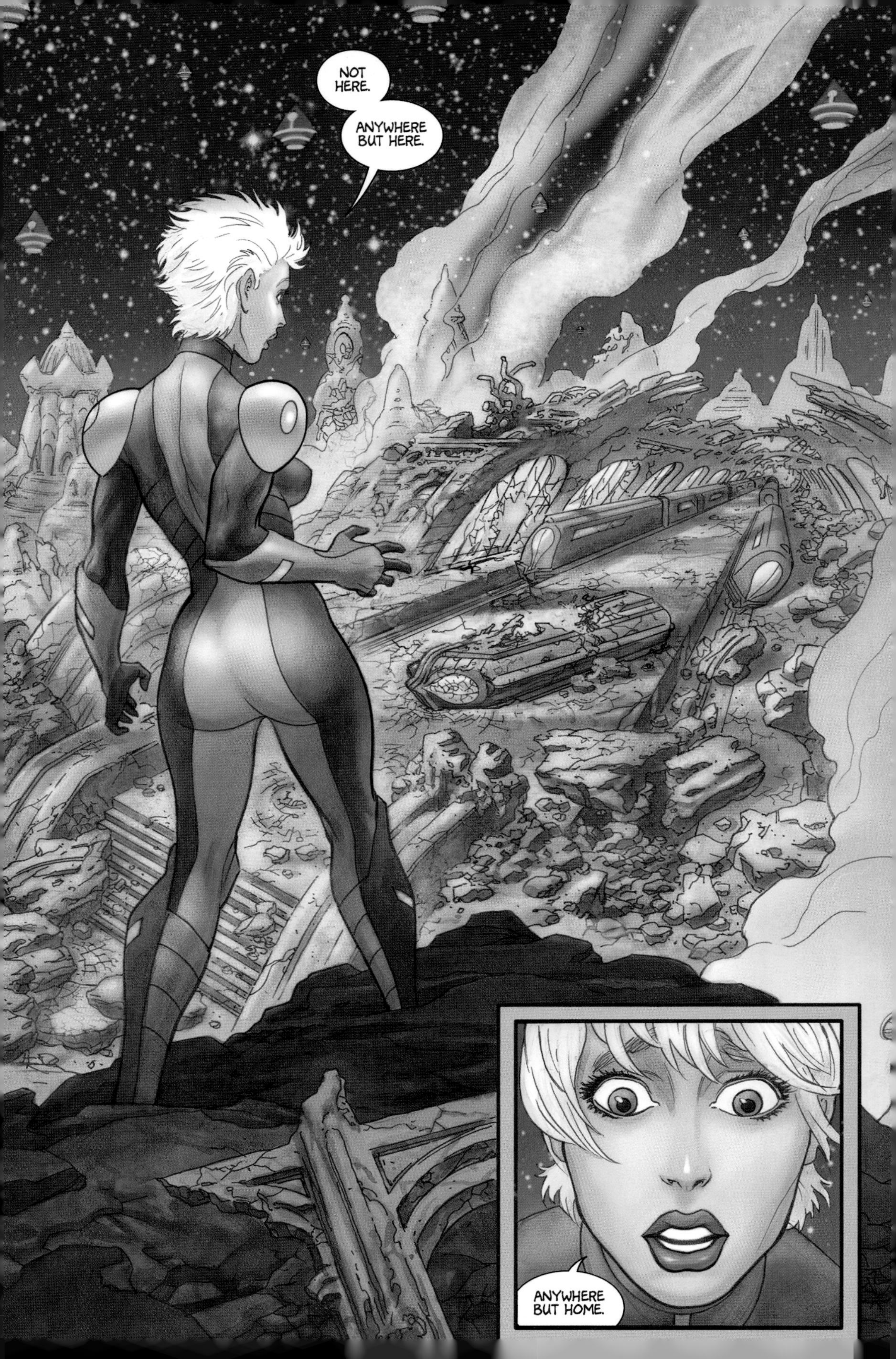
NOT HERE.
ANYWHERE BUT HERE.
ANYWHERE BUT HOME.

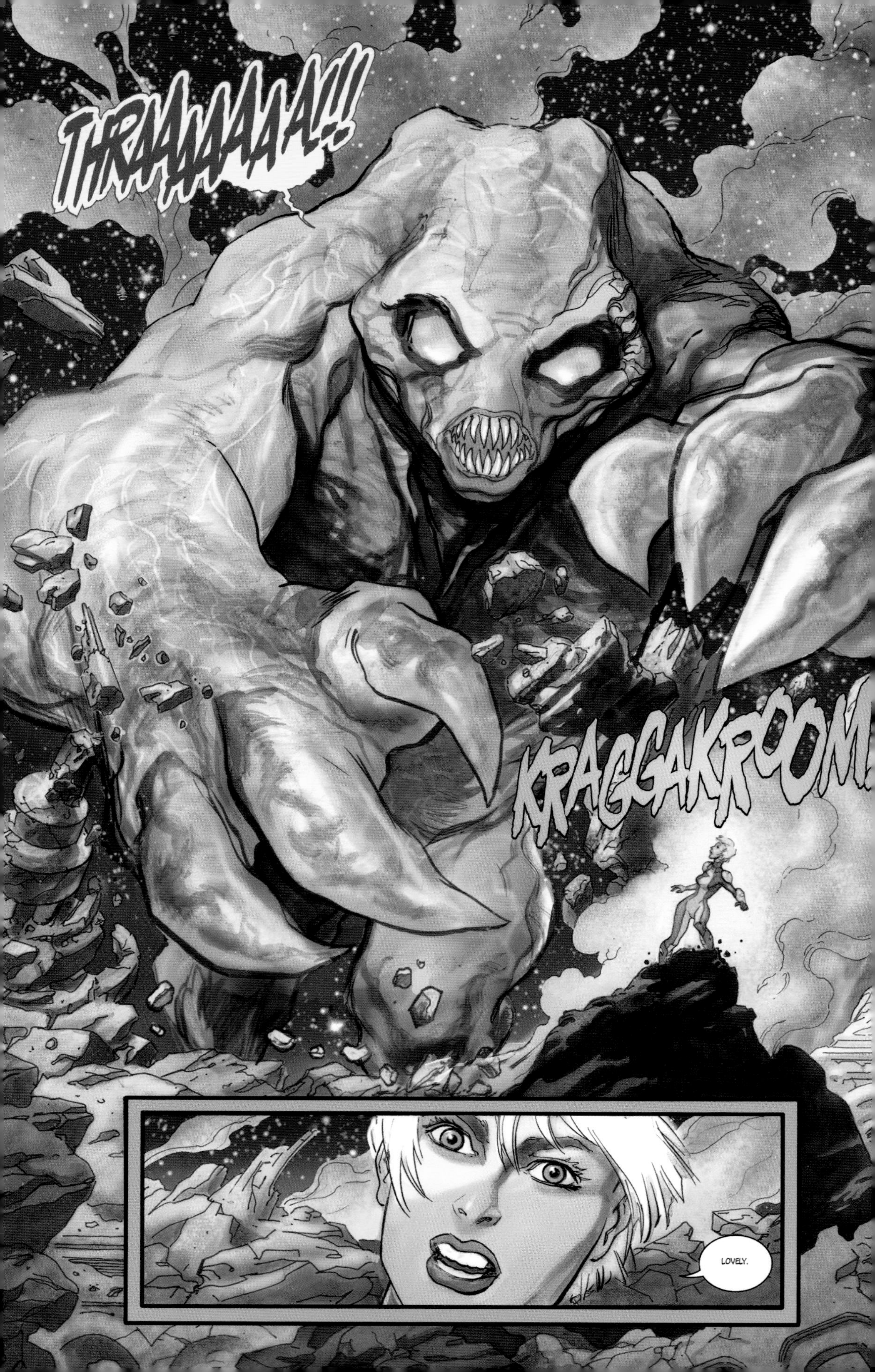
THRAAAAAA!!!
KRAGGAKROOM
LOVELY.

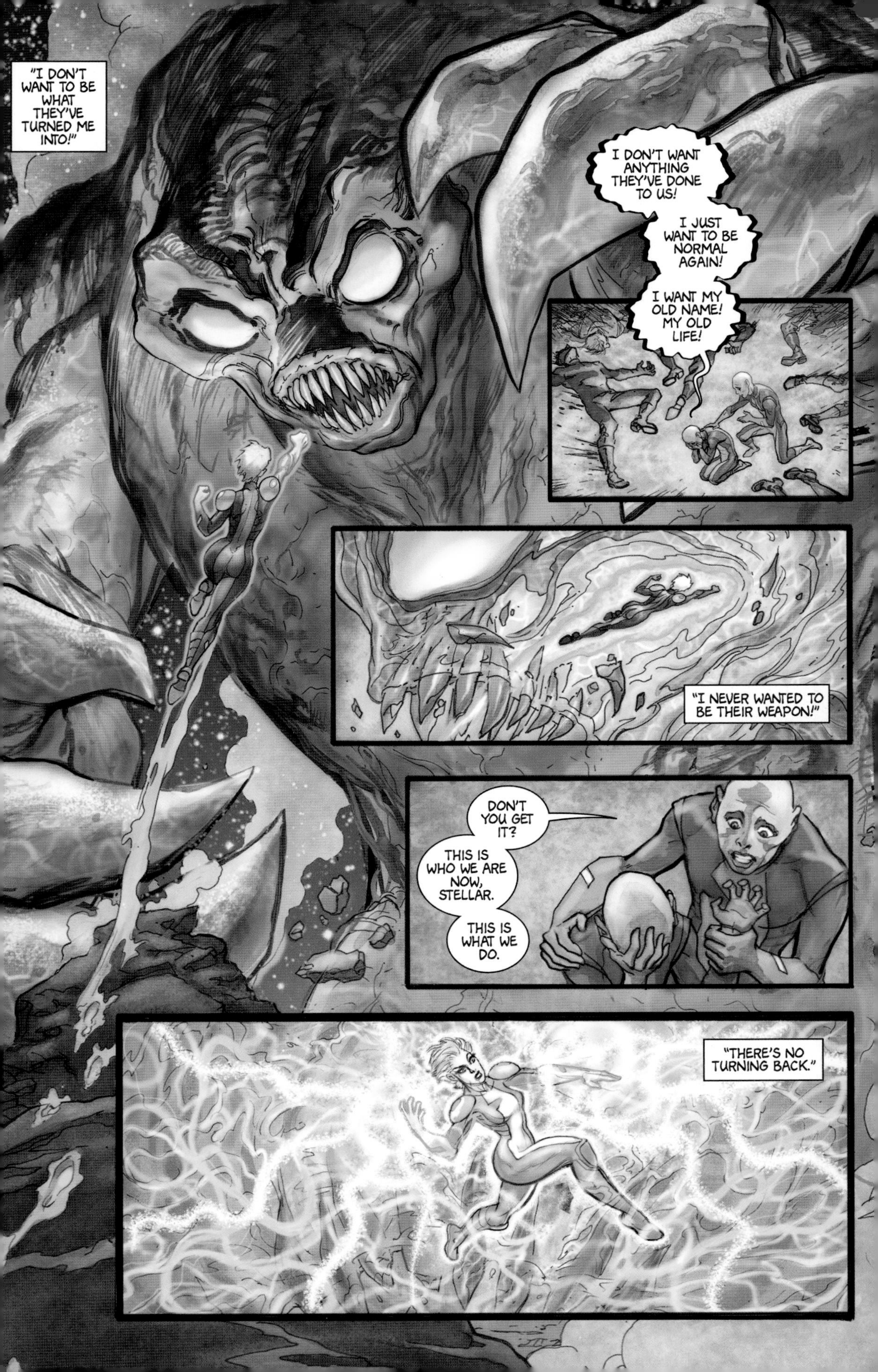
"I DON'T WANT TO BE WHAT THEY'VE TURNED ME INTO!"
I DON'T WANT ANYTHING THEY'VE DONE TO US!
I JUST WANT TO BE NORMAL AGAIN!
I WANT MY OLD NAME! MY OLD LIFE!
"I NEVER WANTED TO BE THEIR WEAPON!"
DON'T YOU GET IT?
THIS IS WHO WE ARE NOW, STELLAR.
THIS IS WHAT WE DO.
"THERE'S NO TURNING BACK."

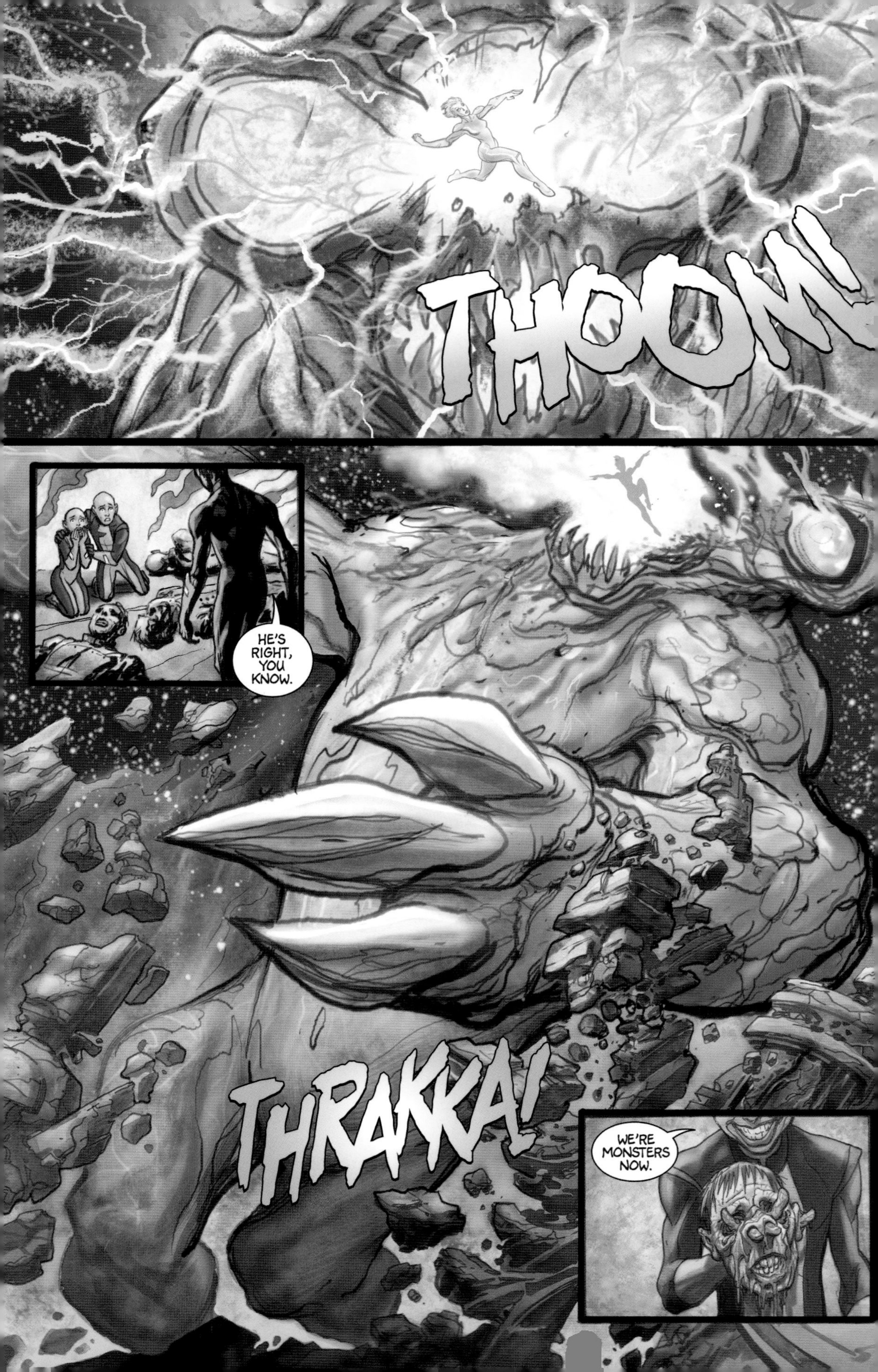
THOOM!
HE'S RIGHT, YOU KNOW.
THRAKKA!
WE'RE MONSTERS NOW.

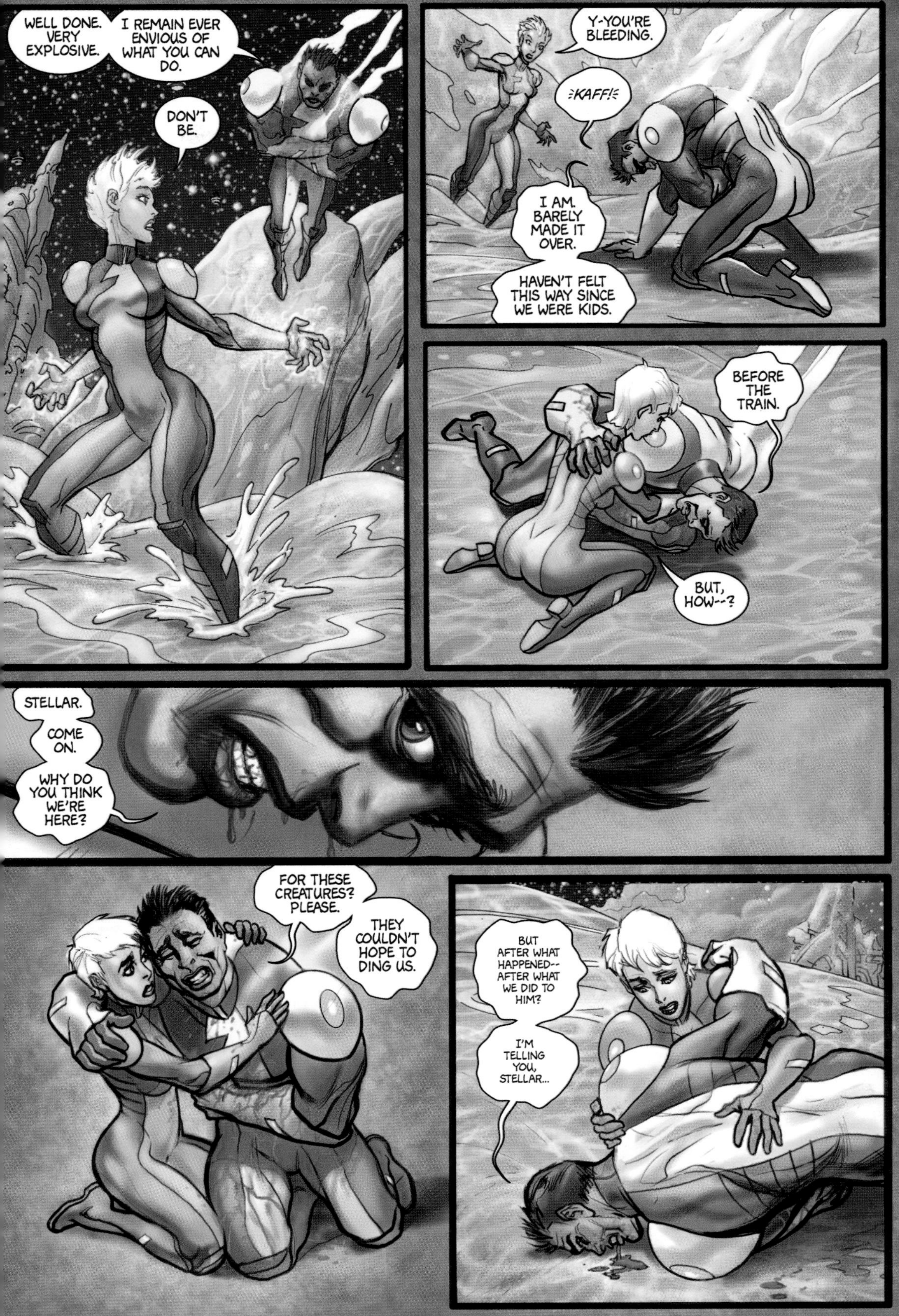
WELL DONE. VERY EXPLOSIVE.
I REMAIN EVER ENVIOUS OF WHAT YOU CAN DO.
DON'T BE.
Y-YOU'RE BLEEDING.
KAFF!
I AM. BARELY MADE IT OVER.
HAVEN'T FELT THIS WAY SINCE WE WERE KIDS.
BEFORE THE TRAIN.
BUT, HOW--?
STELLAR.
COME ON.
WHY DO YOU THINK WE'RE HERE?
FOR THESE CREATURES? PLEASE.
THEY COULDN'T HOPE TO DING US.
BUT AFTER WHAT HAPPENED-- AFTER WHAT WE DID TO HIM?
I'M TELLING YOU, STELLAR...

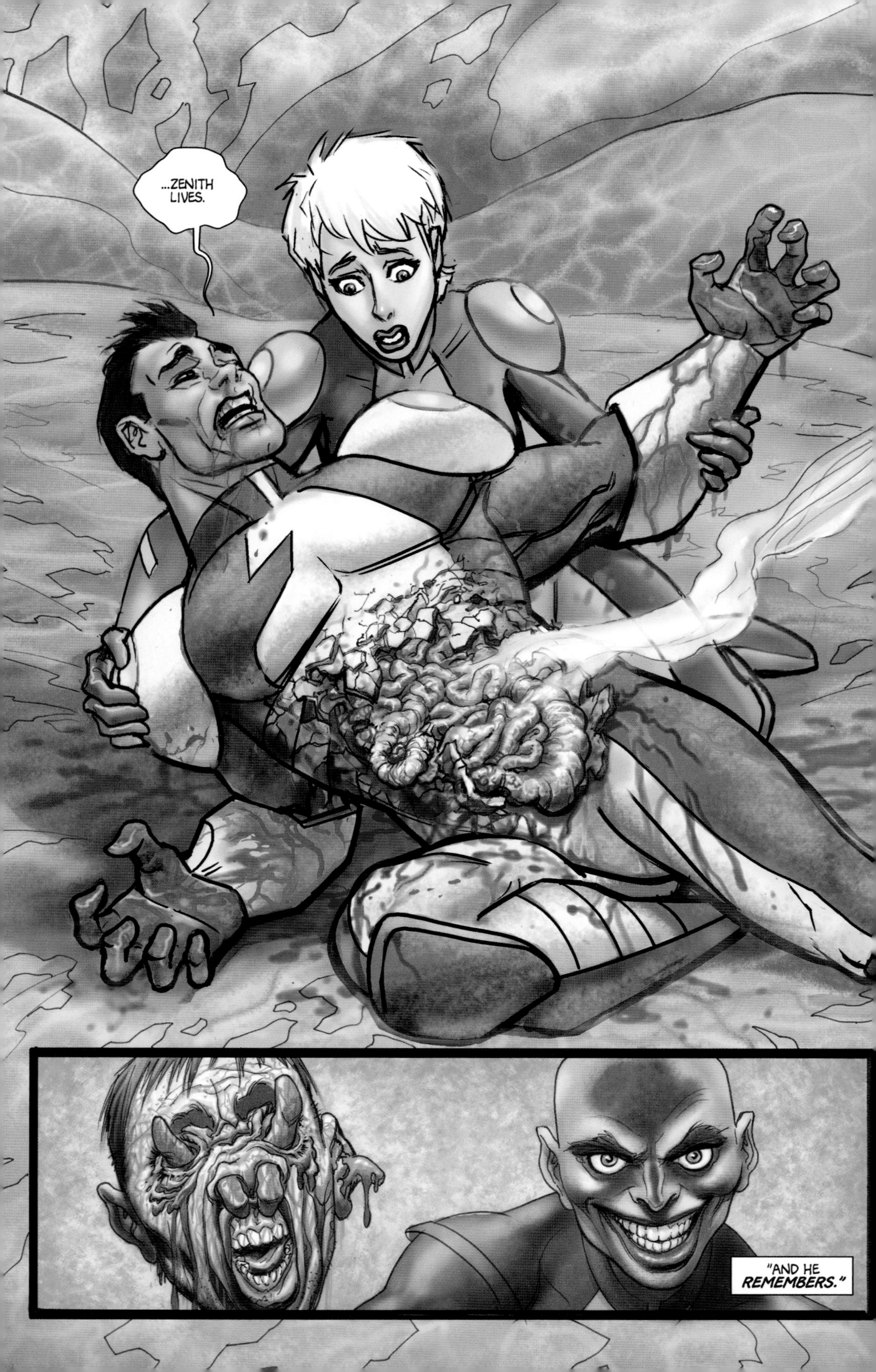
...ZENITH LIVES.
"AND HE REMEMBERS."

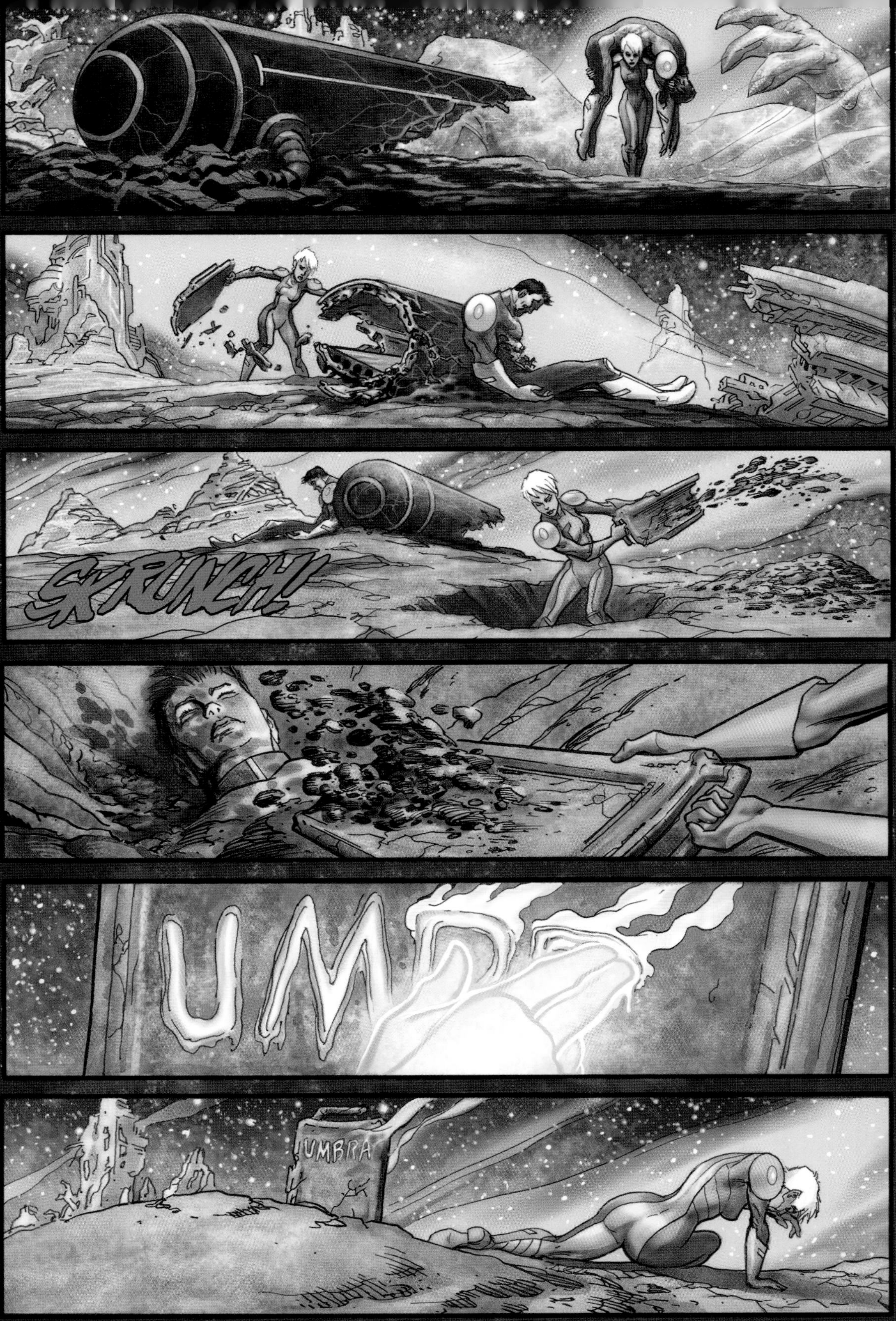
SKRUNCH!
UMB
UMBRA

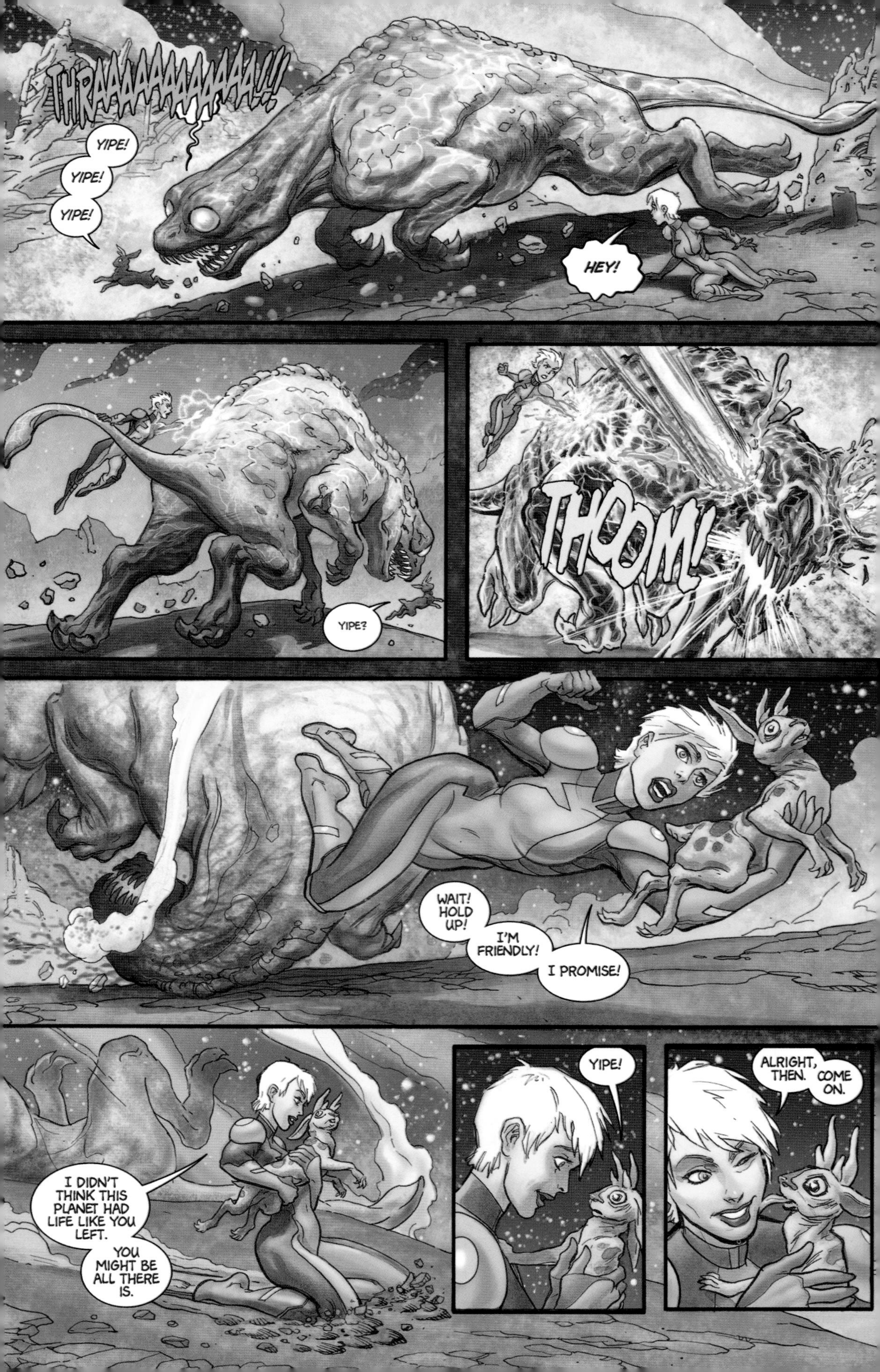
THRAAAAAAAAAA!!!
YIPE!
YIPE!
YIPE!
HEY!
YIPE?
THOOM!
WAIT! HOLD UP!
I'M FRIENDLY!
I PROMISE!
I DIDN'T THINK THIS PLANET HAD LIFE LIKE YOU LEFT.
YOU MIGHT BE ALL THERE IS.
YIPE!
ALRIGHT, THEN.
COME ON.

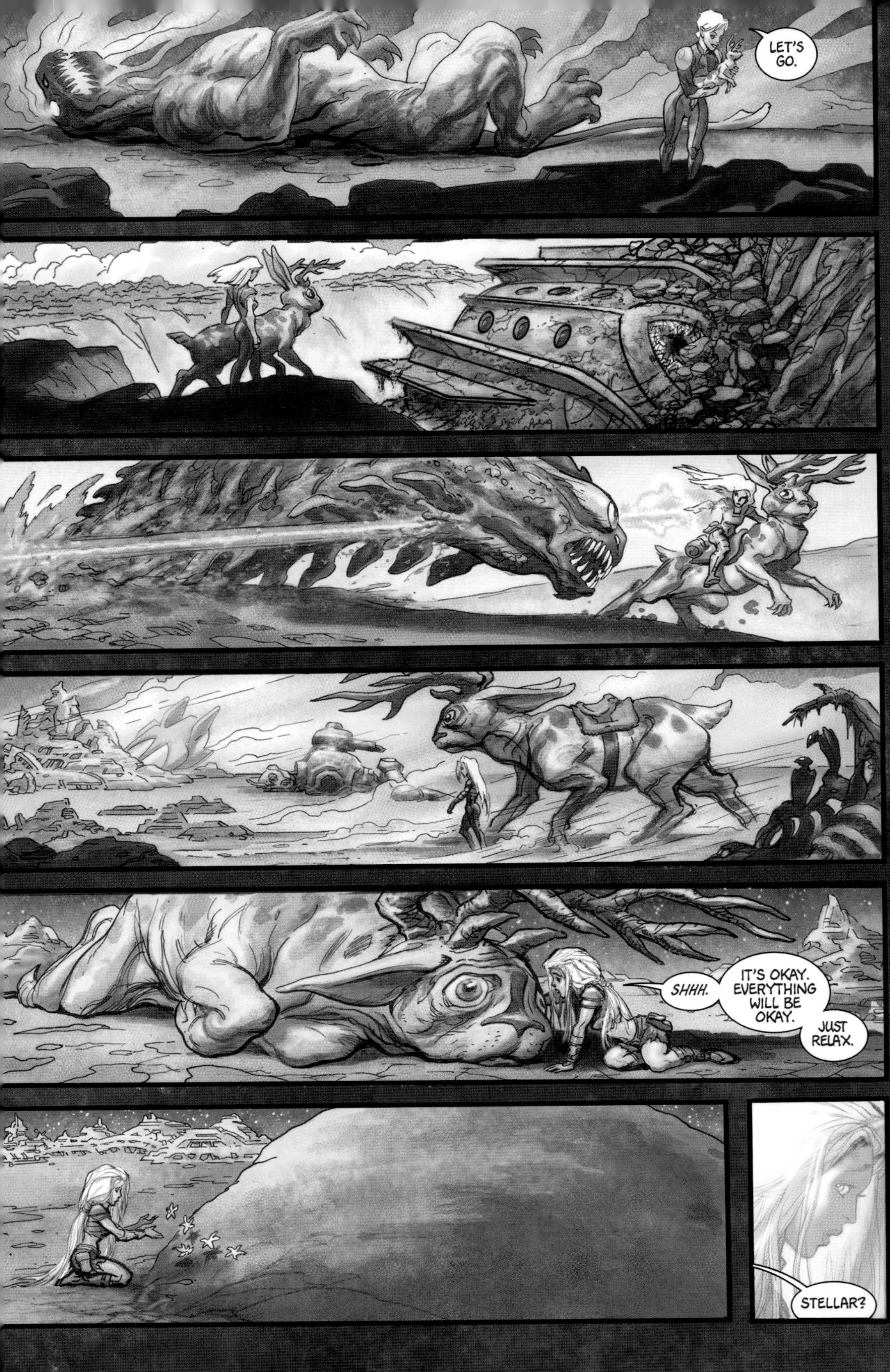
LET'S GO.
SHHH.
IT'S OKAY. EVERYTHING WILL BE OKAY.
JUST RELAX.
STELLAR?

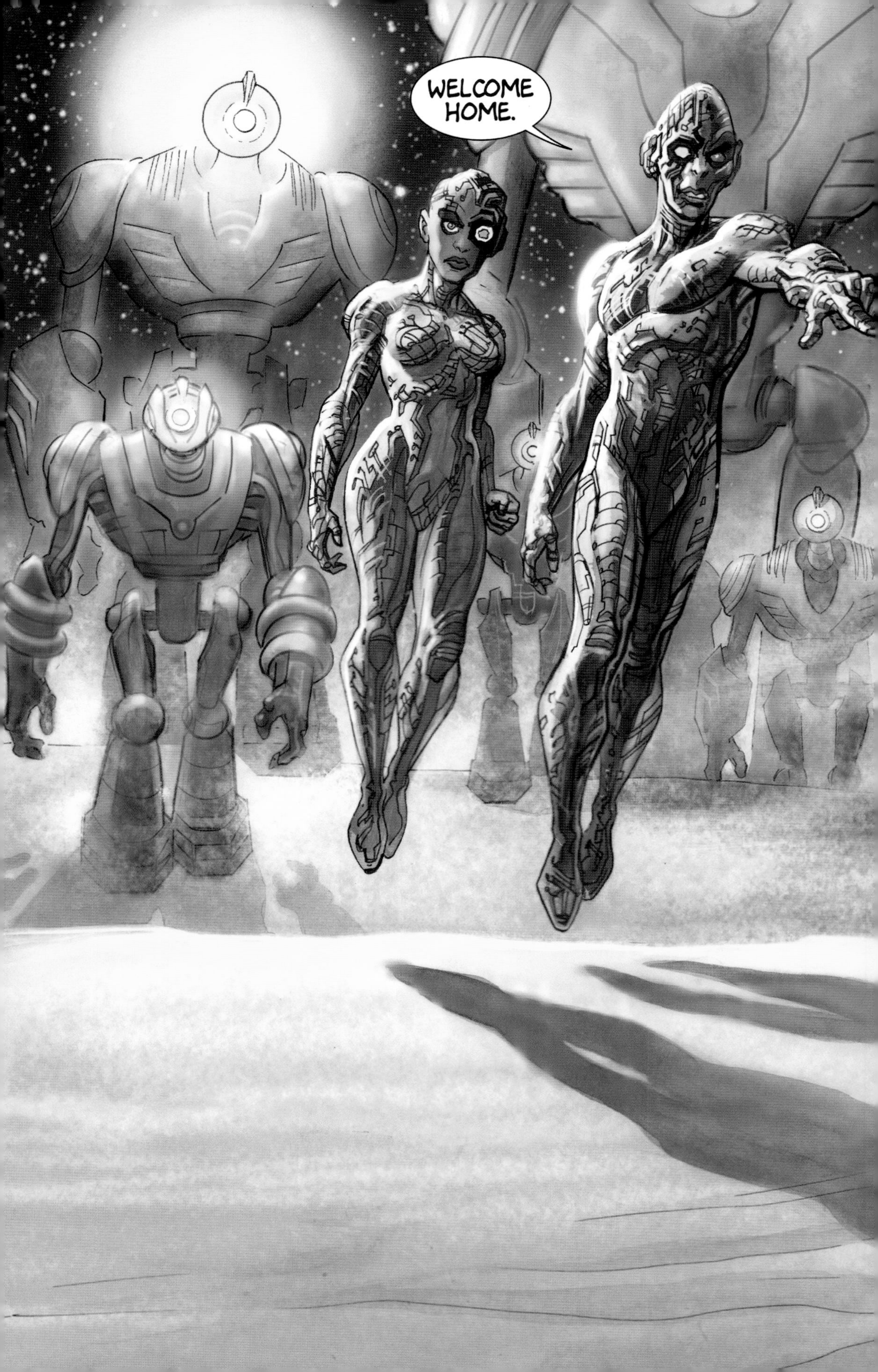
WELCOME HOME.

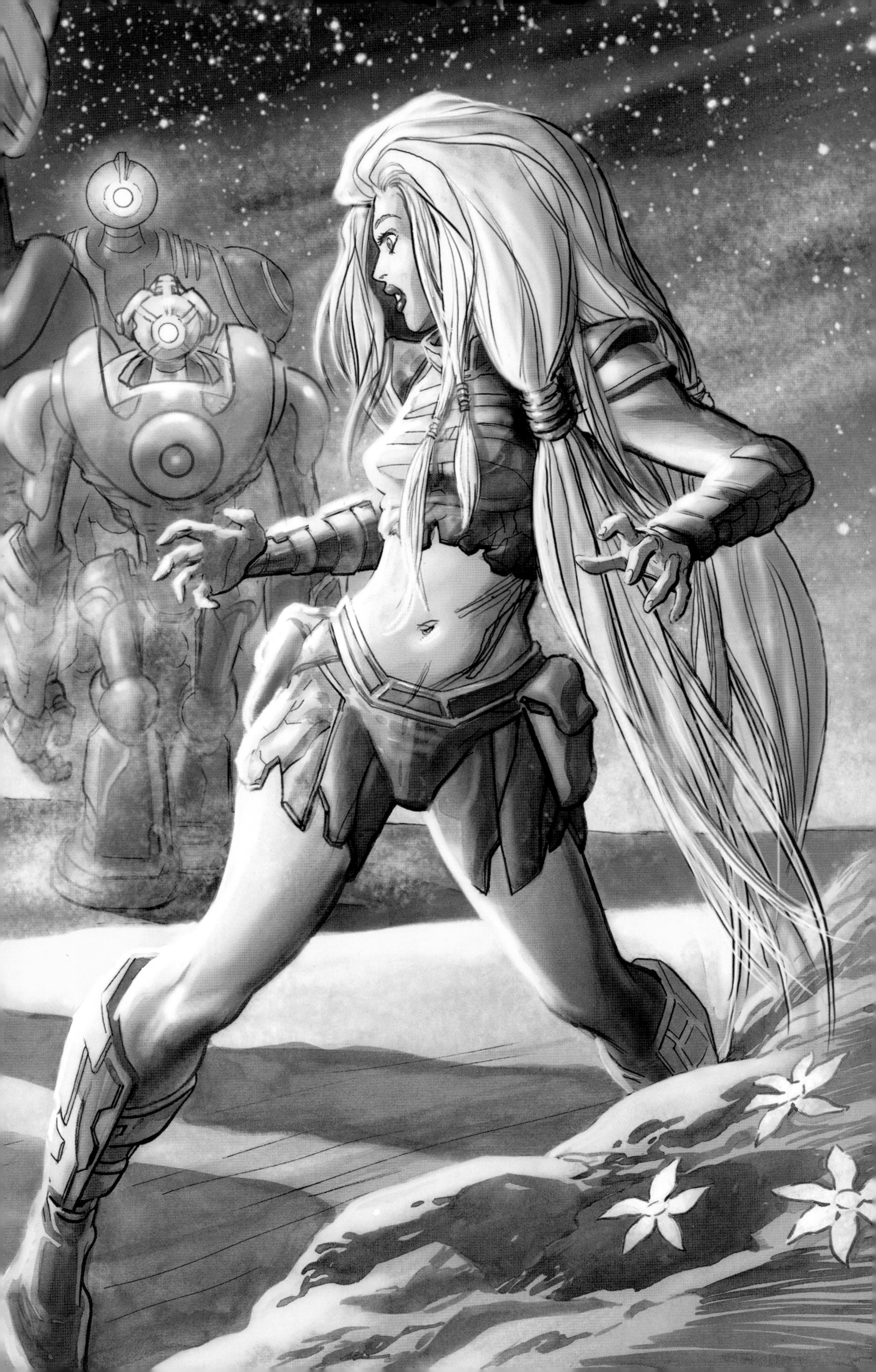

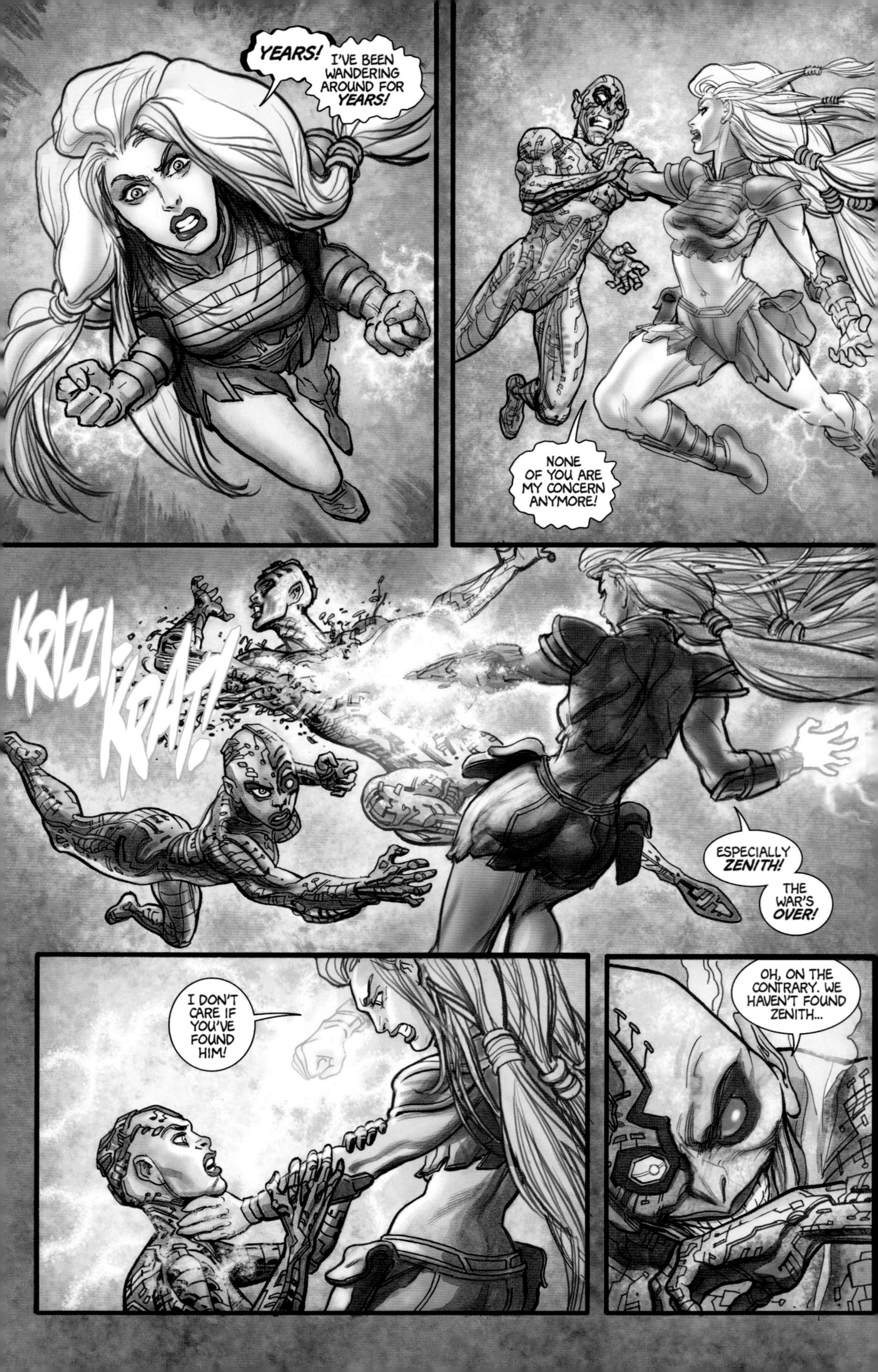
YEARS! I'VE BEEN WANDERING AROUND FOR YEARS!
NONE OF YOU ARE MY CONCERN ANYMORE!
KRIZZI-KRAT!
ESPECIALLY ZENITH!
THE WAR'S OVER!
I DON'T CARE IF YOU'VE FOUND HIM!
OH, ON THE CONTRARY. WE HAVEN'T FOUND ZENITH...

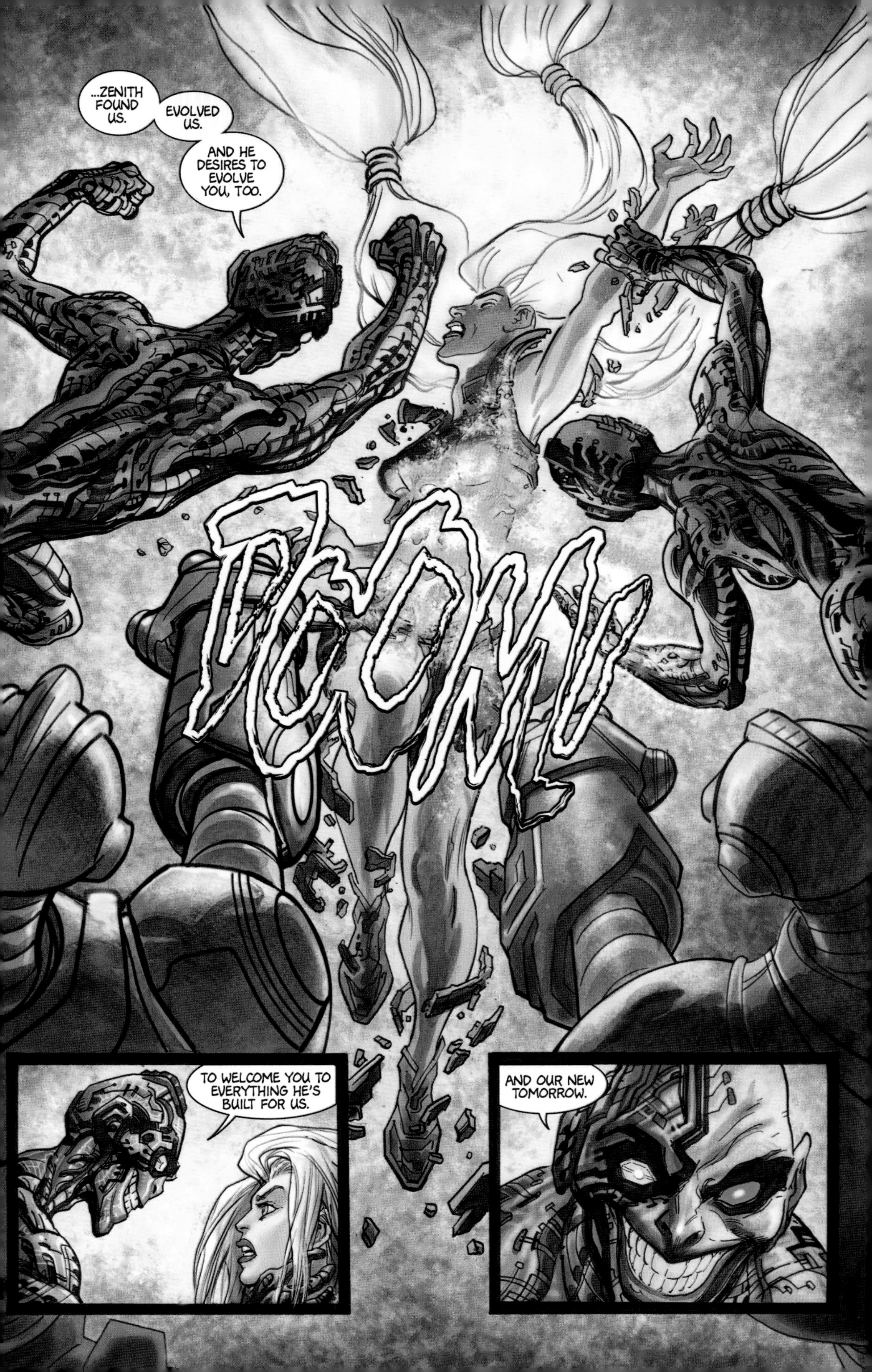
...ZENITH FOUND US.
EVOLVED US.
AND HE DESIRES TO EVOLVE YOU, TOO.
TO WELCOME YOU TO EVERYTHING HE'S BUILT FOR US.
AND OUR NEW TOMORROW.

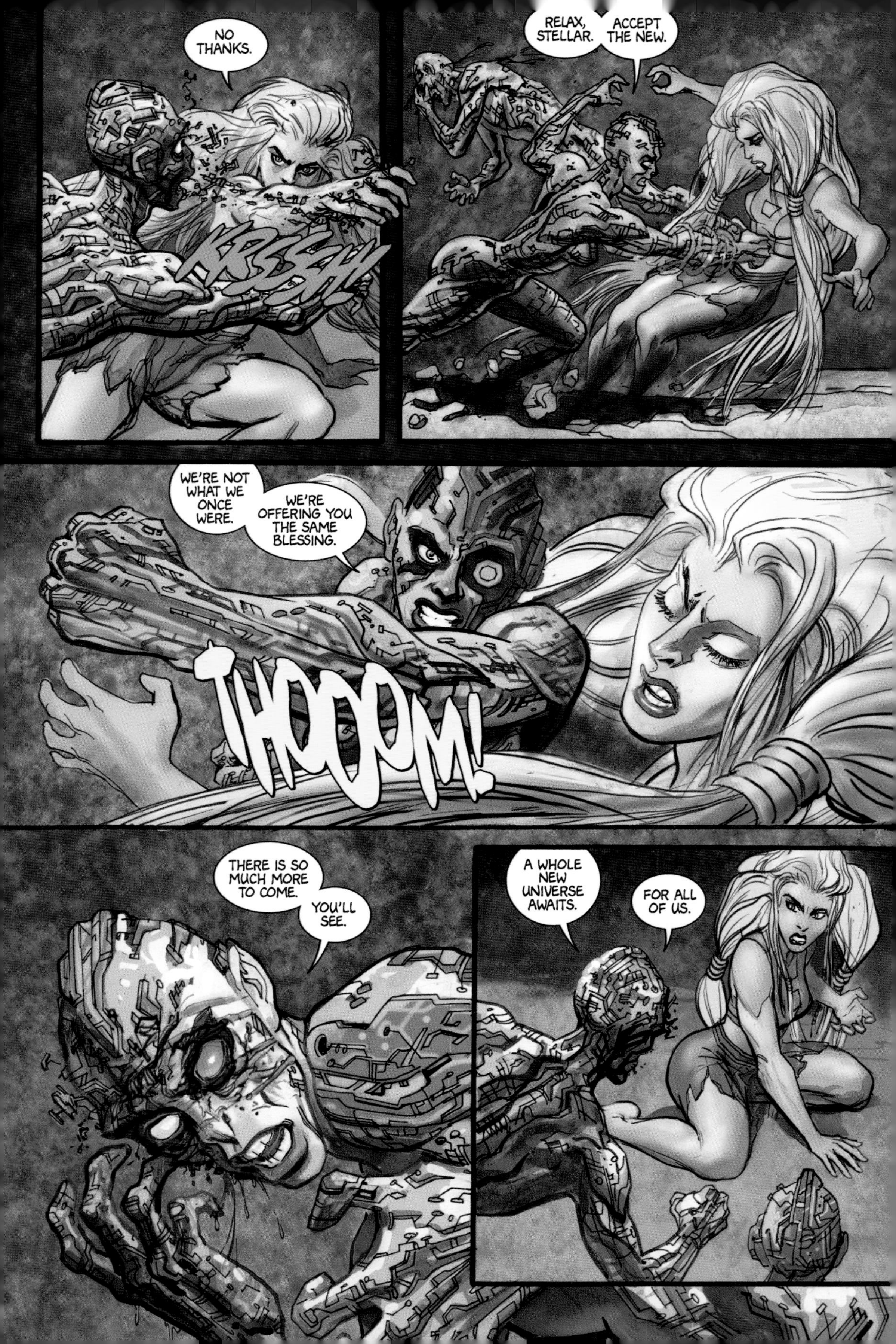
NO THANKS.
KRSSSH!
RELAX, STELLAR.
ACCEPT THE NEW.
WE'RE NOT WHAT WE ONCE WERE.
WE'RE OFFERING YOU THE SAME BLESSING.
THOOOM!
THERE IS SO MUCH MORE TO COME.
YOU'LL SEE.
A WHOLE NEW UNIVERSE AWAITS.
FOR ALL OF US.

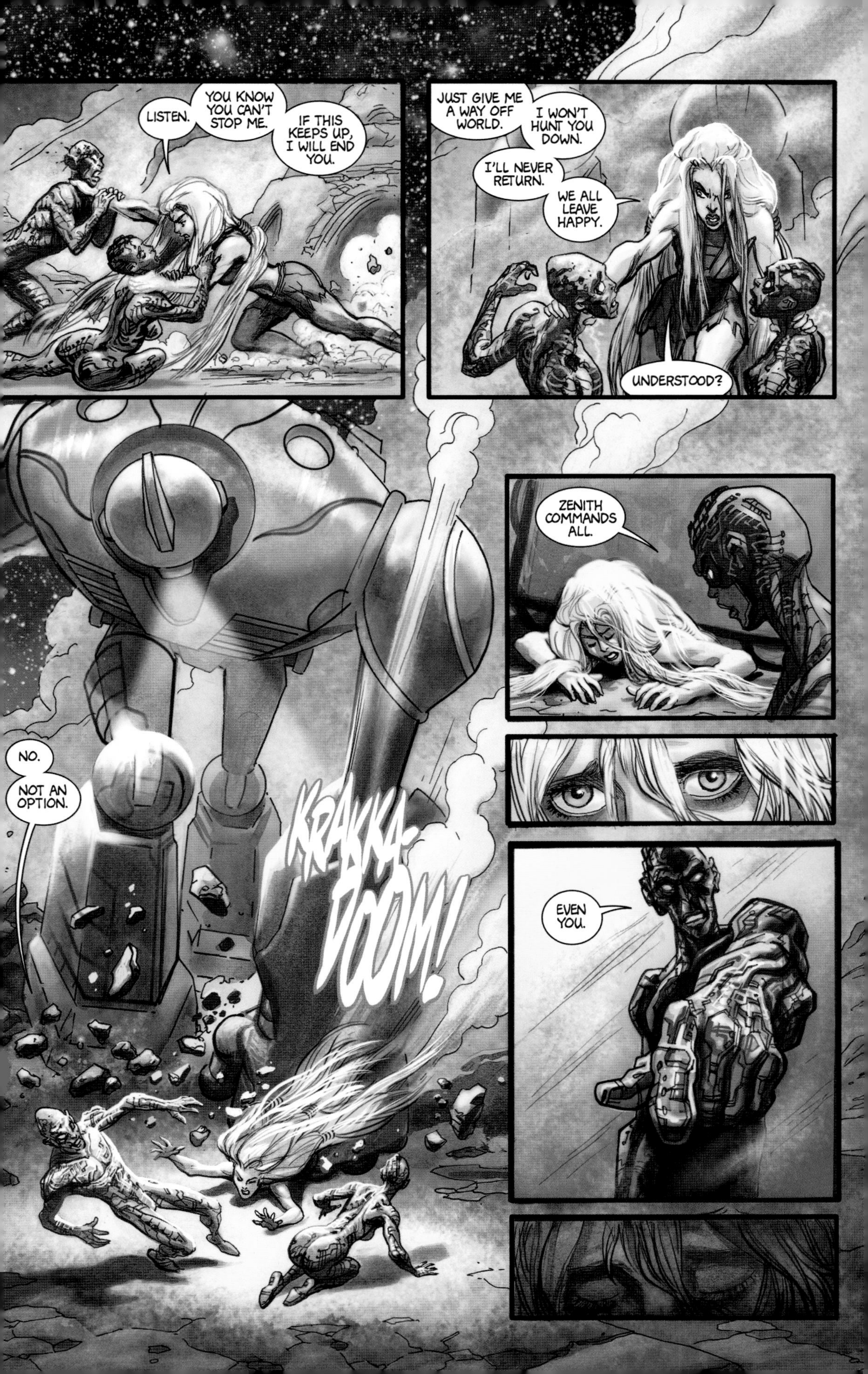
LISTEN.
YOU KNOW YOU CAN'T STOP ME.
IF THIS KEEPS UP, I WILL END YOU.
JUST GIVE ME A WAY OFF WORLD.
I WON'T HUNT YOU DOWN.
I'LL NEVER RETURN.
WE ALL LEAVE HAPPY.
UNDERSTOOD?
NO.
NOT AN OPTION.
KRAKKA-DOOM!
ZENITH COMMANDS ALL.
EVEN YOU.

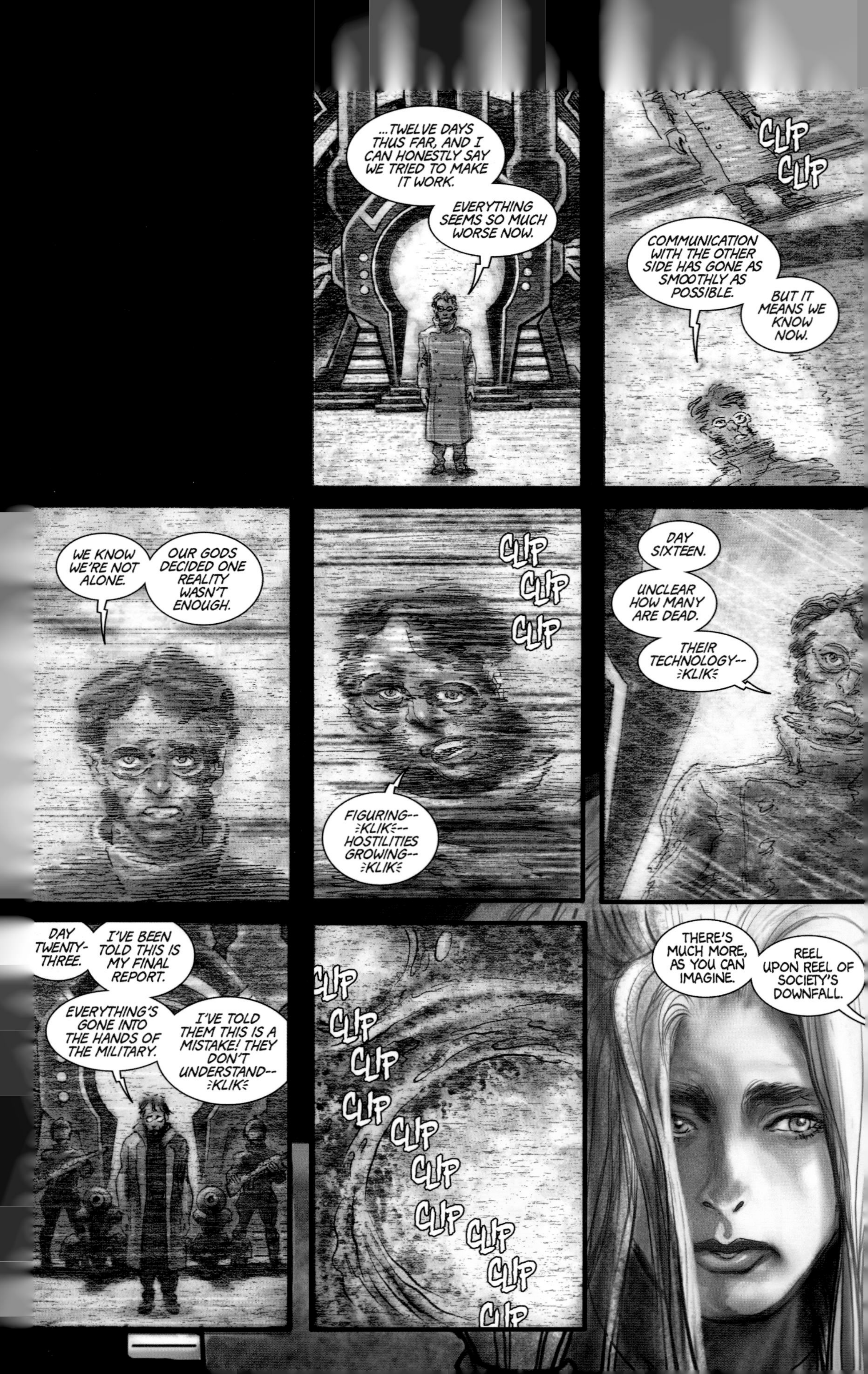
...TWELVE DAYS THUS FAR, AND I CAN HONESTLY SAY WE TRIED TO MAKE IT WORK.
EVERYTHING SEEMS SO MUCH WORSE NOW.
CLIP CLIP
COMMUNICATION WITH THE OTHER SIDE HAS GONE AS SMOOTHLY AS POSSIBLE.
BUT IT MEANS WE KNOW NOW.
WE KNOW WE'RE NOT ALONE.
OUR GODS DECIDED ONE REALITY WASN'T ENOUGH.
CLIP CLIP CLIP
FIGURING-- KLIK-- HOSTILITIES GROWING-- KLIK
DAY SIXTEEN.
UNCLEAR HOW MANY ARE DEAD.
THEIR TECHNOLOGY-- KLIK
DAY TWENTY-THREE.
I'VE BEEN TOLD THIS IS MY FINAL REPORT.
EVERYTHING'S GONE INTO THE HANDS OF THE MILITARY.
I'VE TOLD THEM THIS IS A MISTAKE! THEY DON'T UNDERSTAND-- KLIK
CLIP CLIP CLIP CLIP CLIP CLIP CLIP CLIP CLIP CLIP
THERE'S MUCH MORE, AS YOU CAN IMAGINE.
REEL UPON REEL OF SOCIETY'S DOWNFALL.

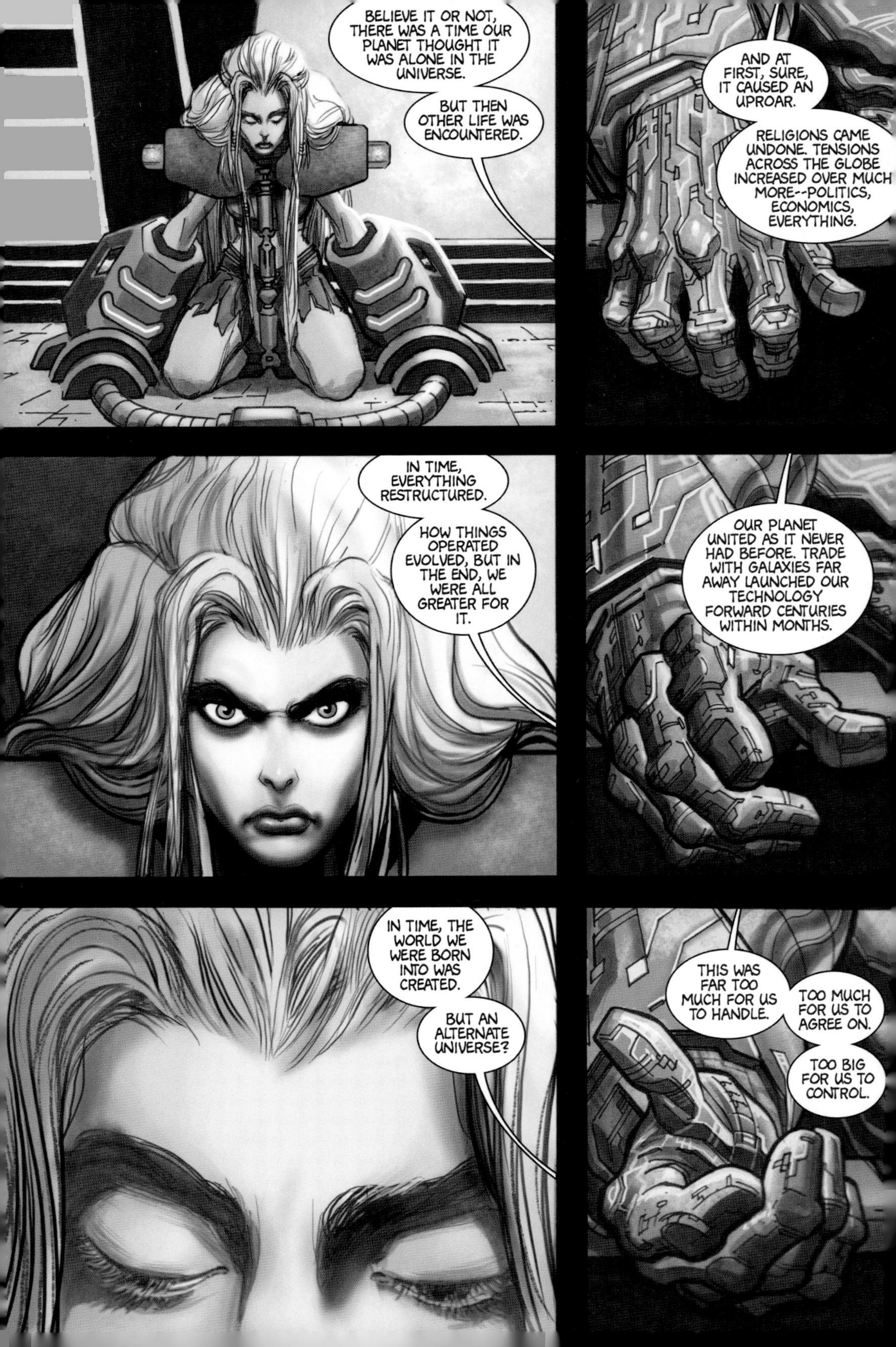
BELIEVE IT OR NOT, THERE WAS A TIME OUR PLANET THOUGHT IT WAS ALONE IN THE UNIVERSE.
BUT THEN OTHER LIFE WAS ENCOUNTERED.
AND AT FIRST, SURE, IT CAUSED AN UPROAR.
RELIGIONS CAME UNDONE. TENSIONS ACROSS THE GLOBE INCREASED OVER MUCH MORE--POLITICS, ECONOMICS, EVERYTHING.
IN TIME, EVERYTHING RESTRUCTURED.
HOW THINGS OPERATED EVOLVED, BUT IN THE END, WE WERE ALL GREATER FOR IT.
OUR PLANET UNITED AS IT NEVER HAD BEFORE. TRADE WITH GALAXIES FAR AWAY LAUNCHED OUR TECHNOLOGY FORWARD CENTURIES WITHIN MONTHS.
IN TIME, THE WORLD WE WERE BORN INTO WAS CREATED.
BUT AN ALTERNATE UNIVERSE?
THIS WAS FAR TOO MUCH FOR US TO HANDLE.
TOO MUCH FOR US TO AGREE ON.
TOO BIG FOR US TO CONTROL.

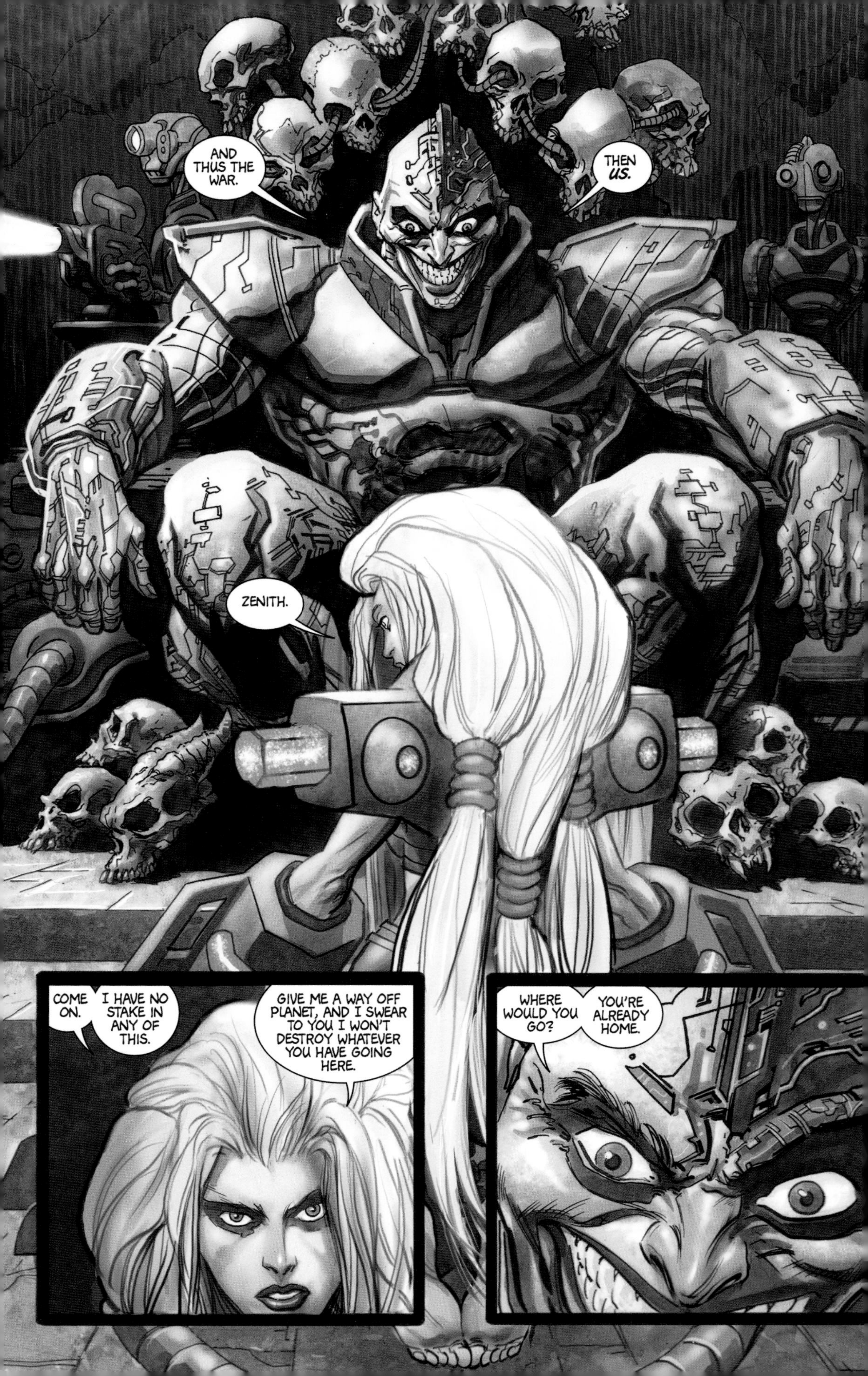
AND THUS THE WAR.
THEN US.
ZENITH.
COME ON.
I HAVE NO STAKE IN ANY OF THIS.
GIVE ME A WAY OFF PLANET, AND I SWEAR TO YOU I WON'T DESTROY WHATEVER YOU HAVE GOING HERE.
WHERE WOULD YOU GO?
YOU'RE ALREADY HOME.

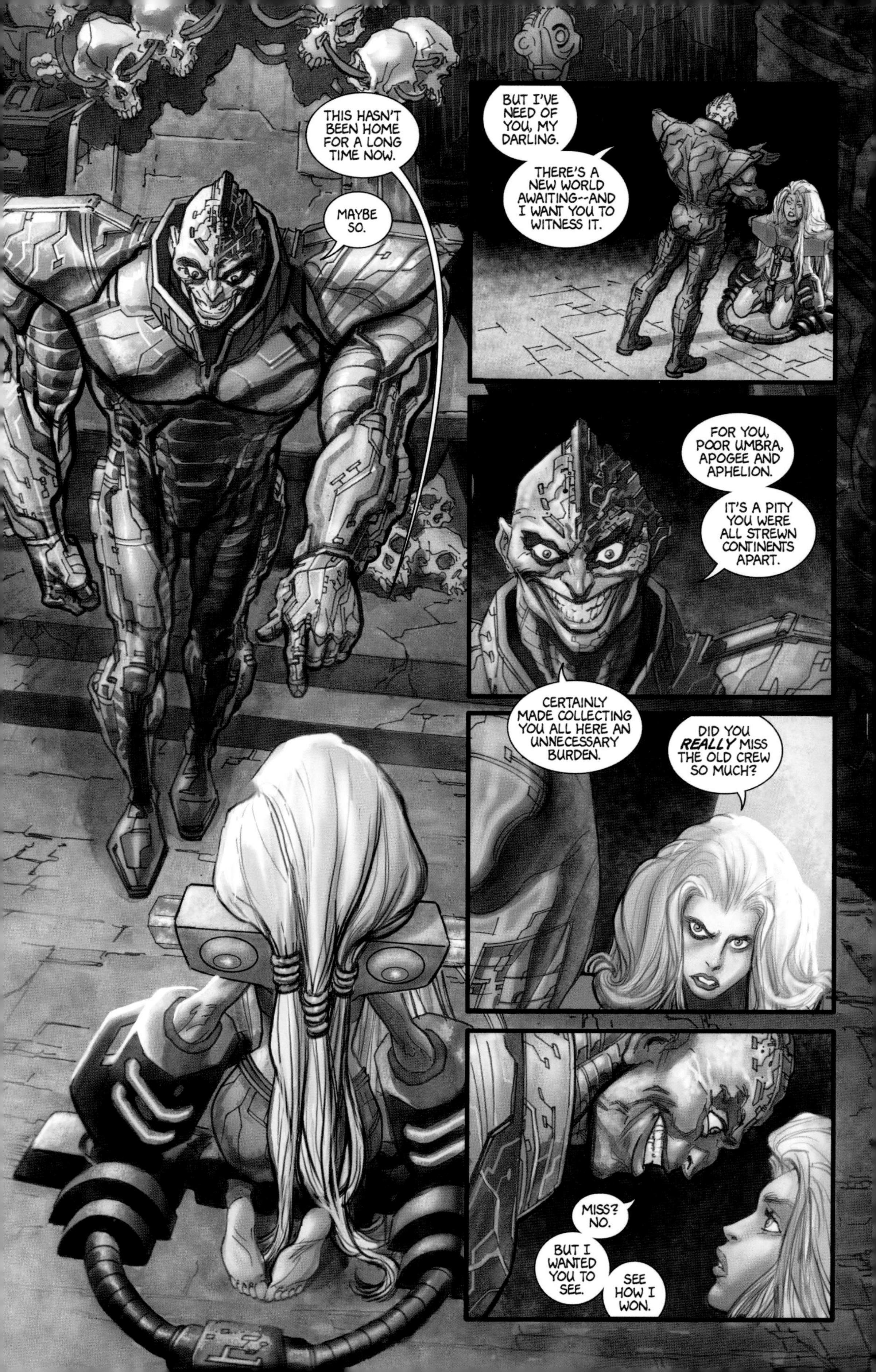
THIS HASN'T BEEN HOME FOR A LONG TIME NOW.
MAYBE SO.
BUT I'VE NEED OF YOU, MY DARLING.
THERE'S A NEW WORLD AWAITING--AND I WANT YOU TO WITNESS IT.
FOR YOU, POOR UMBRA, APOGEE AND APHELION.
IT'S A PITY YOU WERE ALL STREWN CONTINENTS APART.
CERTAINLY MADE COLLECTING YOU ALL HERE AN UNNECESSARY BURDEN.
DID YOU *REALLY* MISS THE OLD CREW SO MUCH?
MISS? NO.
BUT I WANTED YOU TO SEE.
SEE HOW I WON.

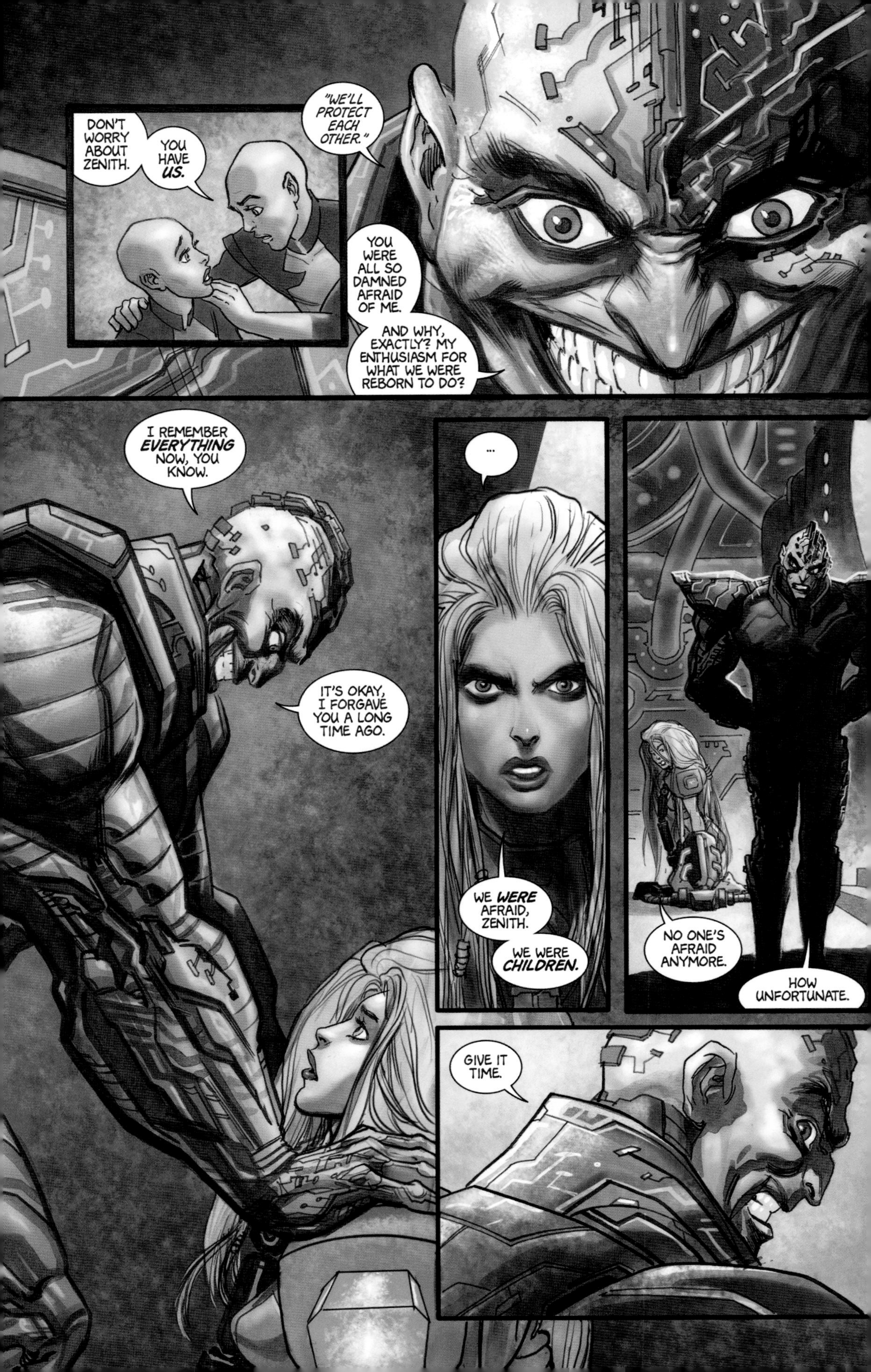
DON'T WORRY ABOUT ZENITH.
YOU HAVE US.
"WE'LL PROTECT EACH OTHER."
YOU WERE ALL SO DAMNED AFRAID OF ME.
AND WHY, EXACTLY? MY ENTHUSIASM FOR WHAT WE WERE REBORN TO DO?
I REMEMBER EVERYTHING NOW, YOU KNOW.
IT'S OKAY, I FORGAVE YOU A LONG TIME AGO.
...
WE WERE AFRAID, ZENITH.
WE WERE CHILDREN.
NO ONE'S AFRAID ANYMORE.
HOW UNFORTUNATE.
GIVE IT TIME.

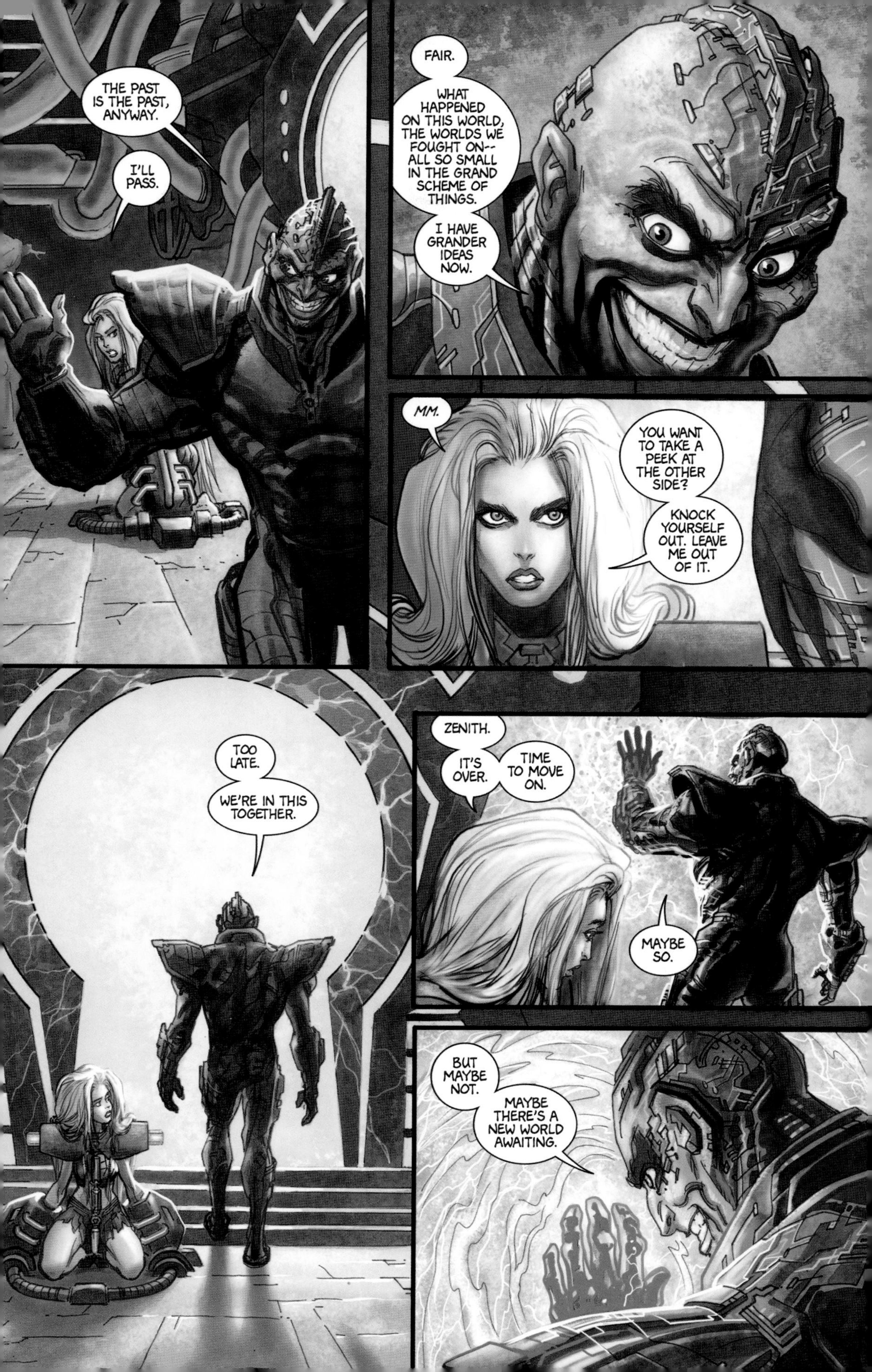
THE PAST IS THE PAST, ANYWAY.
I'LL PASS.
FAIR.
WHAT HAPPENED ON THIS WORLD, THE WORLDS WE FOUGHT ON-- ALL SO SMALL IN THE GRAND SCHEME OF THINGS.
I HAVE GRANDER IDEAS NOW.
MM.
YOU WANT TO TAKE A PEEK AT THE OTHER SIDE?
KNOCK YOURSELF OUT. LEAVE ME OUT OF IT.
TOO LATE.
WE'RE IN THIS TOGETHER.
ZENITH.
IT'S OVER.
TIME TO MOVE ON.
MAYBE SO.
BUT MAYBE NOT.
MAYBE THERE'S A NEW WORLD AWAITING.

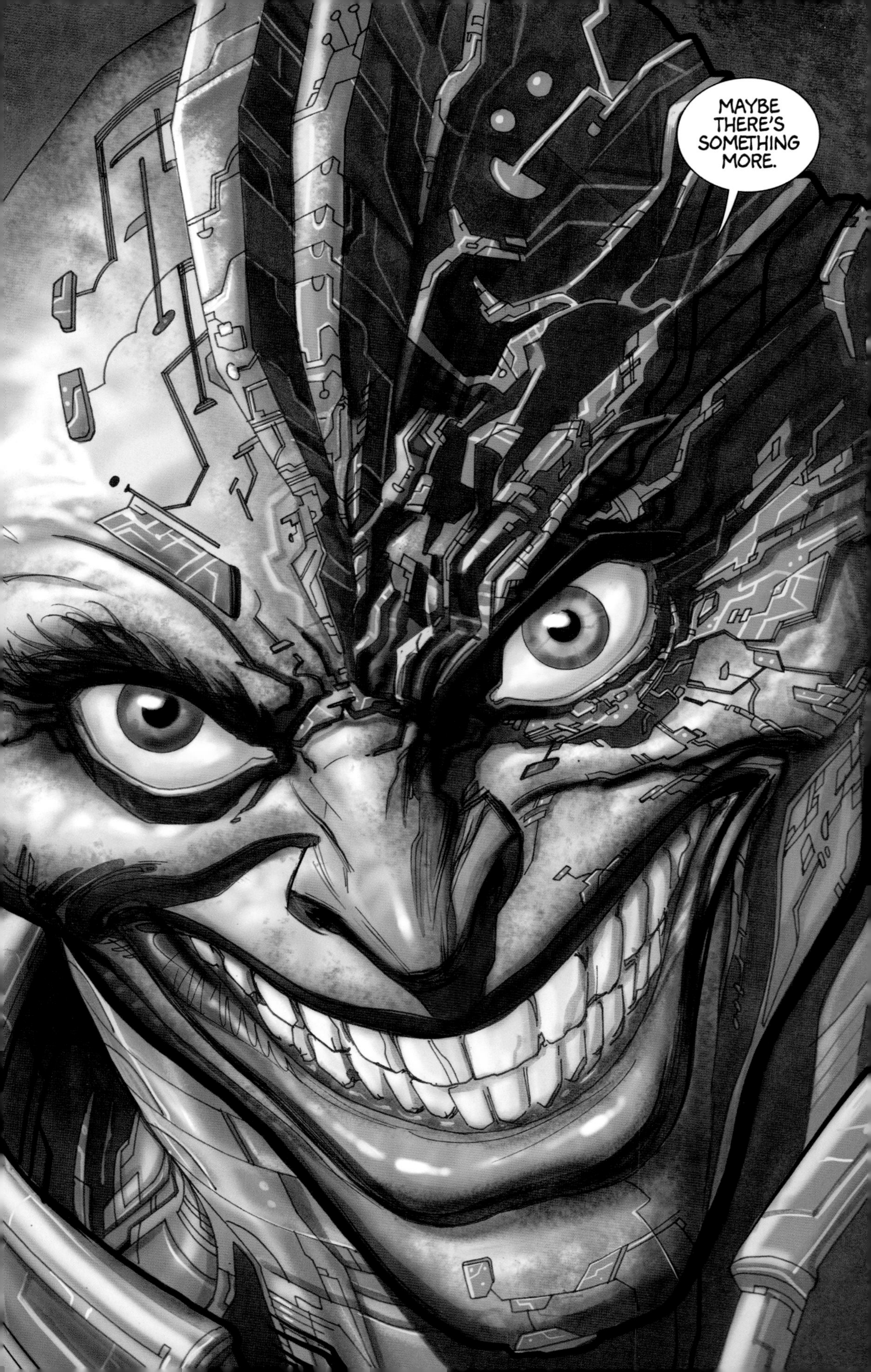
MAYBE THERE'S SOMETHING MORE.

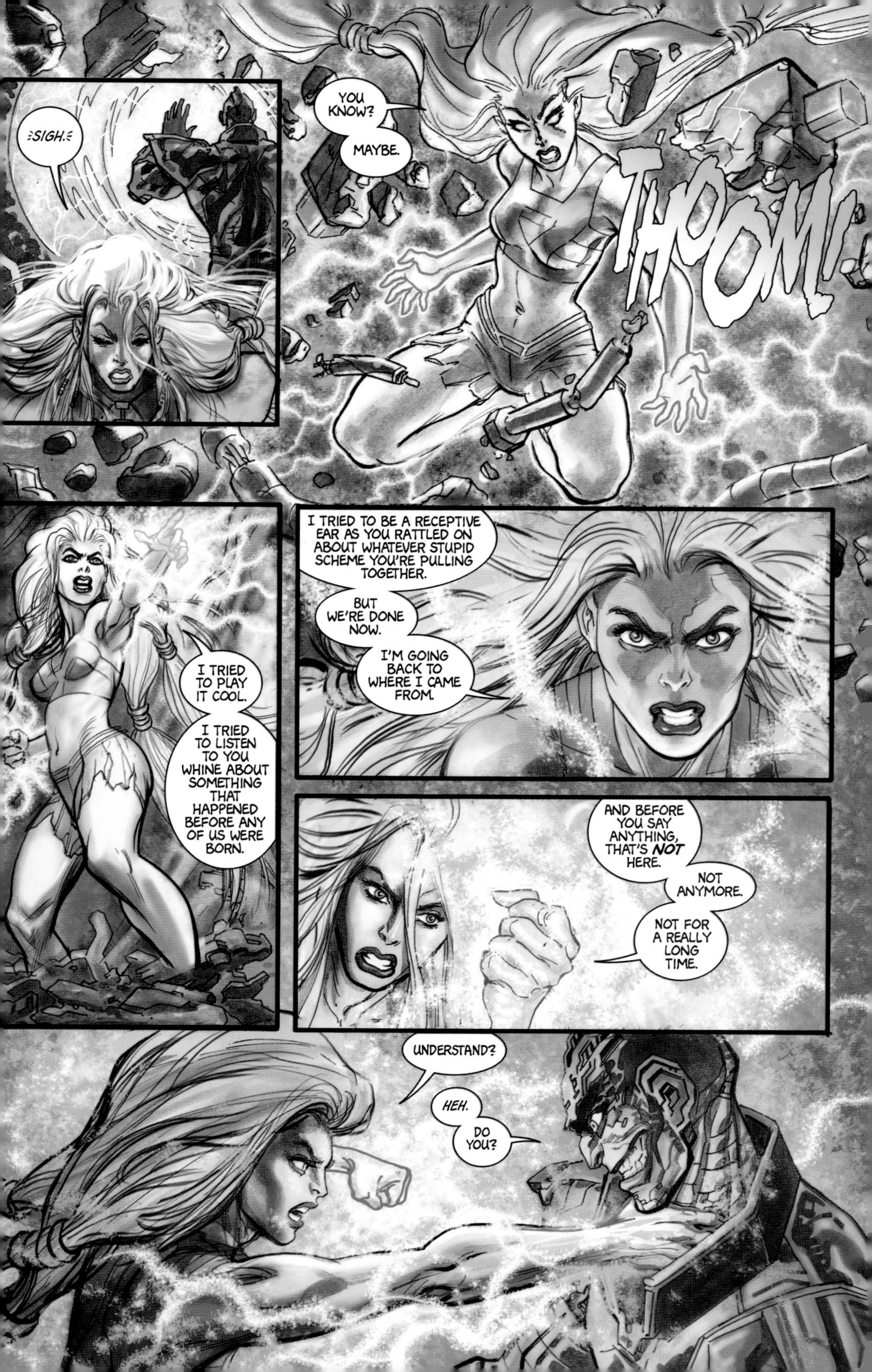

SIGH.
YOU KNOW?
MAYBE.
THOOM!
I TRIED TO BE A RECEPTIVE EAR AS YOU RATTLED ON ABOUT WHATEVER STUPID SCHEME YOU'RE PULLING TOGETHER.
BUT WE'RE DONE NOW.
I'M GOING BACK TO WHERE I CAME FROM.
I TRIED TO PLAY IT COOL.
I TRIED TO LISTEN TO YOU WHINE ABOUT SOMETHING THAT HAPPENED BEFORE ANY OF US WERE BORN.
AND BEFORE YOU SAY ANYTHING, THAT'S ***NOT*** HERE.
NOT ANYMORE.
NOT FOR A REALLY LONG TIME.
UNDERSTAND?
HEH.
DO YOU?

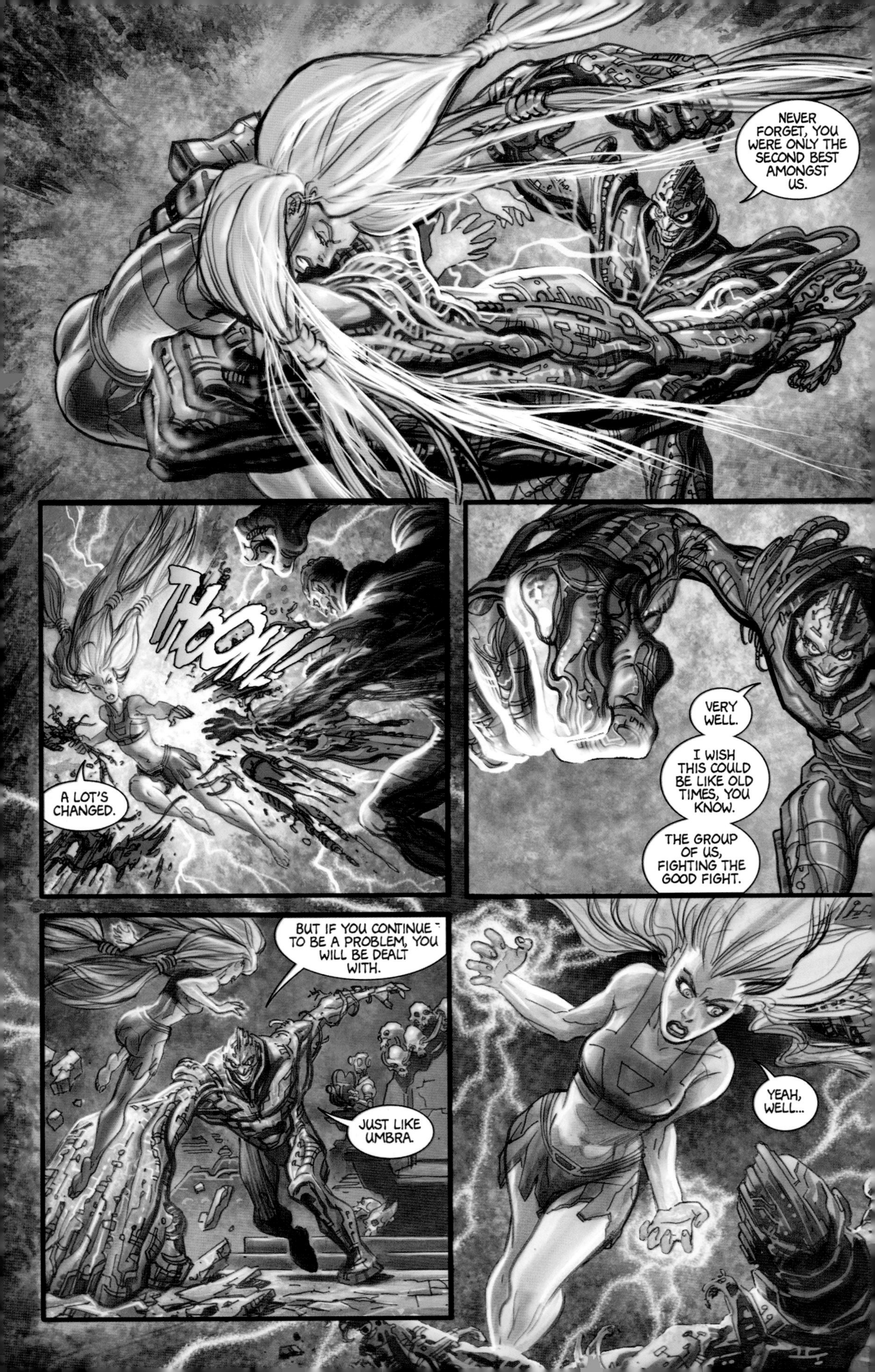
NEVER FORGET, YOU WERE ONLY THE SECOND BEST AMONGST US.
THOOM!
A LOT'S CHANGED.
VERY WELL.
I WISH THIS COULD BE LIKE OLD TIMES, YOU KNOW.
THE GROUP OF US, FIGHTING THE GOOD FIGHT.
BUT IF YOU CONTINUE TO BE A PROBLEM, YOU WILL BE DEALT WITH.
JUST LIKE UMBRA.
YEAH, WELL...

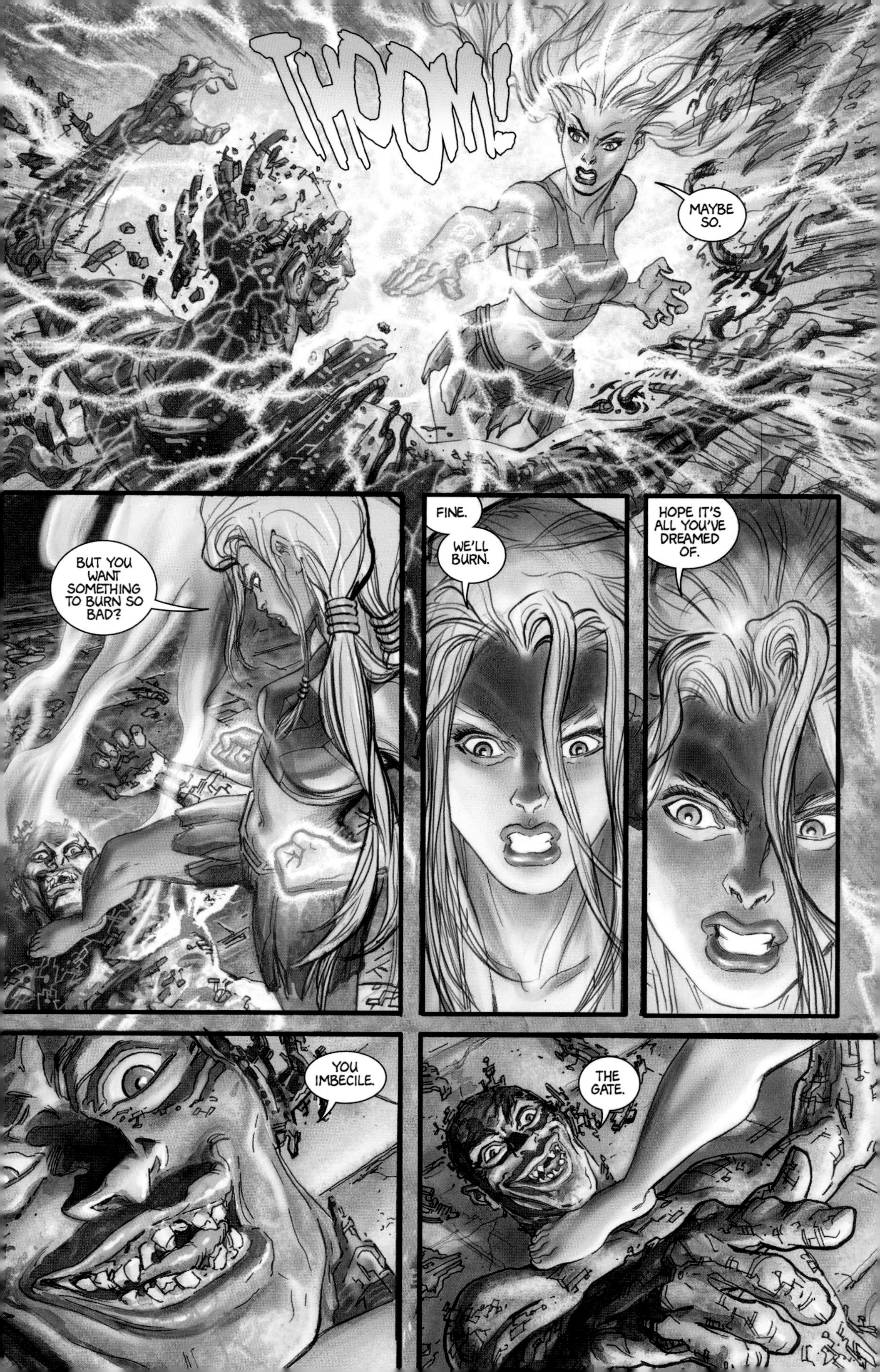
THOOM!
MAYBE SO.
BUT YOU WANT SOMETHING TO BURN SO BAD?
FINE.
WE'LL BURN.
HOPE IT'S ALL YOU'VE DREAMED OF.
YOU IMBECILE.
THE GATE.

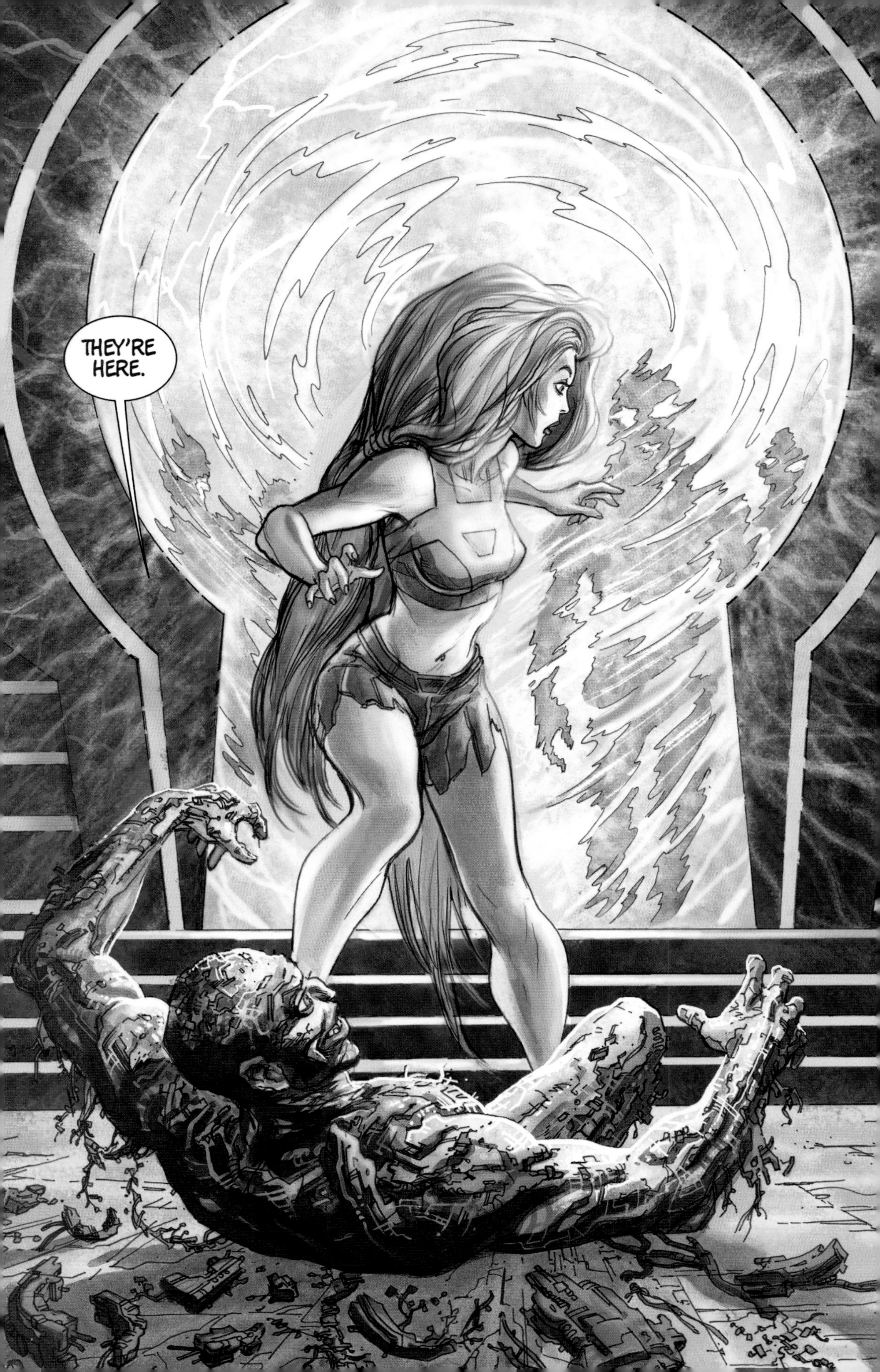
THEY'RE HERE.

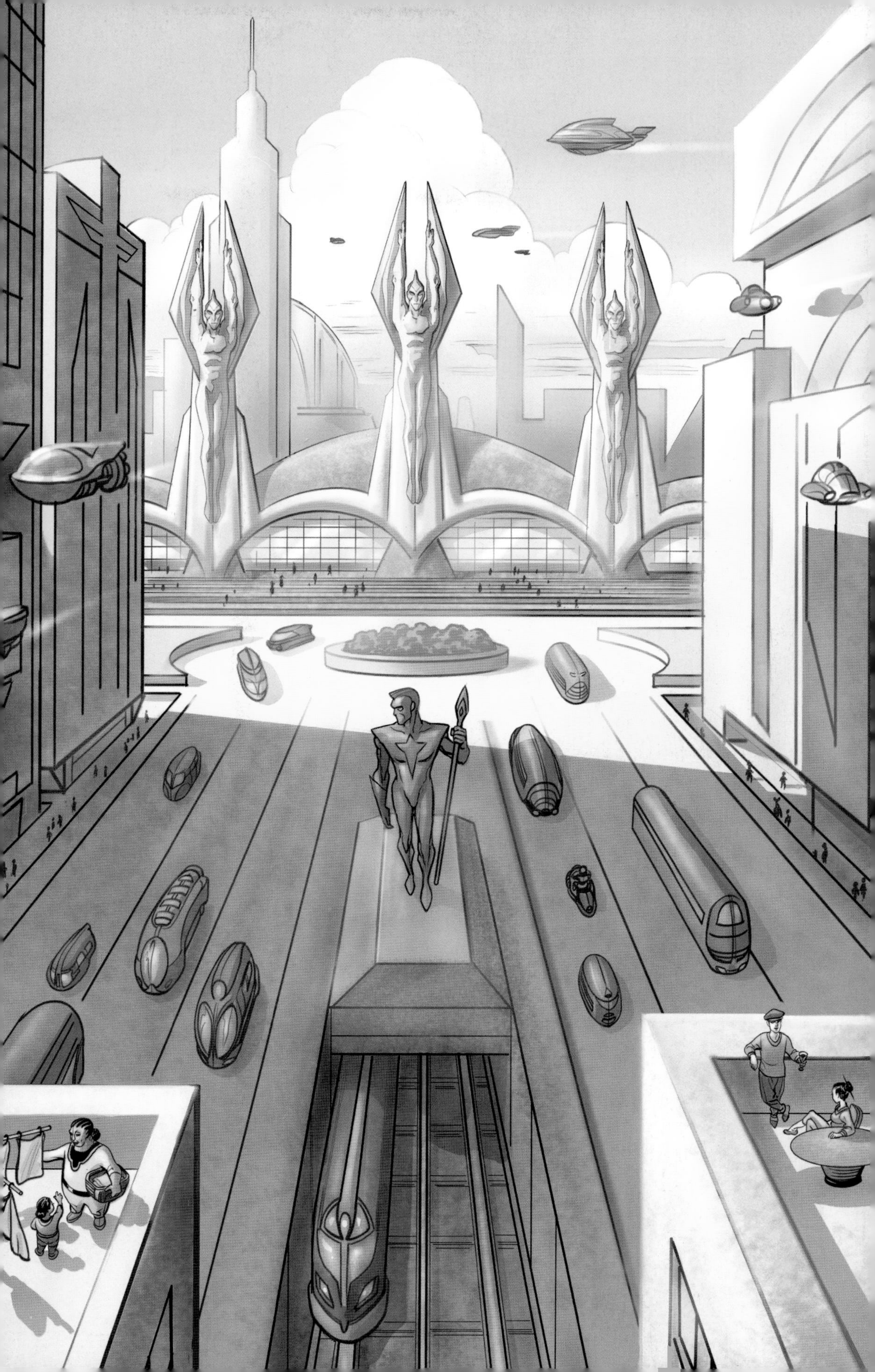

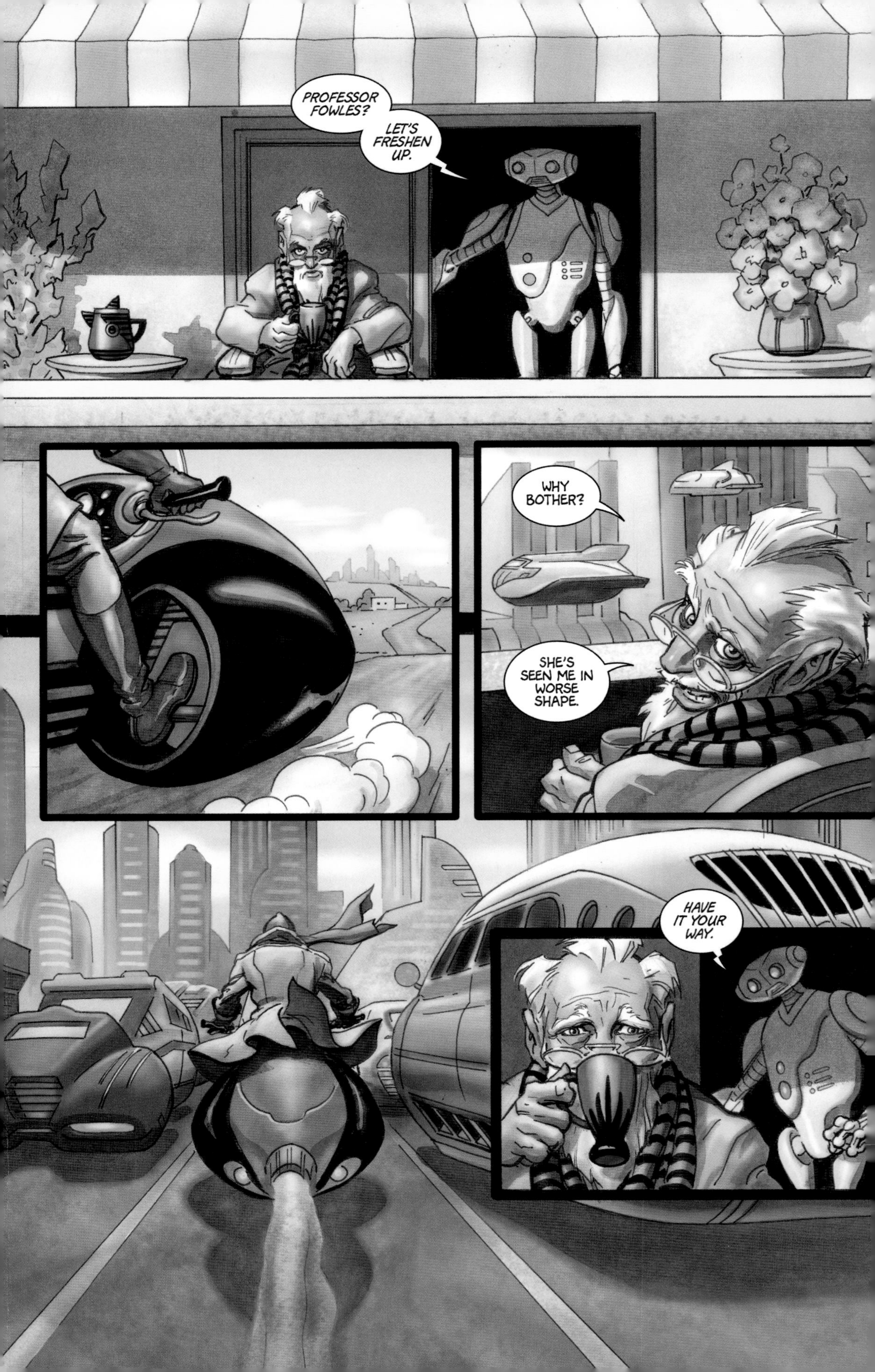
PROFESSOR FOWLES?
LET'S FRESHEN UP.
WHY BOTHER?
SHE'S SEEN ME IN WORSE SHAPE.
HAVE IT YOUR WAY.

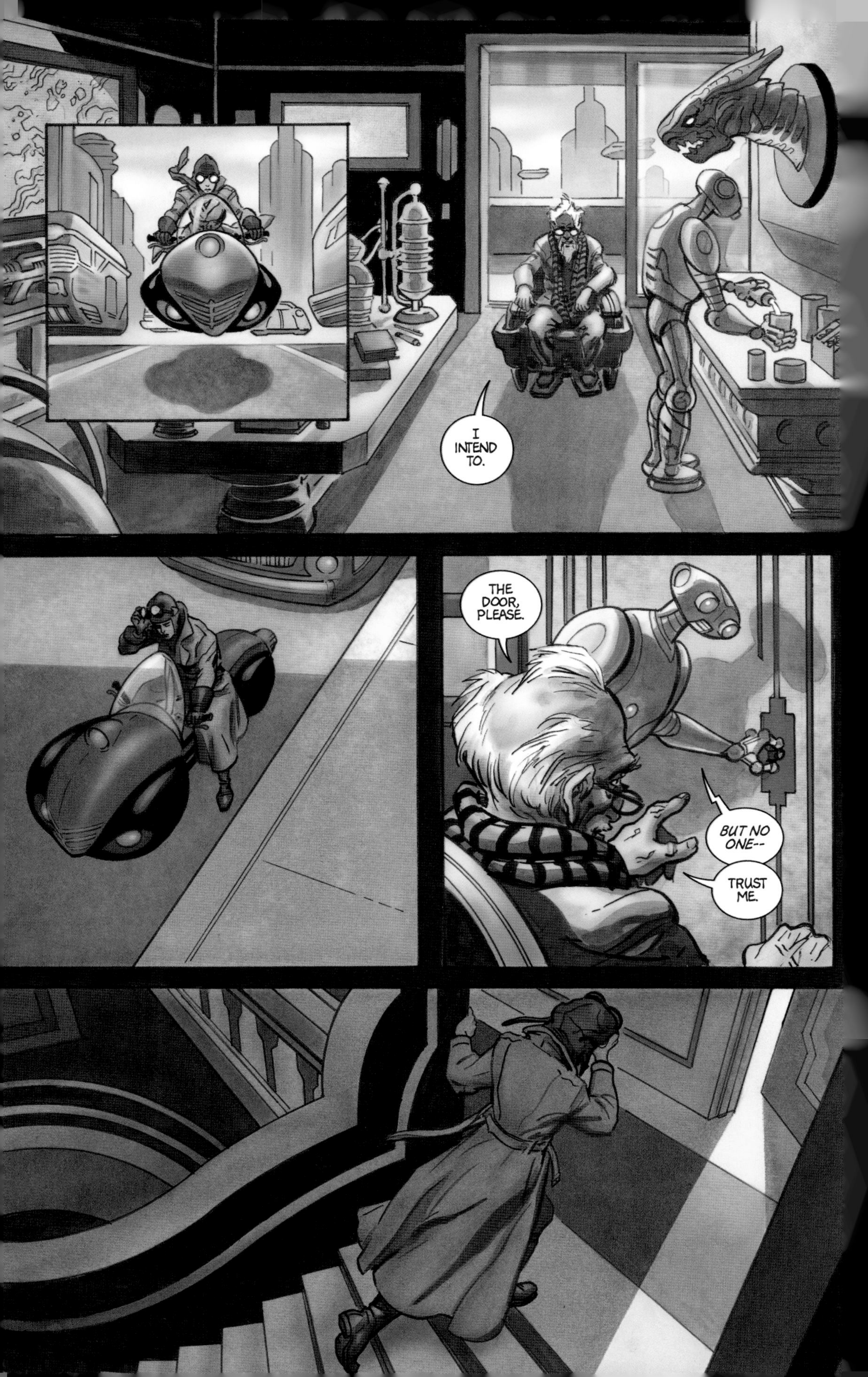
I INTEND TO.
THE DOOR, PLEASE.
BUT NO ONE--
TRUST ME.

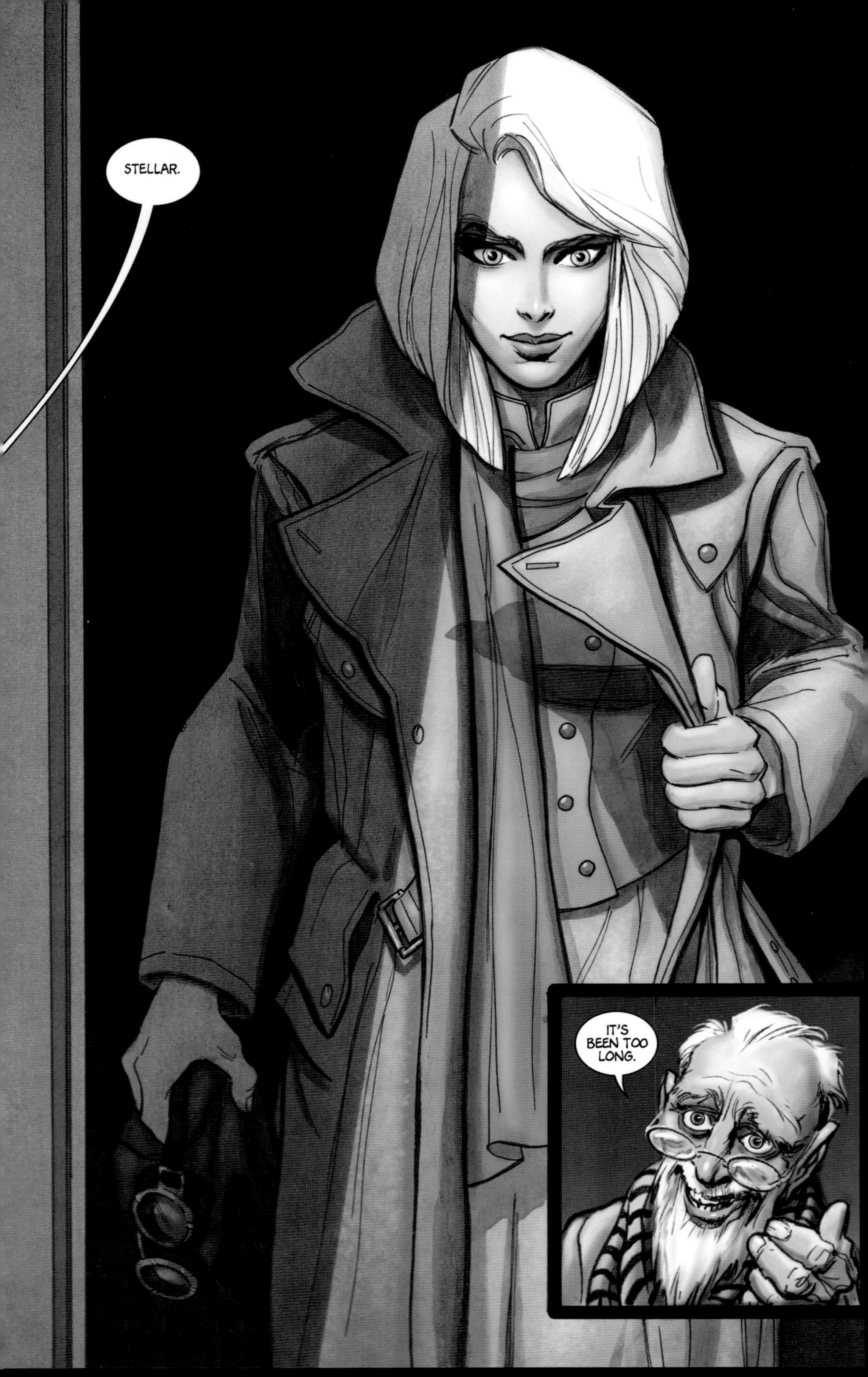
STELLAR.
IT'S BEEN TOO LONG.

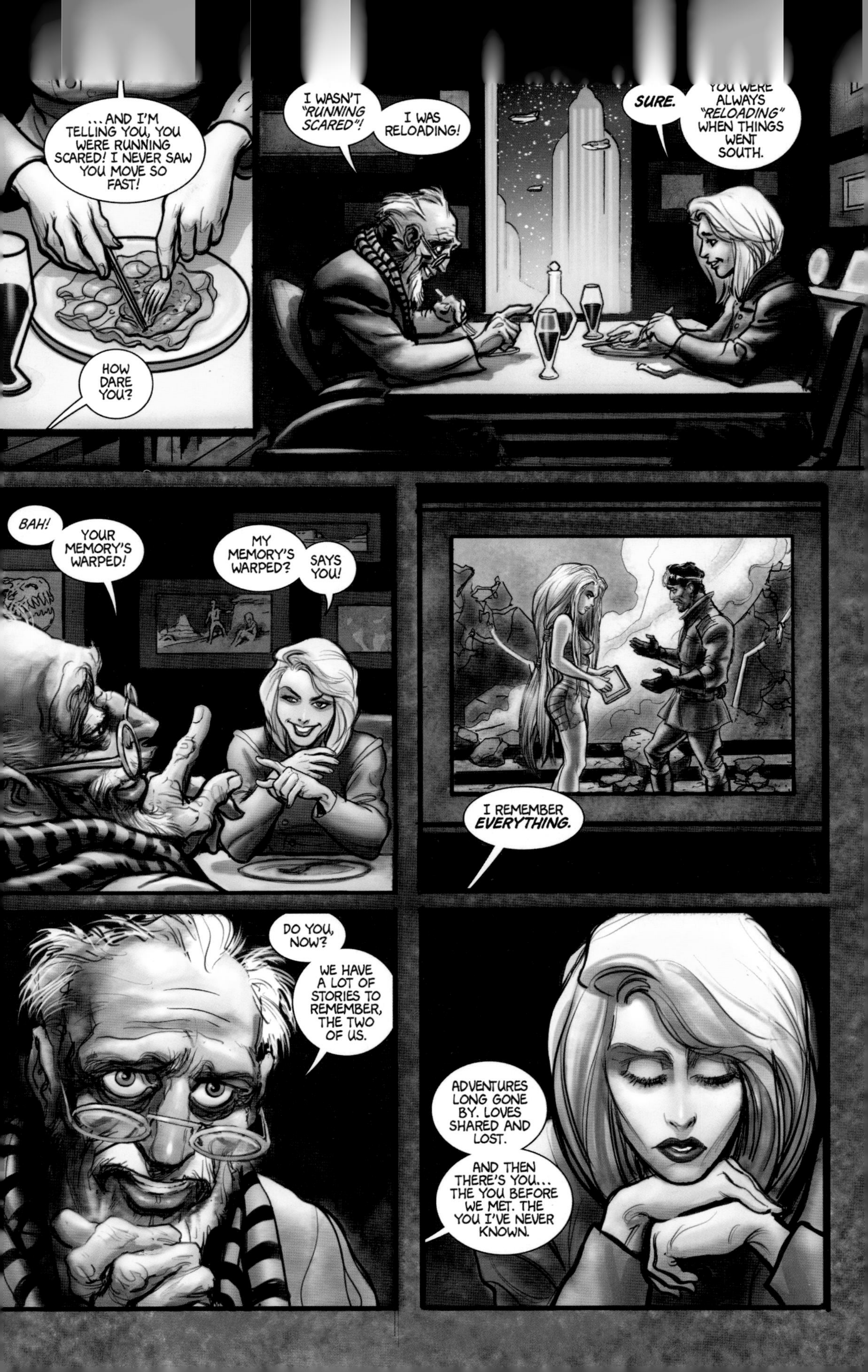
...AND I'M TELLING YOU, YOU WERE RUNNING SCARED! I NEVER SAW YOU MOVE SO FAST!
HOW DARE YOU?
I WASN'T "RUNNING SCARED"!
I WAS RELOADING!
SURE.
YOU WERE ALWAYS "RELOADING" WHEN THINGS WENT SOUTH.
BAH!
YOUR MEMORY'S WARPED!
MY MEMORY'S WARPED?
SAYS YOU!
I REMEMBER EVERYTHING.
DO YOU, NOW?
WE HAVE A LOT OF STORIES TO REMEMBER, THE TWO OF US.
ADVENTURES LONG GONE BY. LOVES SHARED AND LOST.
AND THEN THERE'S YOU... THE YOU BEFORE WE MET. THE YOU I'VE NEVER KNOWN.

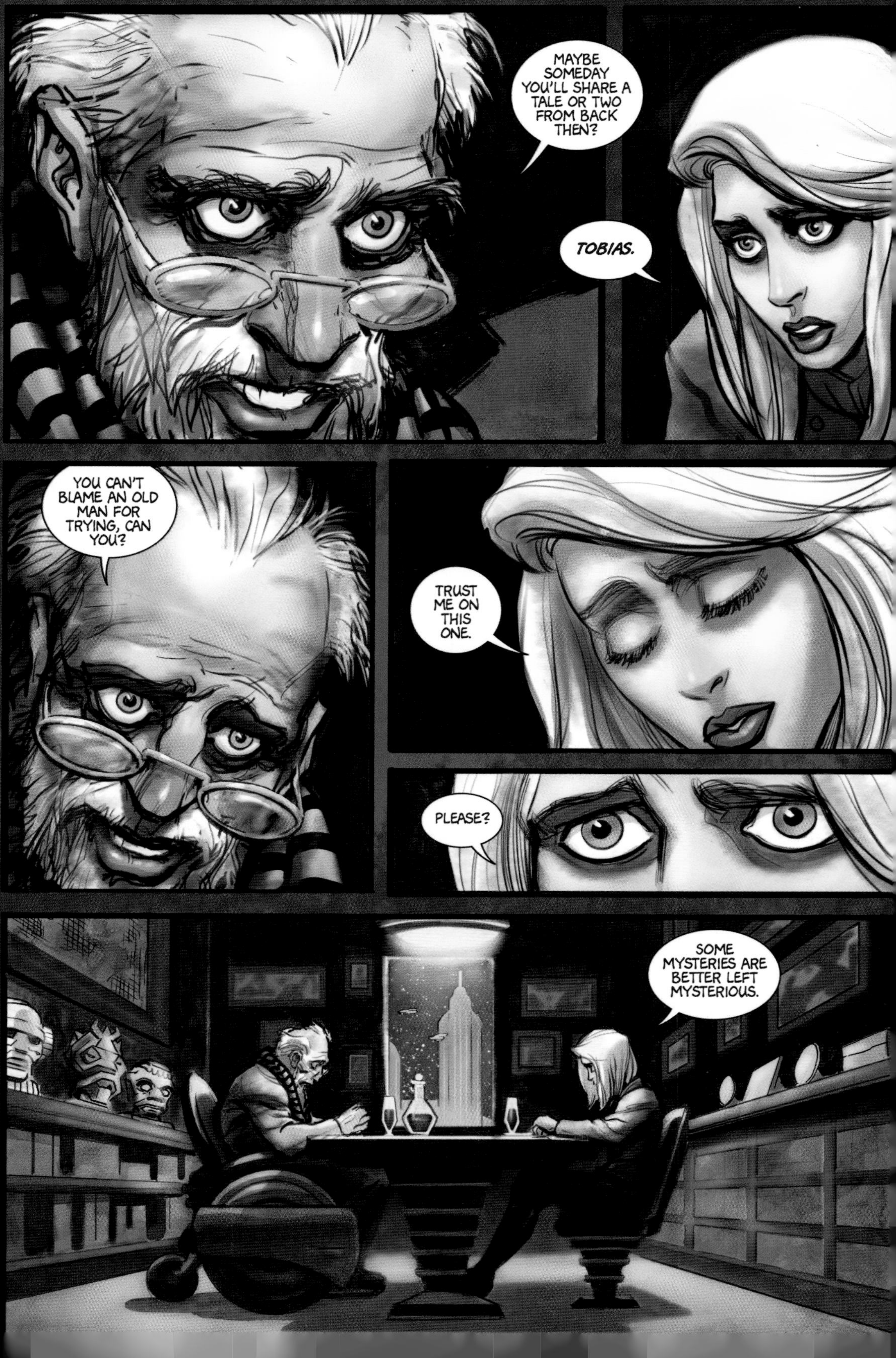
MAYBE SOMEDAY YOU'LL SHARE A TALE OR TWO FROM BACK THEN?
TOBIAS.
YOU CAN'T BLAME AN OLD MAN FOR TRYING, CAN YOU?
TRUST ME ON THIS ONE.
PLEASE?
SOME MYSTERIES ARE BETTER LEFT MYSTERIOUS.

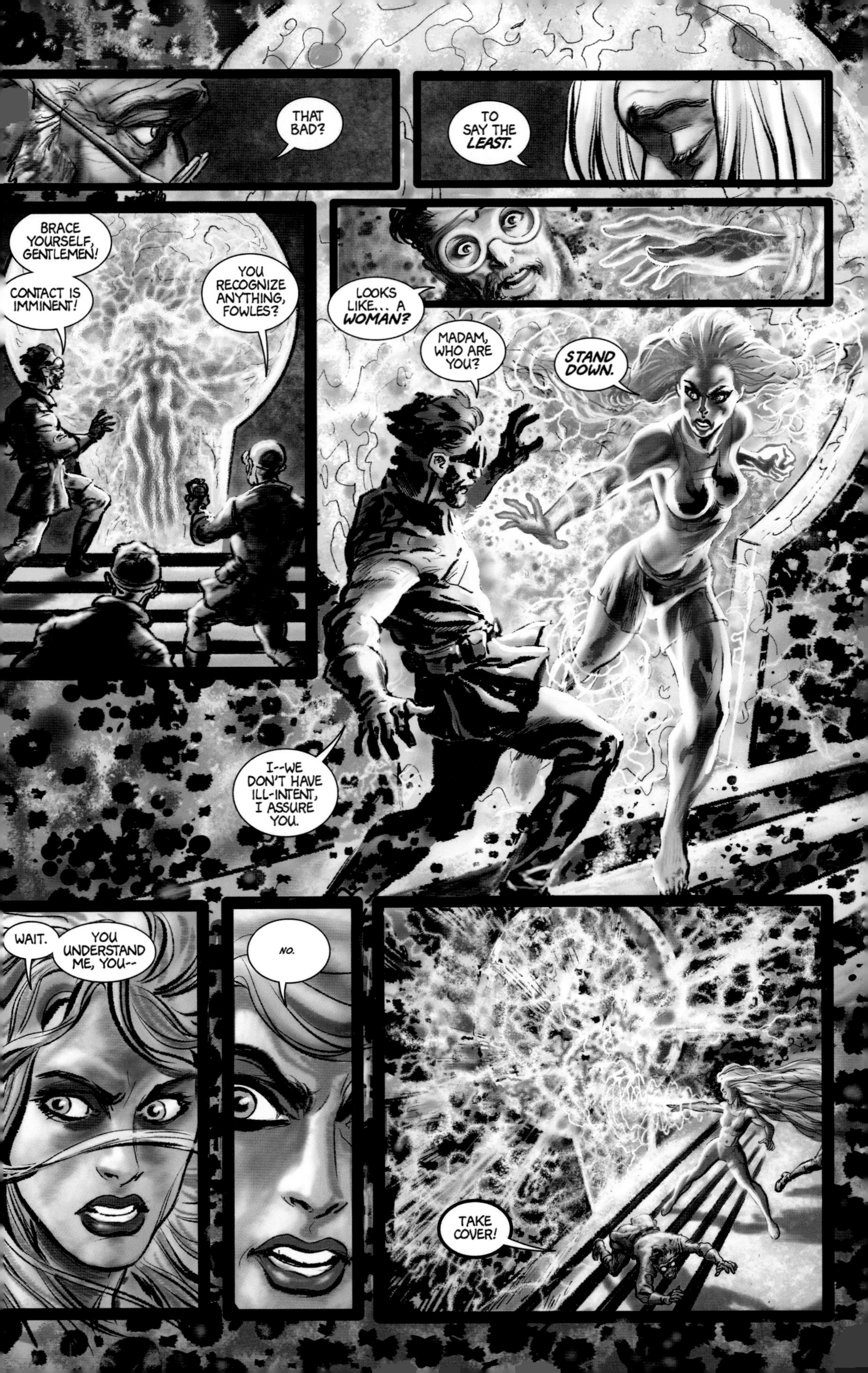

THAT BAD?
TO SAY THE **LEAST**.
BRACE YOURSELF, GENTLEMEN!
CONTACT IS IMMINENT!
YOU RECOGNIZE ANYTHING, FOWLES?
LOOKS LIKE... A **WOMAN?**
MADAM, WHO ARE YOU?
STAND DOWN.
I--WE DON'T HAVE ILL-INTENT, I ASSURE YOU.
WAIT.
YOU UNDERSTAND ME, YOU--
NO.
TAKE COVER!

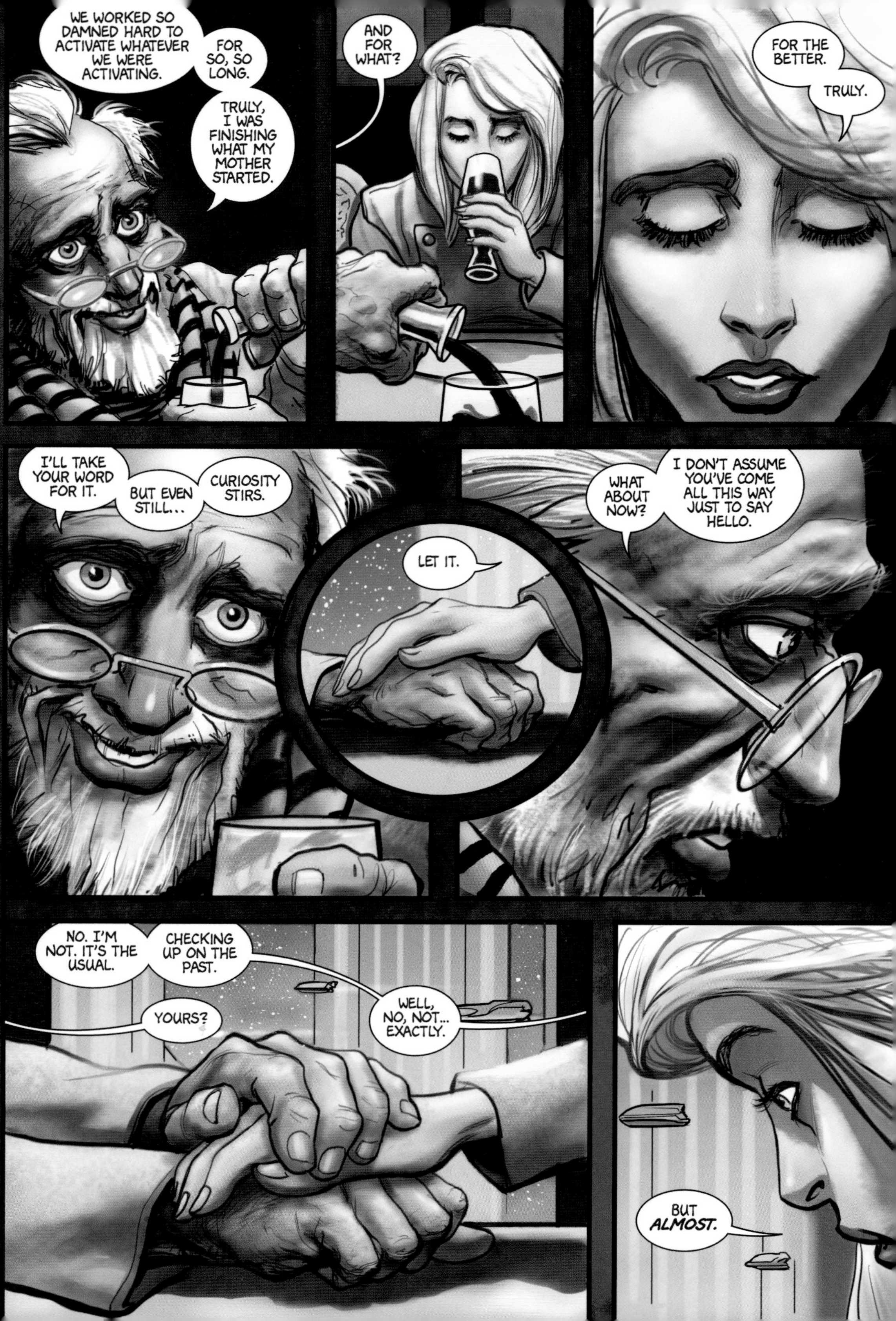
WE WORKED SO DAMNED HARD TO ACTIVATE WHATEVER WE WERE ACTIVATING.
FOR SO, SO LONG.
TRULY, I WAS FINISHING WHAT MY MOTHER STARTED.
AND FOR WHAT?
FOR THE BETTER.
TRULY.
I'LL TAKE YOUR WORD FOR IT.
BUT EVEN STILL...
CURIOSITY STIRS.
LET IT.
WHAT ABOUT NOW?
I DON'T ASSUME YOU'VE COME ALL THIS WAY JUST TO SAY HELLO.
NO. I'M NOT. IT'S THE USUAL.
CHECKING UP ON THE PAST.
YOURS?
WELL, NO, NOT... EXACTLY.
BUT *ALMOST.*

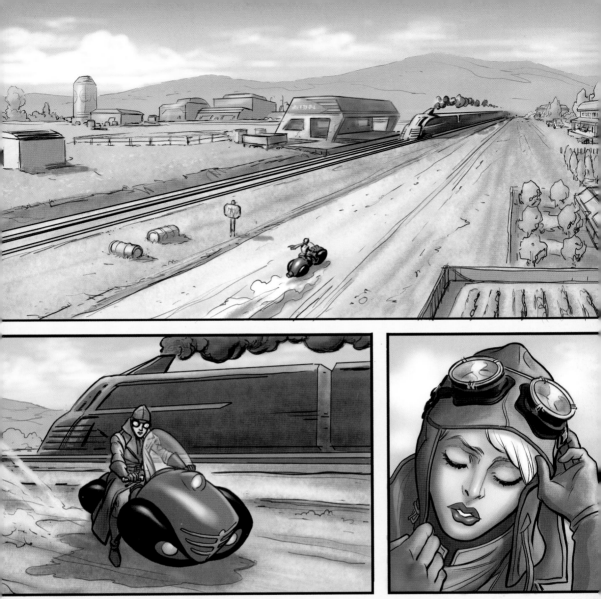

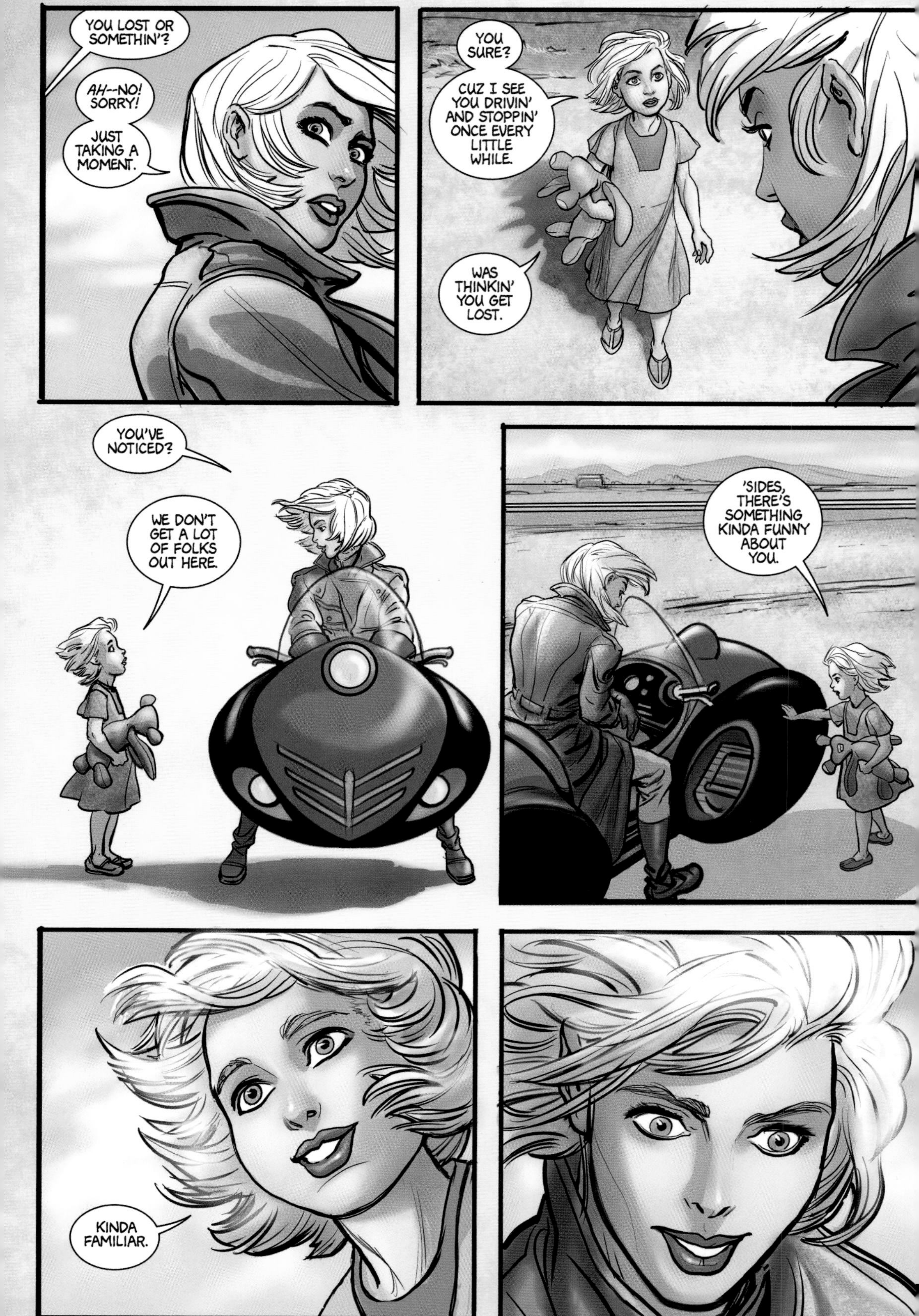
YOU LOST OR SOMETHIN'?
AH--NO! SORRY!
JUST TAKING A MOMENT.
YOU SURE?
CUZ I SEE YOU DRIVIN' AND STOPPIN' ONCE EVERY LITTLE WHILE.
WAS THINKIN' YOU GET LOST.
YOU'VE NOTICED?
WE DON'T GET A LOT OF FOLKS OUT HERE.
'SIDES, THERE'S SOMETHING KINDA FUNNY ABOUT YOU.
KINDA FAMILIAR.

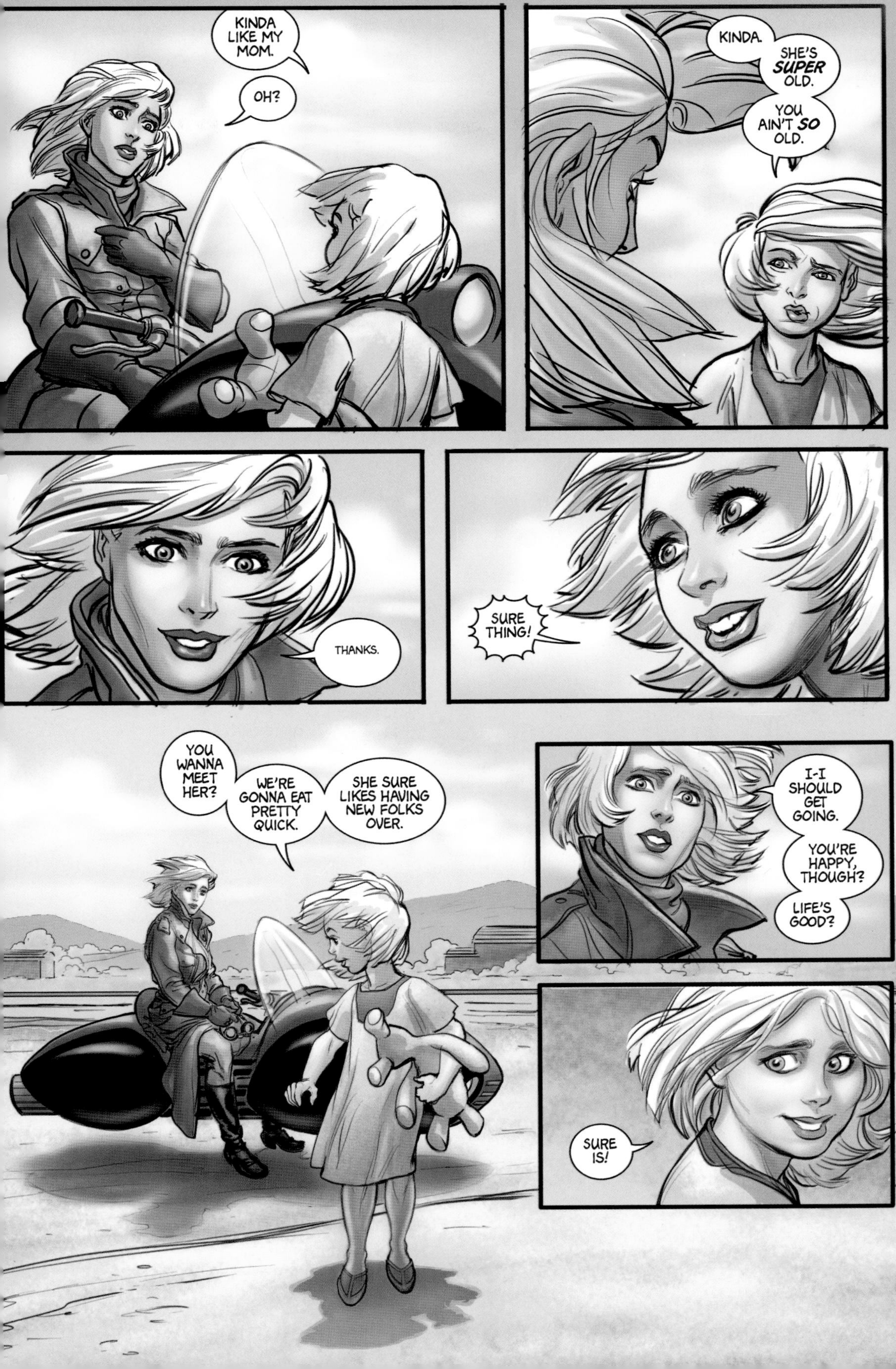
KINDA LIKE MY MOM.
OH?
KINDA.
SHE'S SUPER OLD.
YOU AIN'T SO OLD.
THANKS.
SURE THING!
YOU WANNA MEET HER?
WE'RE GONNA EAT PRETTY QUICK.
SHE SURE LIKES HAVING NEW FOLKS OVER.
I-I SHOULD GET GOING.
YOU'RE HAPPY, THOUGH?
LIFE'S GOOD?
SURE IS!

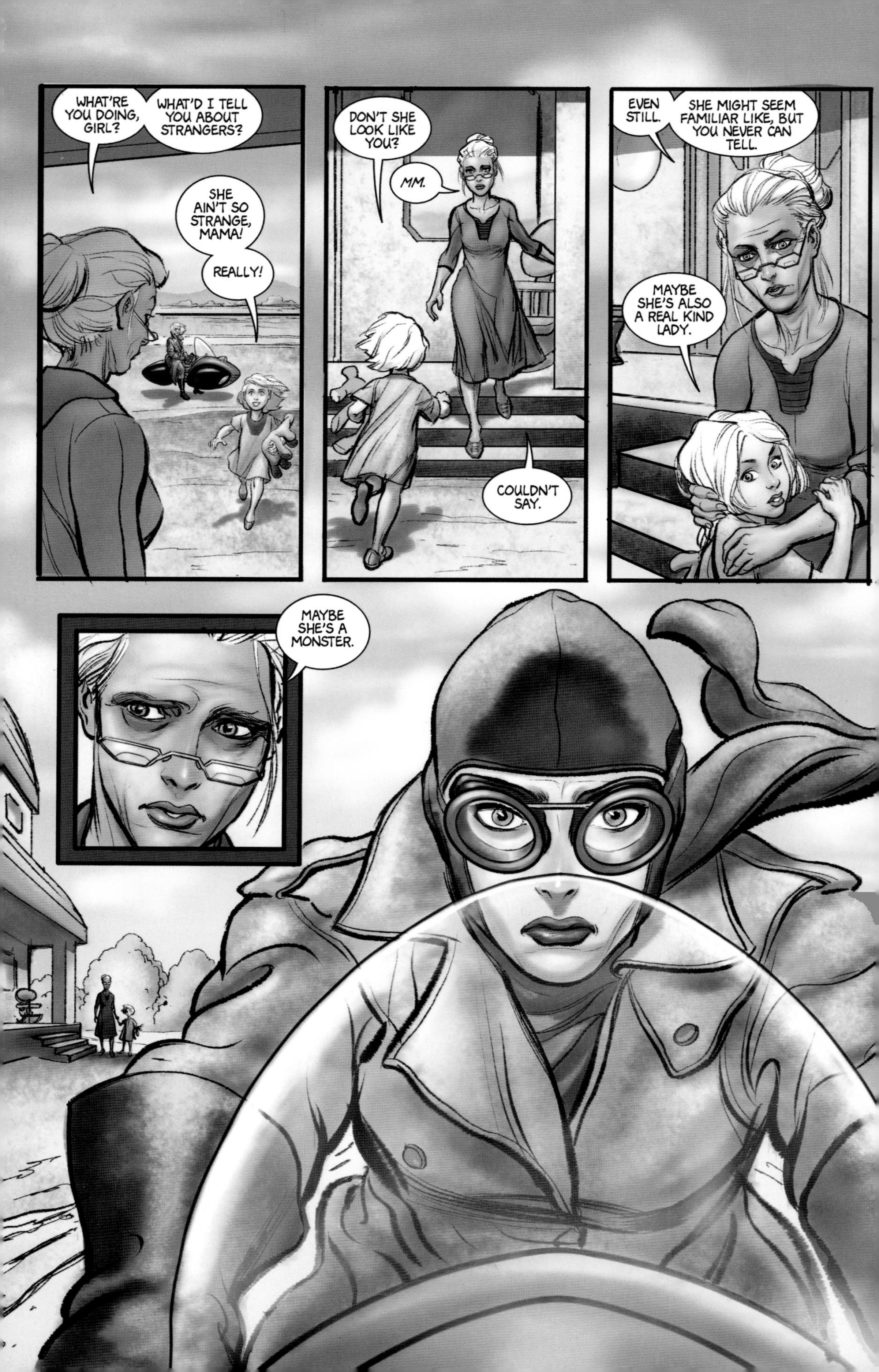
WHAT'RE YOU DOING, GIRL?
WHAT'D I TELL YOU ABOUT STRANGERS?
SHE AIN'T SO STRANGE, MAMA!
REALLY!
DON'T SHE LOOK LIKE YOU?
MM.
COULDN'T SAY.
EVEN STILL.
SHE MIGHT SEEM FAMILIAR LIKE, BUT YOU NEVER CAN TELL.
MAYBE SHE'S ALSO A REAL KIND LADY.
MAYBE SHE'S A MONSTER.

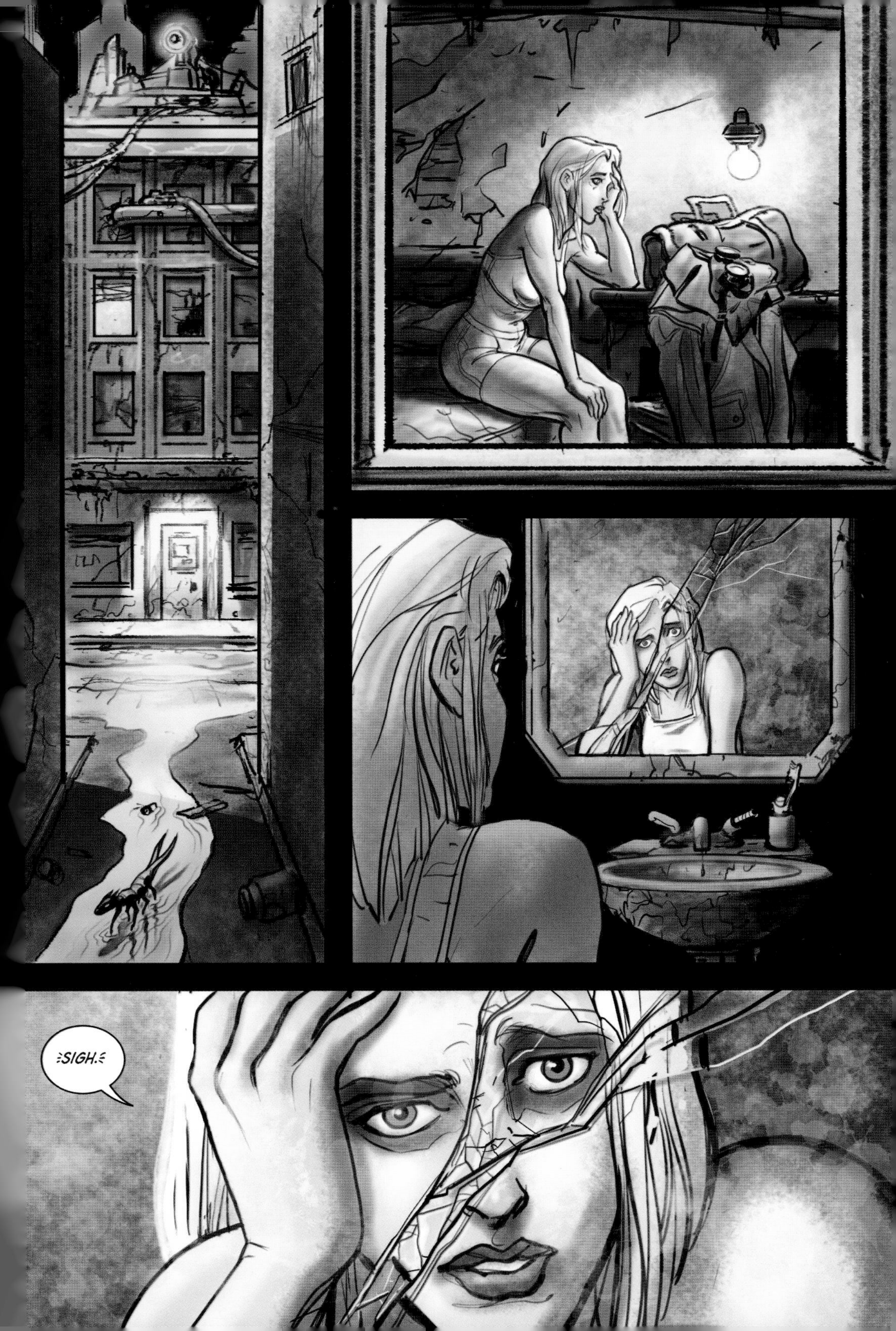

SIGH.

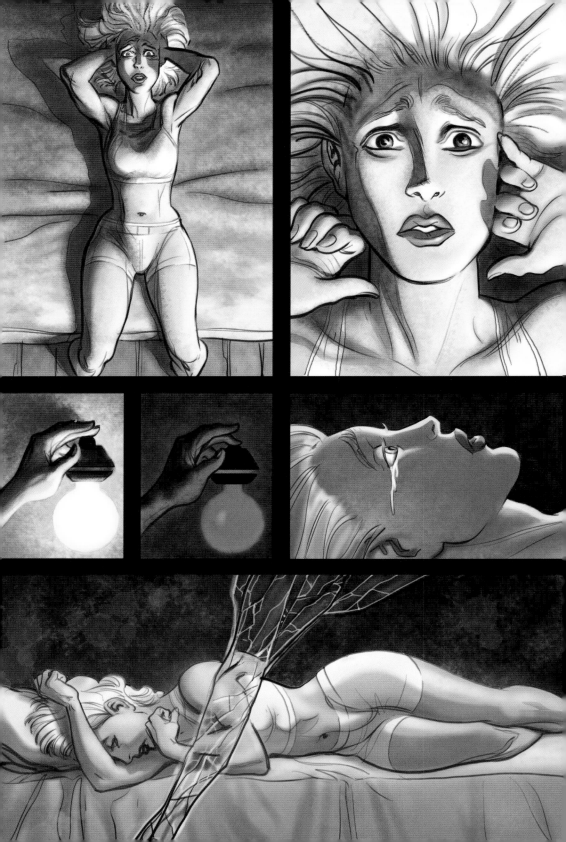

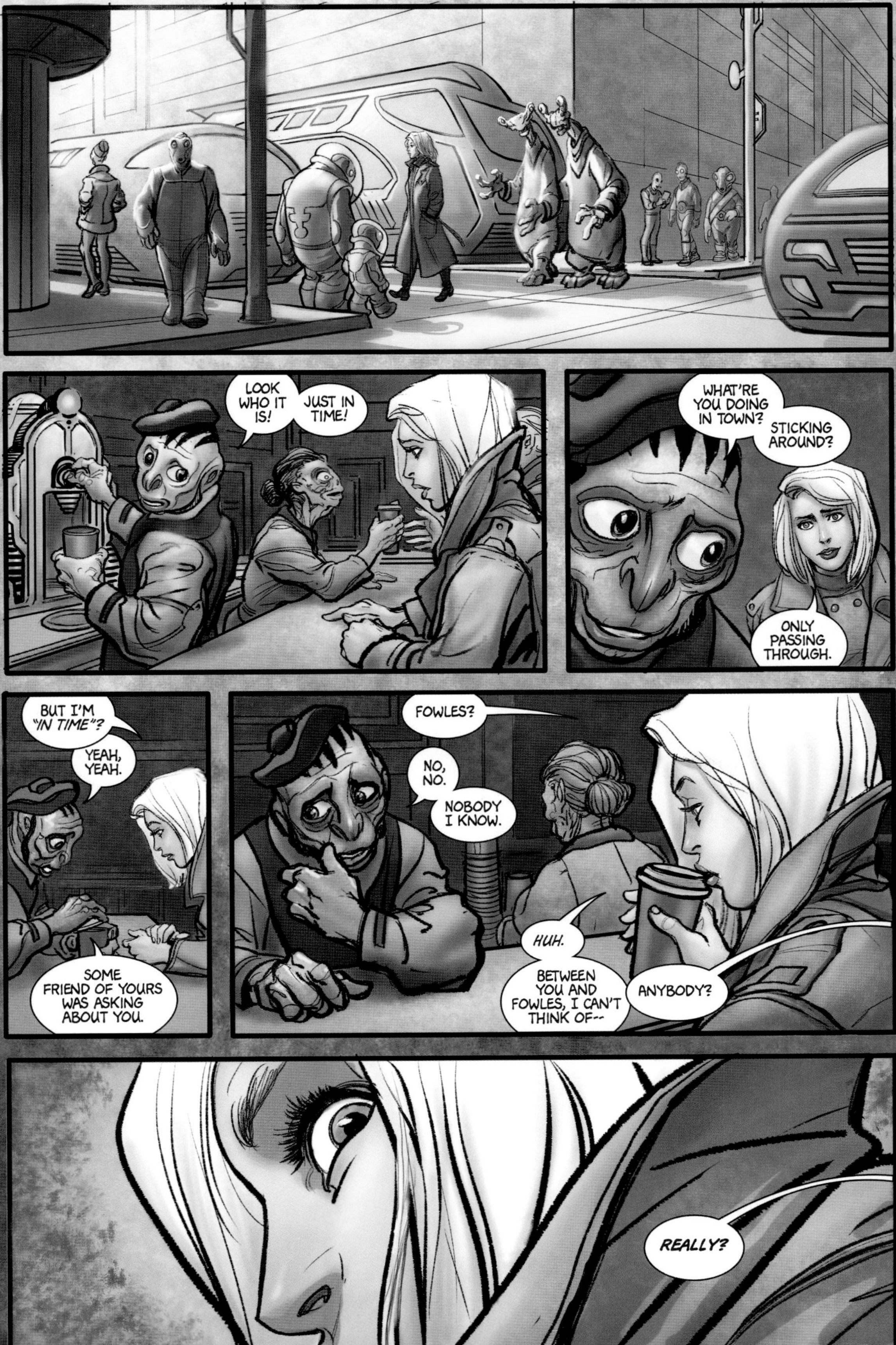
LOOK WHO IT IS!
JUST IN TIME!
WHAT'RE YOU DOING IN TOWN?
STICKING AROUND?
ONLY PASSING THROUGH.
BUT I'M "IN TIME"?
YEAH, YEAH.
SOME FRIEND OF YOURS WAS ASKING ABOUT YOU.
FOWLES?
NO, NO.
NOBODY I KNOW.
HUH.
BETWEEN YOU AND FOWLES, I CAN'T THINK OF--
ANYBODY?
REALLY?

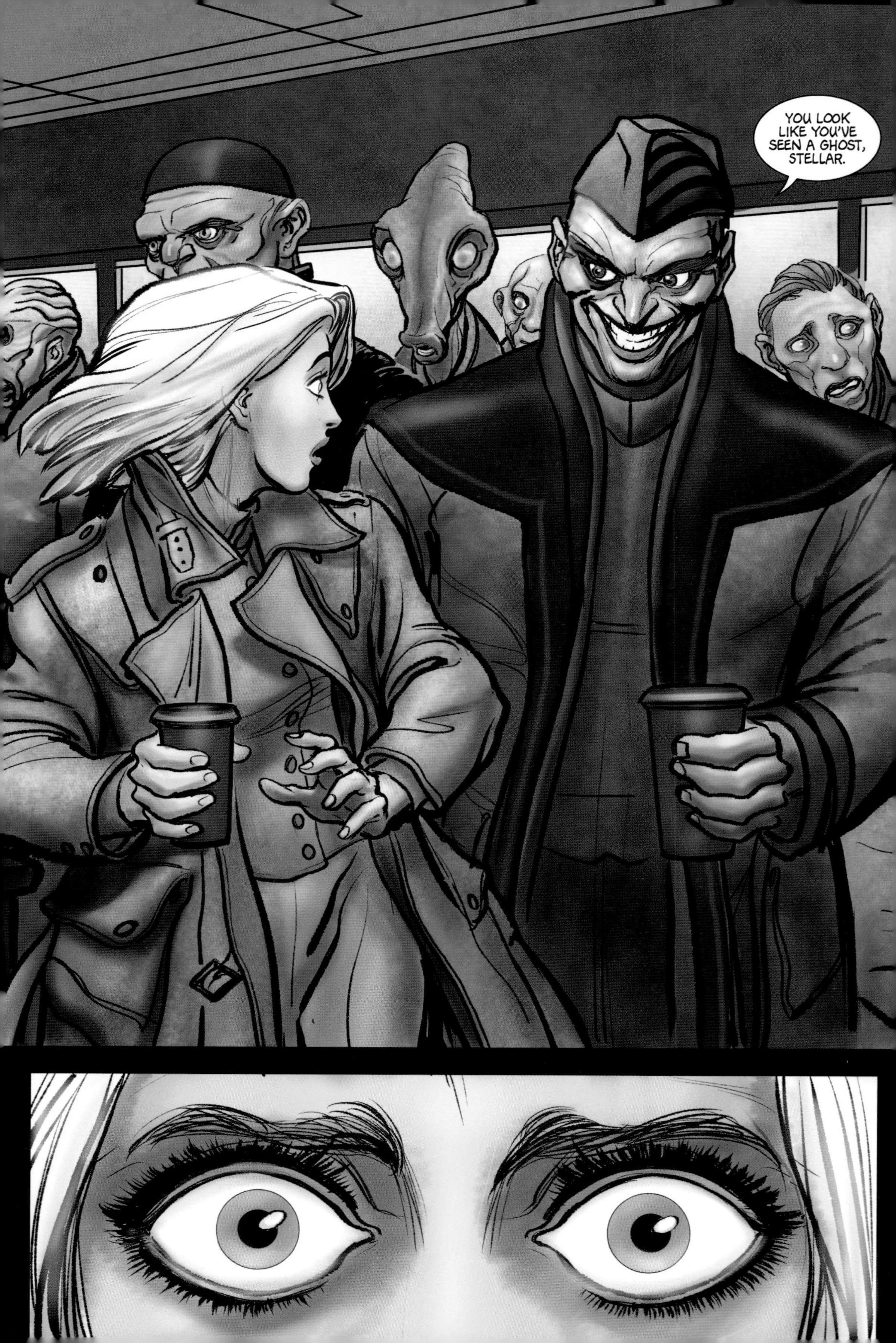
YOU LOOK LIKE YOU'VE SEEN A GHOST, STELLAR.

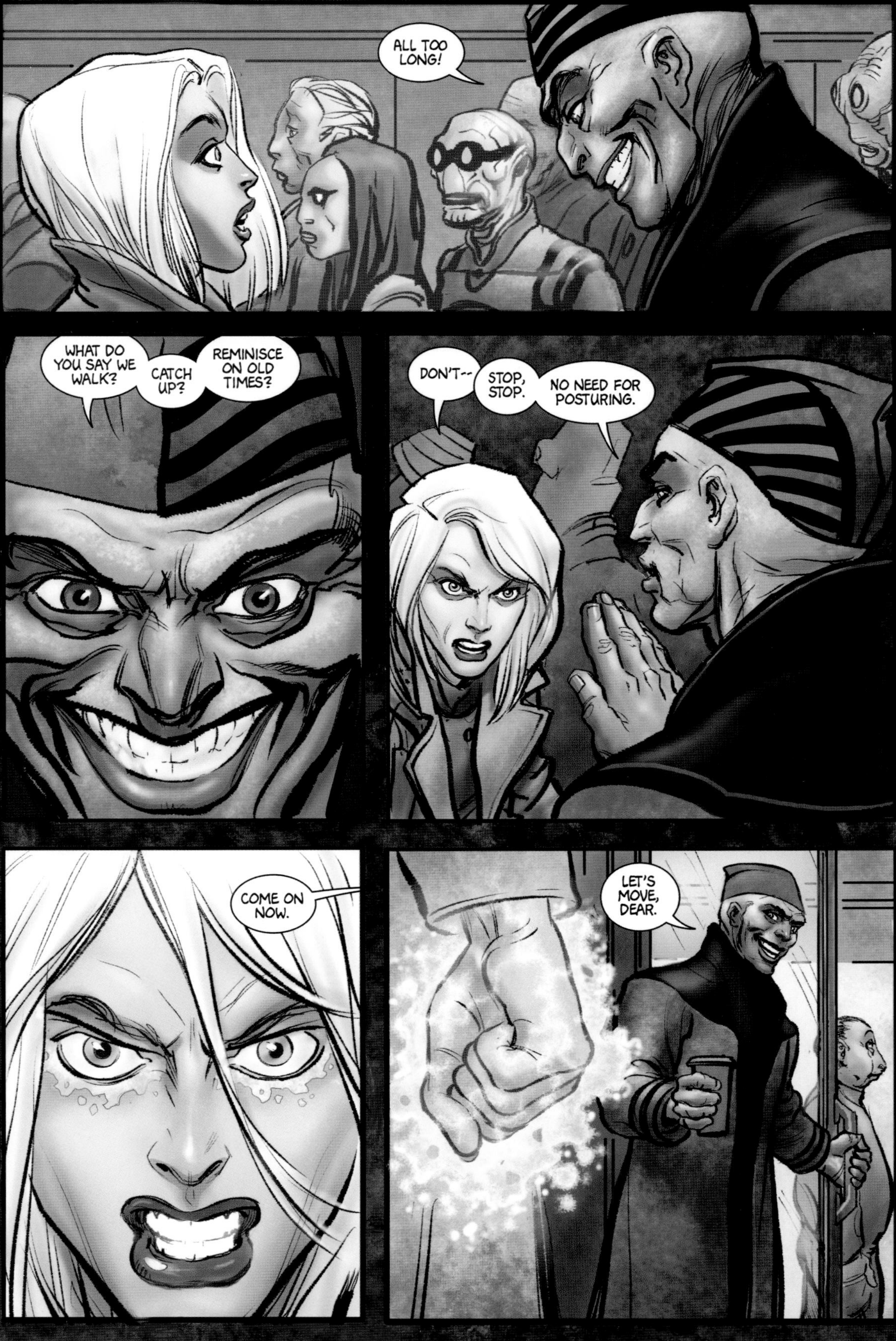
ALL TOO LONG!
WHAT DO YOU SAY WE WALK?
CATCH UP?
REMINISCE ON OLD TIMES?
DON'T--
STOP, STOP.
NO NEED FOR POSTURING.
COME ON NOW.
LET'S MOVE, DEAR.

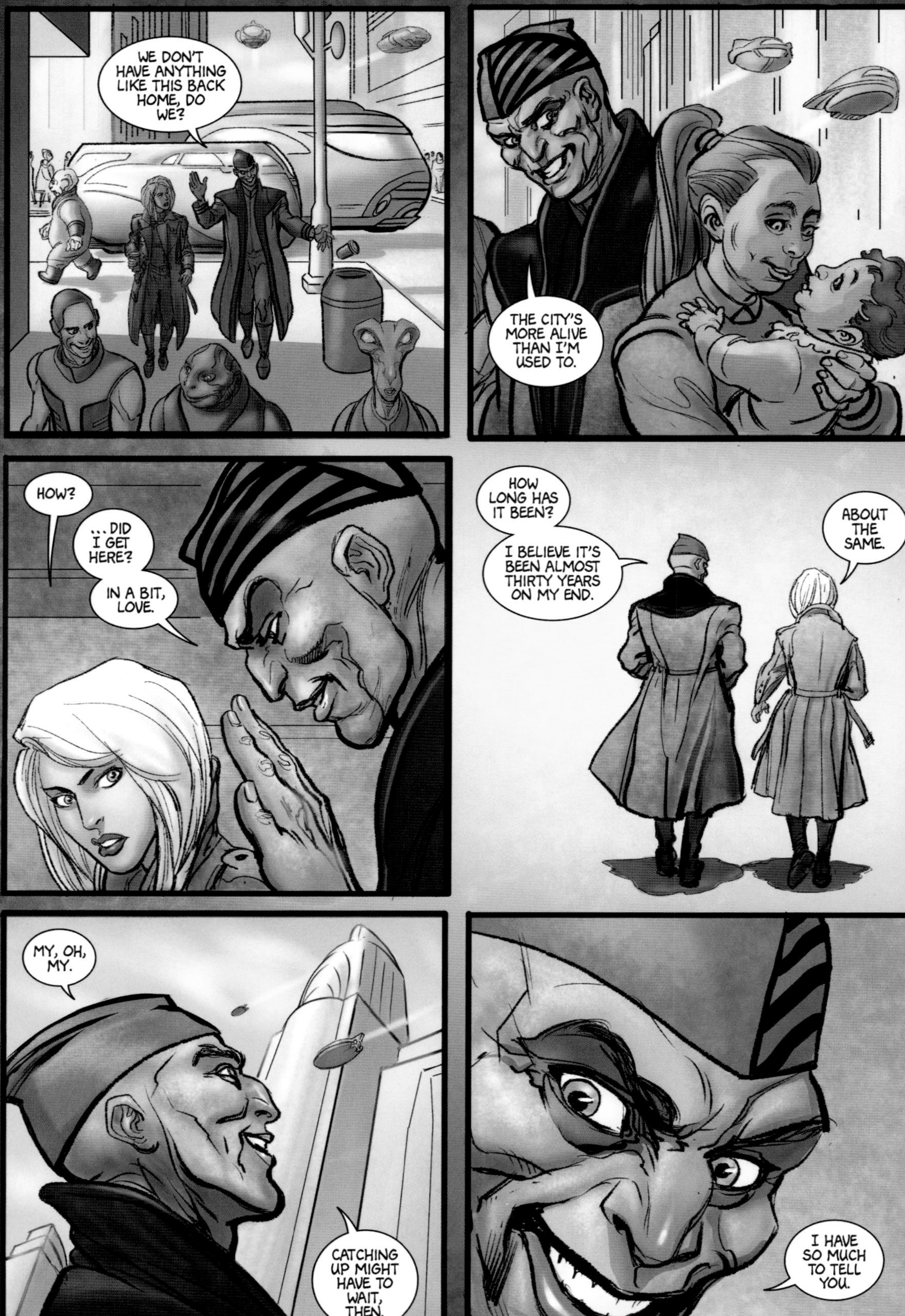
WE DON'T HAVE ANYTHING LIKE THIS BACK HOME, DO WE?
THE CITY'S MORE ALIVE THAN I'M USED TO.
HOW?
...DID I GET HERE?
IN A BIT, LOVE.
HOW LONG HAS IT BEEN?
I BELIEVE IT'S BEEN ALMOST THIRTY YEARS ON MY END.
ABOUT THE SAME.
MY, OH, MY.
CATCHING UP MIGHT HAVE TO WAIT, THEN.
I HAVE SO MUCH TO TELL YOU.

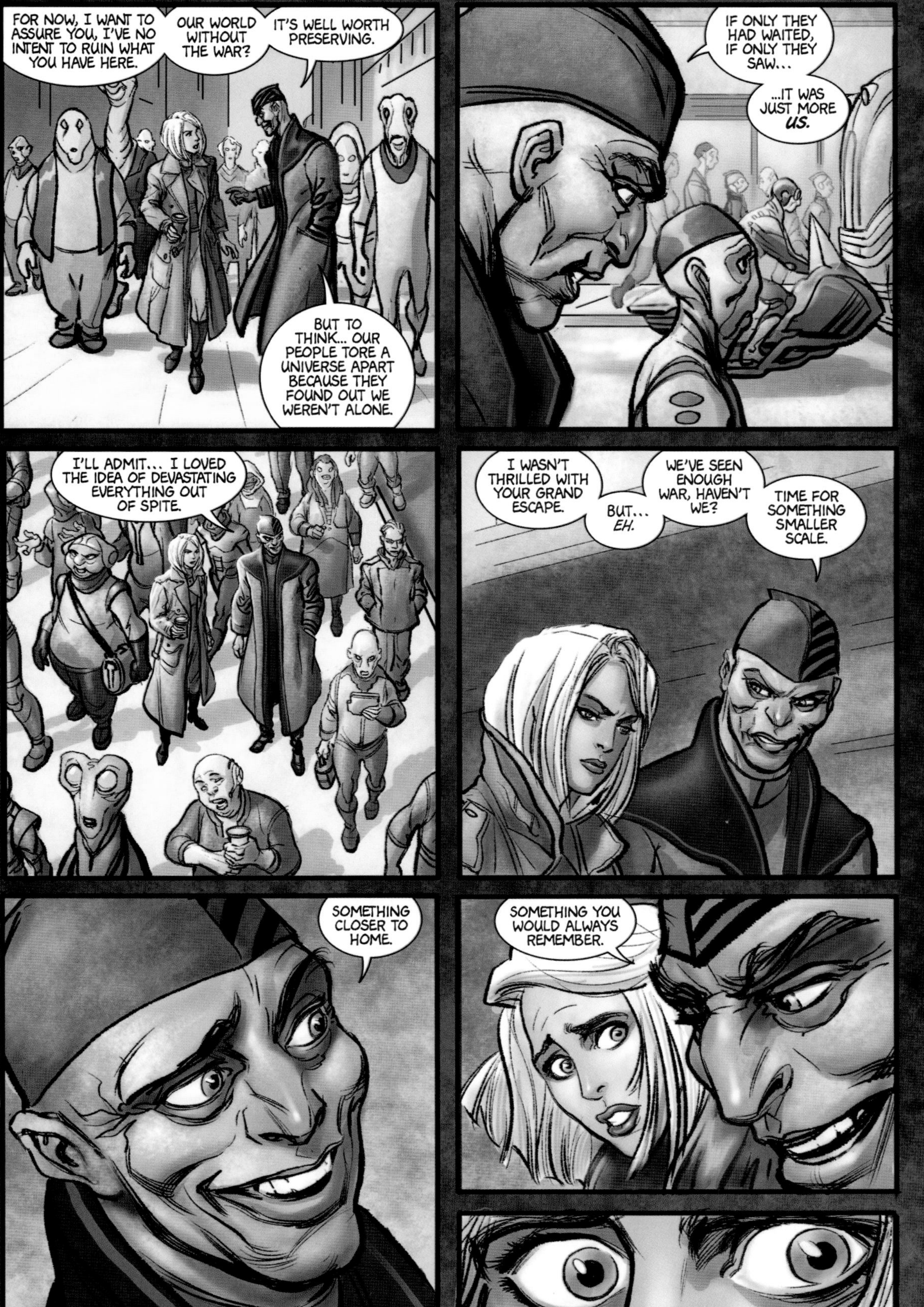
FOR NOW, I WANT TO ASSURE YOU, I'VE NO INTENT TO RUIN WHAT YOU HAVE HERE.
OUR WORLD WITHOUT THE WAR?
IT'S WELL WORTH PRESERVING.
BUT TO THINK... OUR PEOPLE TORE A UNIVERSE APART BECAUSE THEY FOUND OUT WE WEREN'T ALONE.
IF ONLY THEY HAD WAITED, IF ONLY THEY SAW...
...IT WAS JUST MORE *US.*
I'LL ADMIT... I LOVED THE IDEA OF DEVASTATING EVERYTHING OUT OF SPITE.
I WASN'T THRILLED WITH YOUR GRAND ESCAPE.
BUT... *EH.*
WE'VE SEEN ENOUGH WAR, HAVEN'T WE?
TIME FOR SOMETHING SMALLER SCALE.
SOMETHING CLOSER TO HOME.
SOMETHING YOU WOULD ALWAYS REMEMBER.

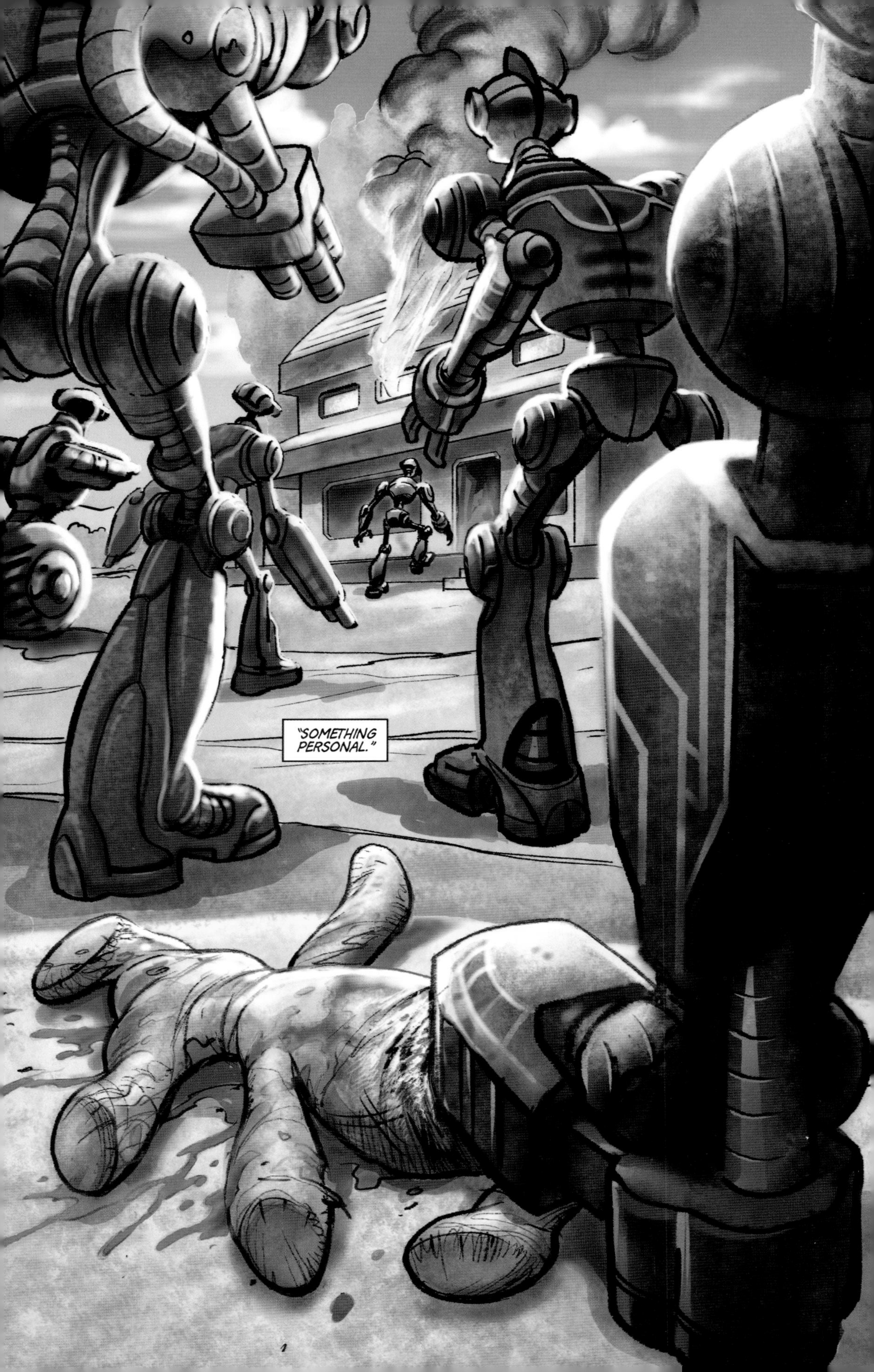
"SOMETHING PERSONAL."

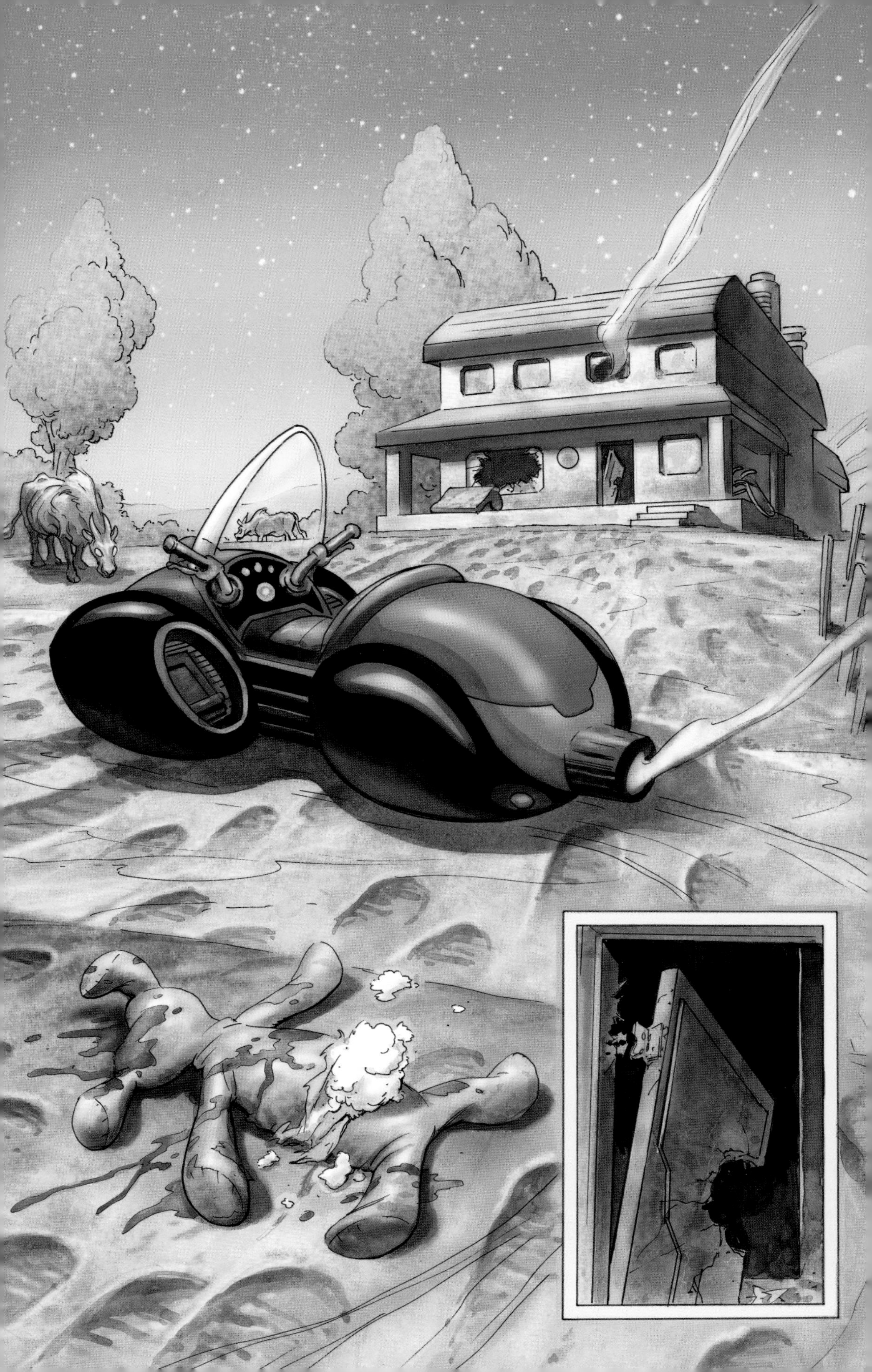

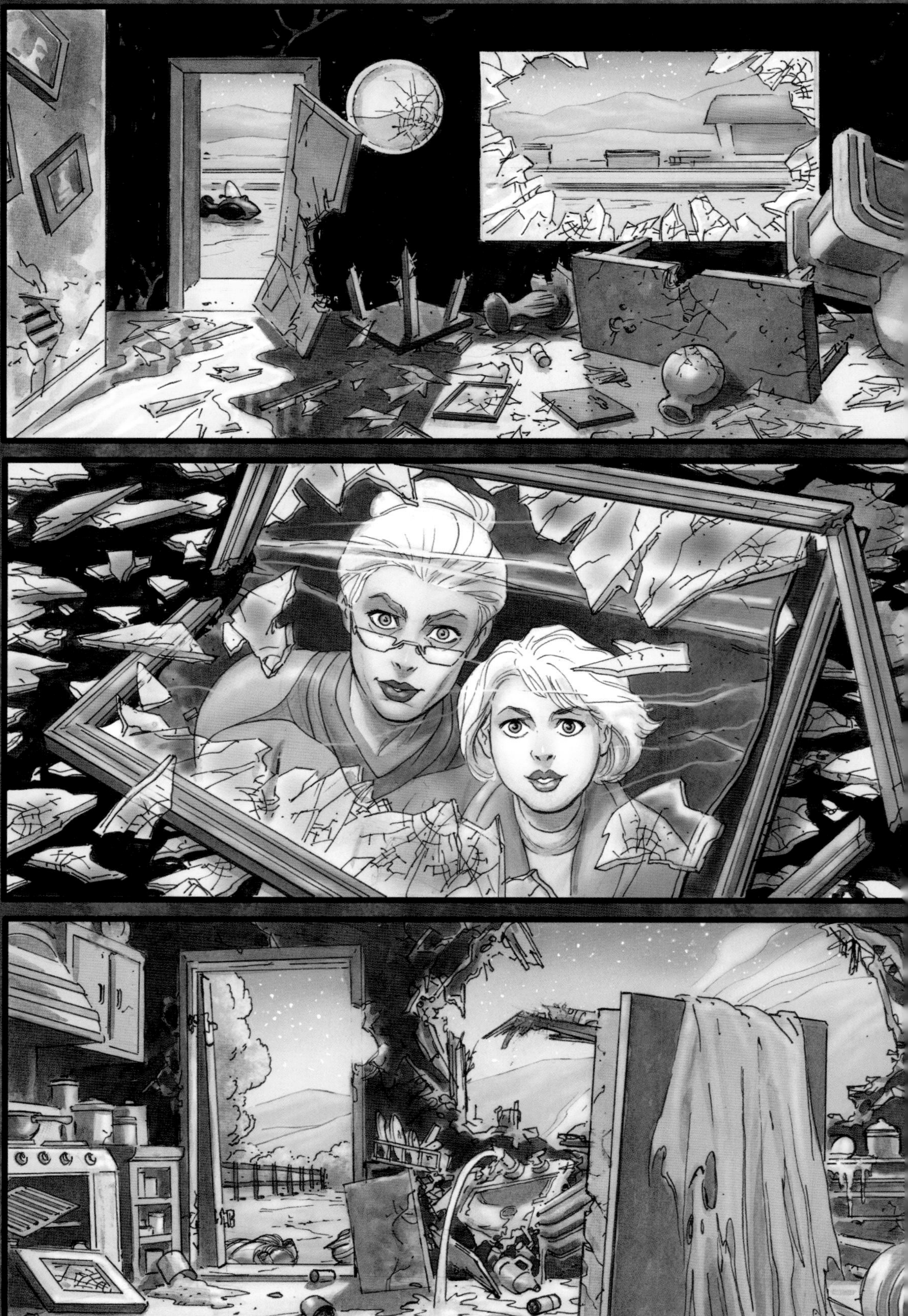

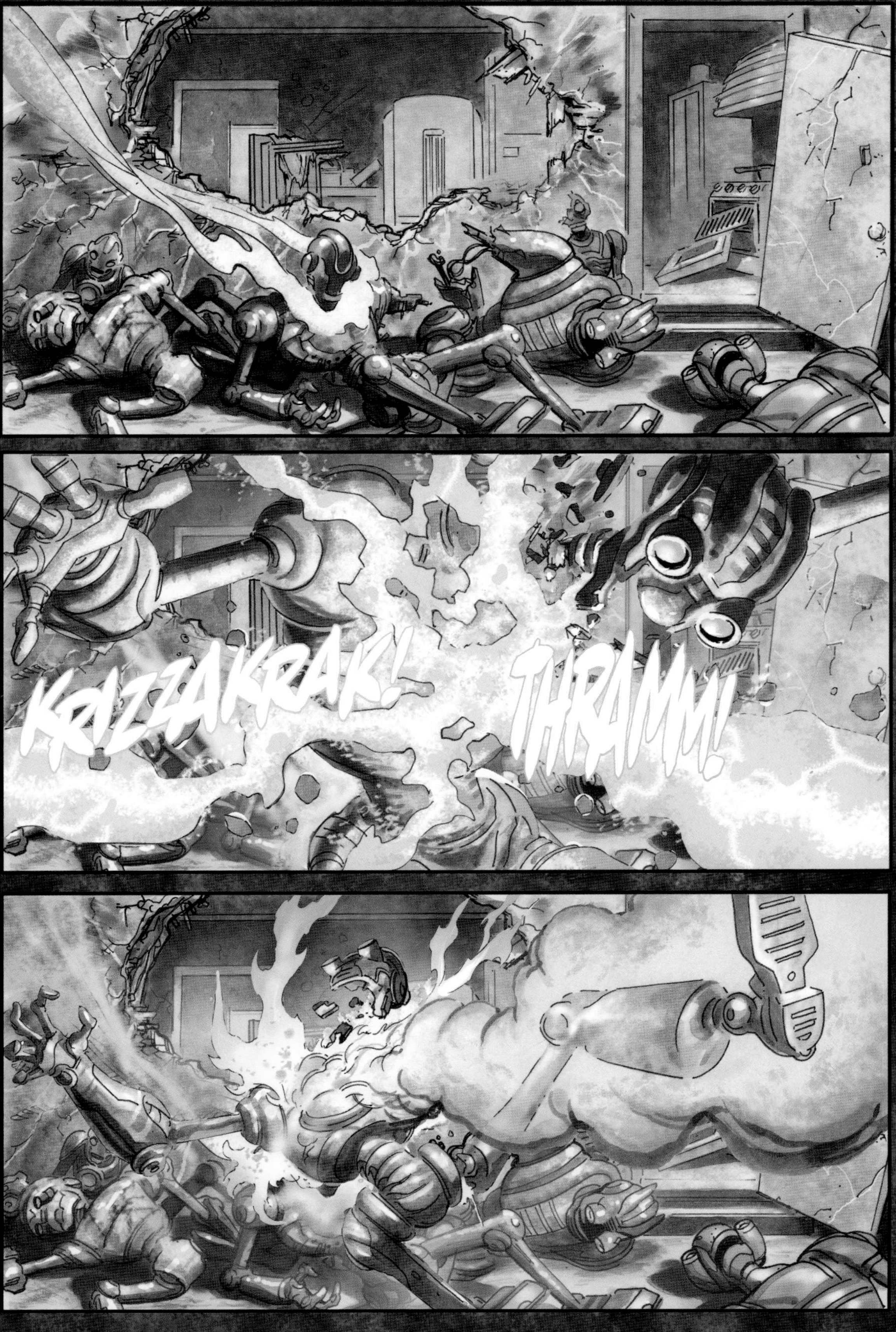
KRIZZAKRAK!
THRAMM!

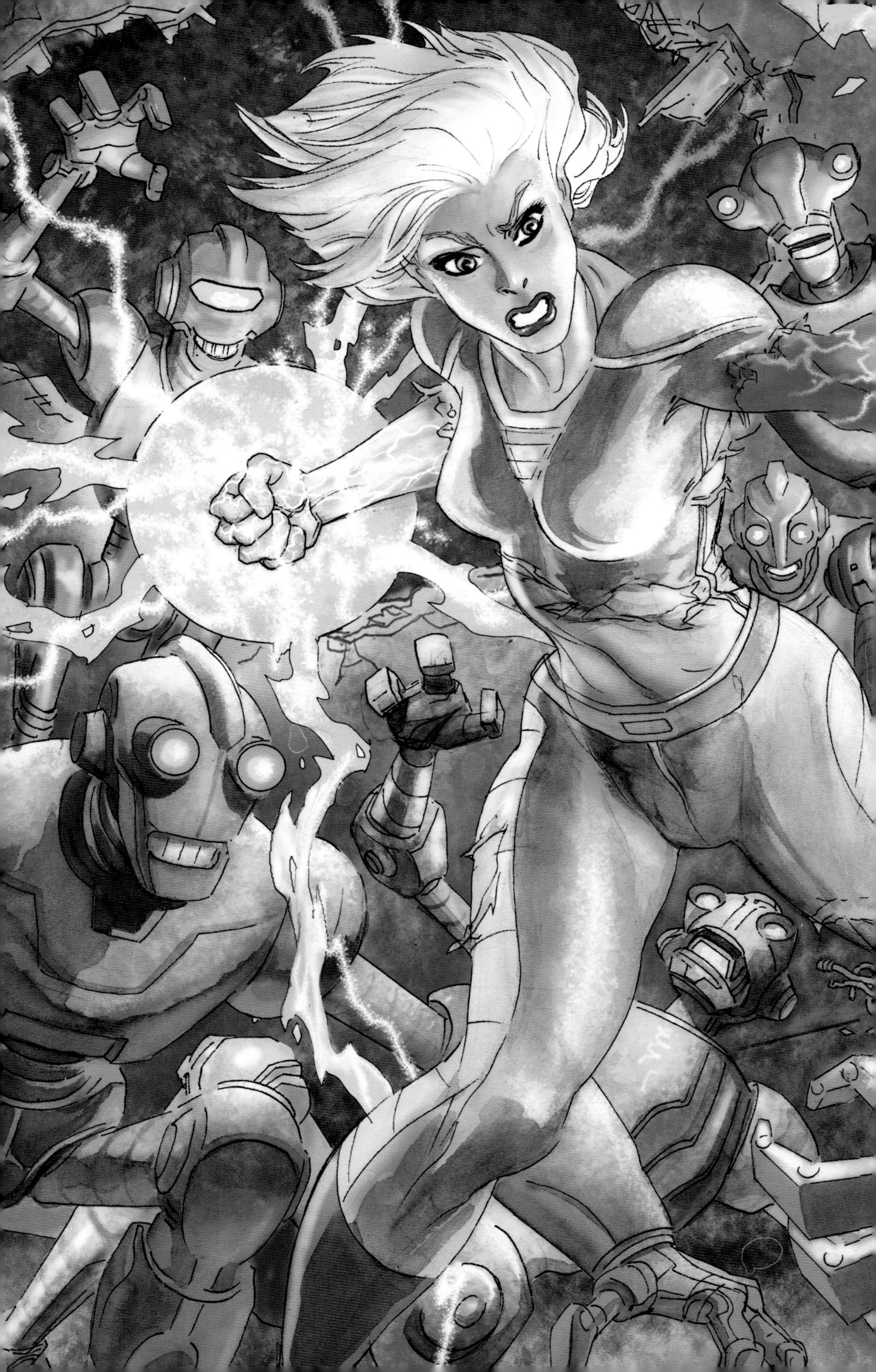

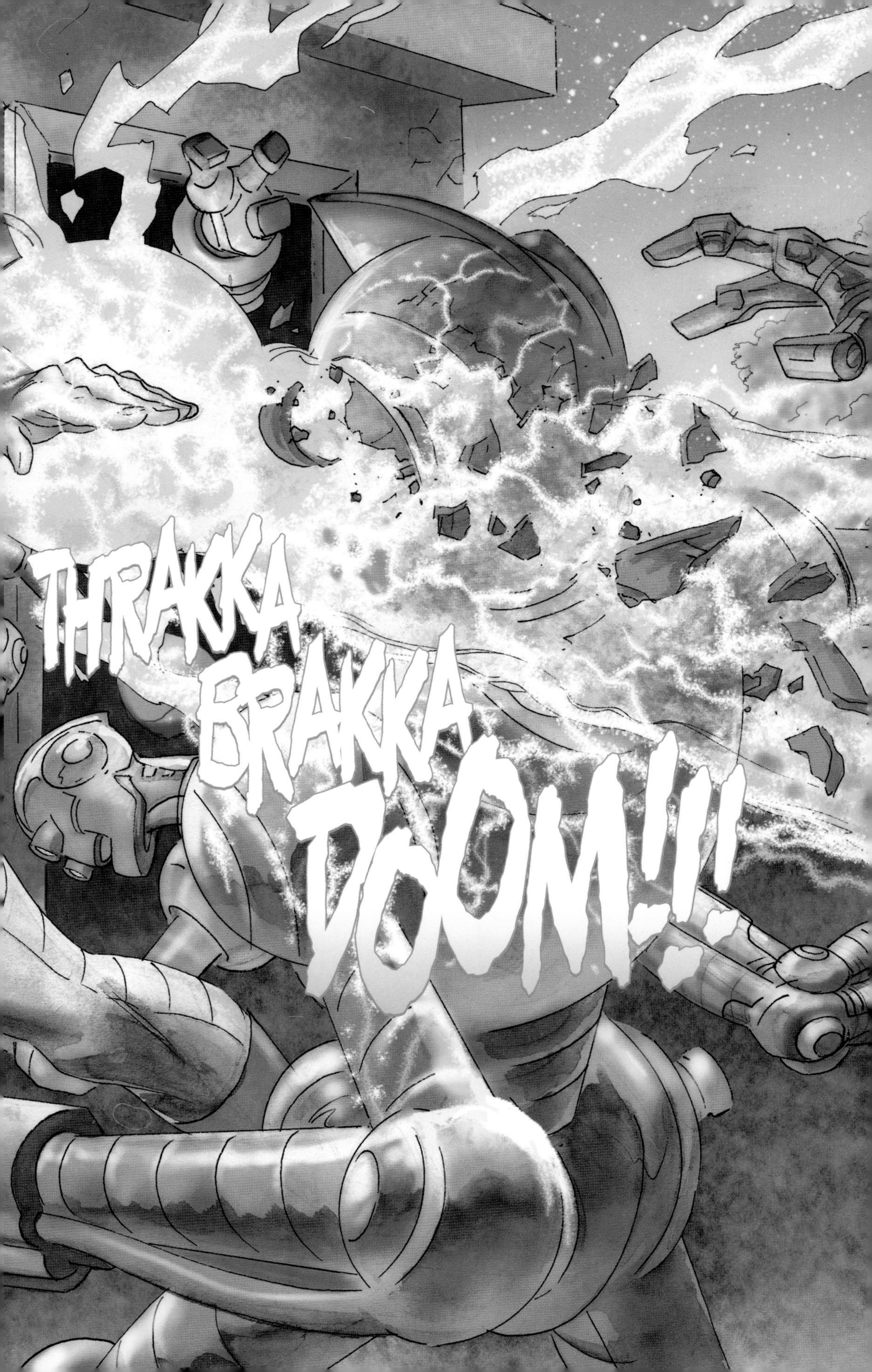
THRAKKA
BRAKKA
DOOM!!!

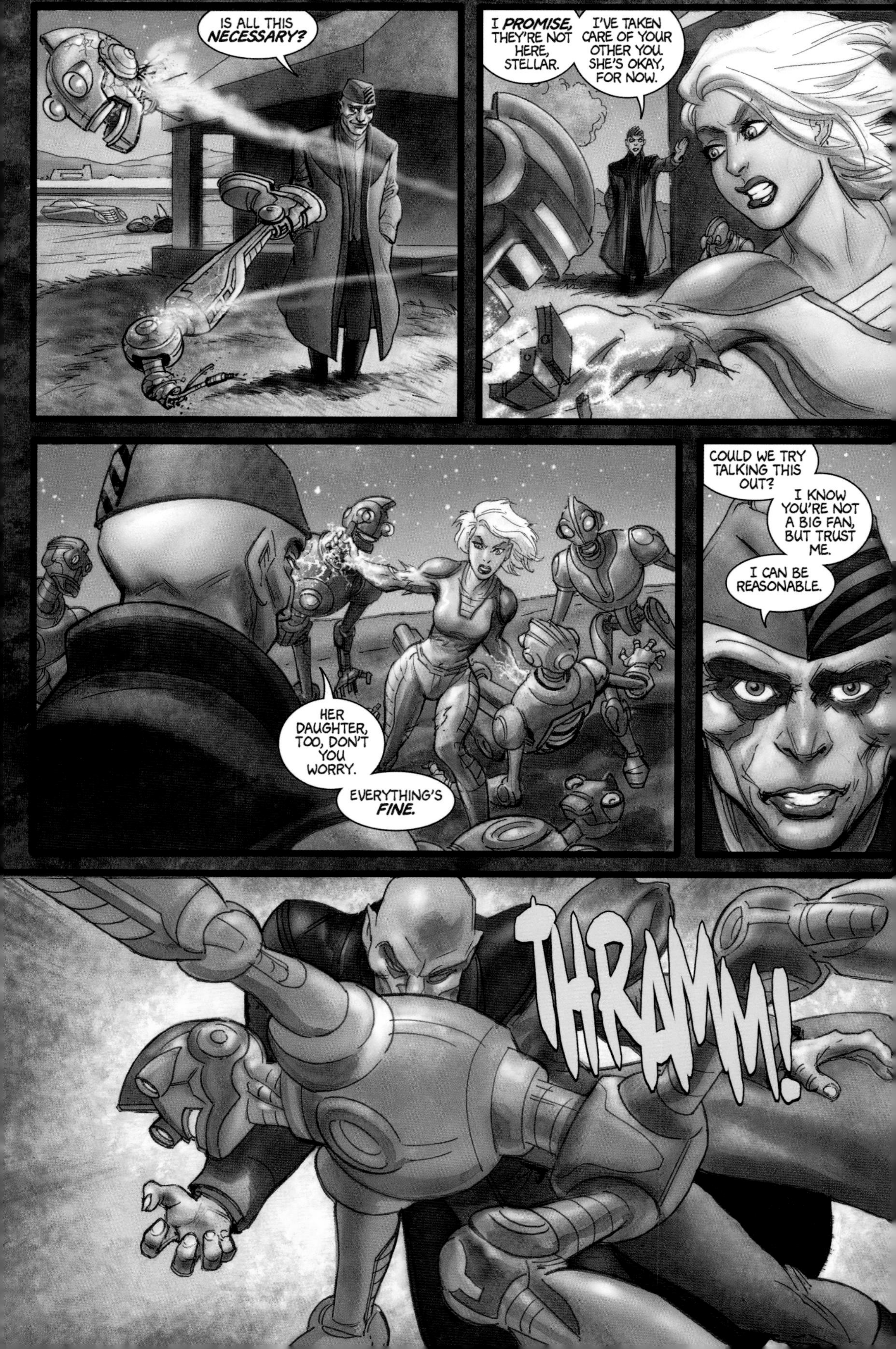
IS ALL THIS *NECESSARY?*
I *PROMISE,* THEY'RE NOT HERE, STELLAR.
I'VE TAKEN CARE OF YOUR OTHER YOU. SHE'S OKAY, FOR NOW.
HER DAUGHTER, TOO, DON'T YOU WORRY.
EVERYTHING'S *FINE.*
COULD WE TRY TALKING THIS OUT?
I KNOW YOU'RE NOT A BIG FAN, BUT TRUST ME.
I CAN BE REASONABLE.
THRAMM!

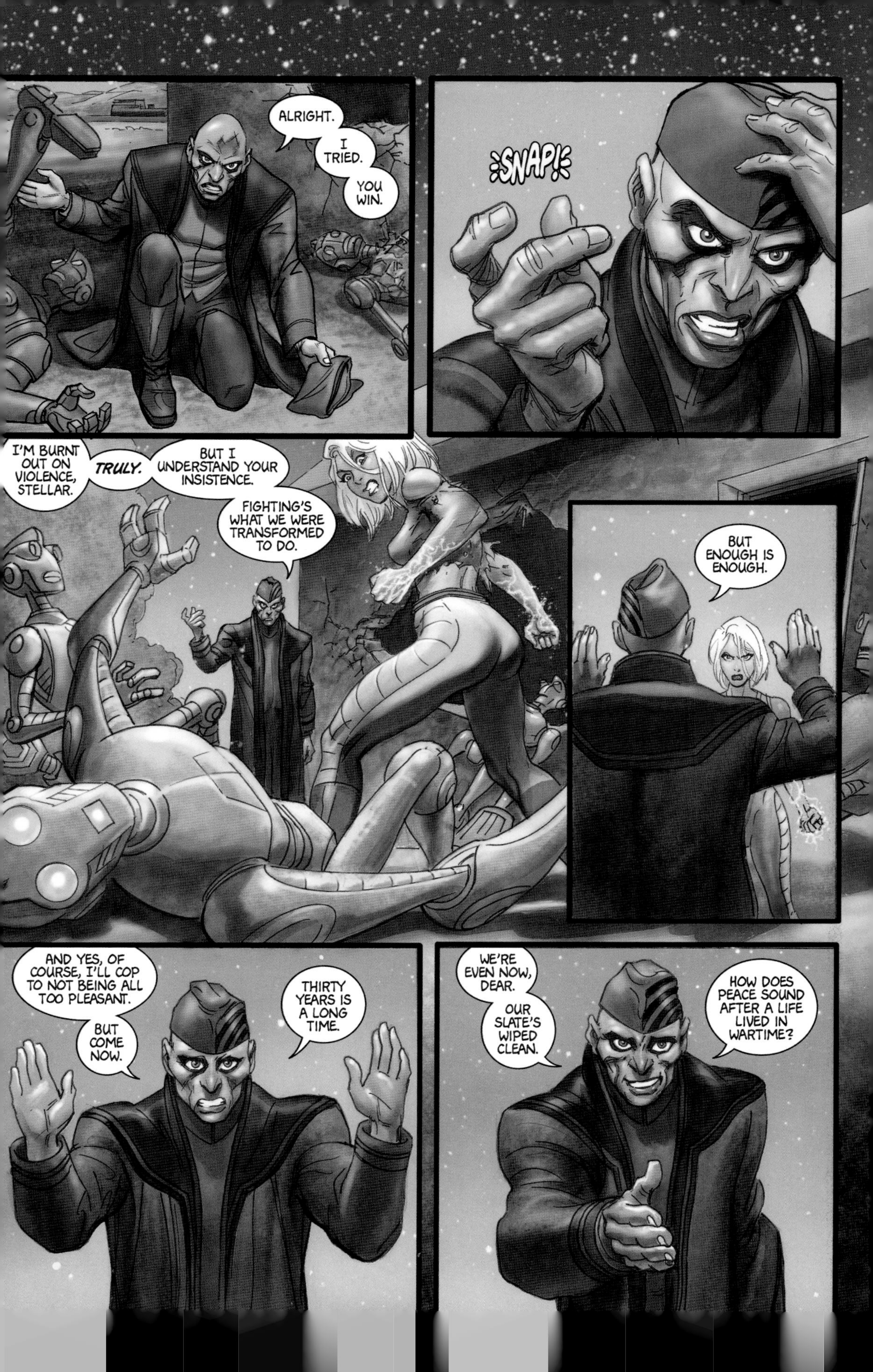
ALRIGHT.
I TRIED.
YOU WIN.
SNAP!
I'M BURNT OUT ON VIOLENCE, STELLAR.
TRULY.
BUT I UNDERSTAND YOUR INSISTENCE.
FIGHTING'S WHAT WE WERE TRANSFORMED TO DO.
BUT ENOUGH IS ENOUGH.
AND YES, OF COURSE, I'LL COP TO NOT BEING ALL TOO PLEASANT.
BUT COME NOW.
THIRTY YEARS IS A LONG TIME.
WE'RE EVEN NOW, DEAR.
OUR SLATE'S WIPED CLEAN.
HOW DOES PEACE SOUND AFTER A LIFE LIVED IN WARTIME?

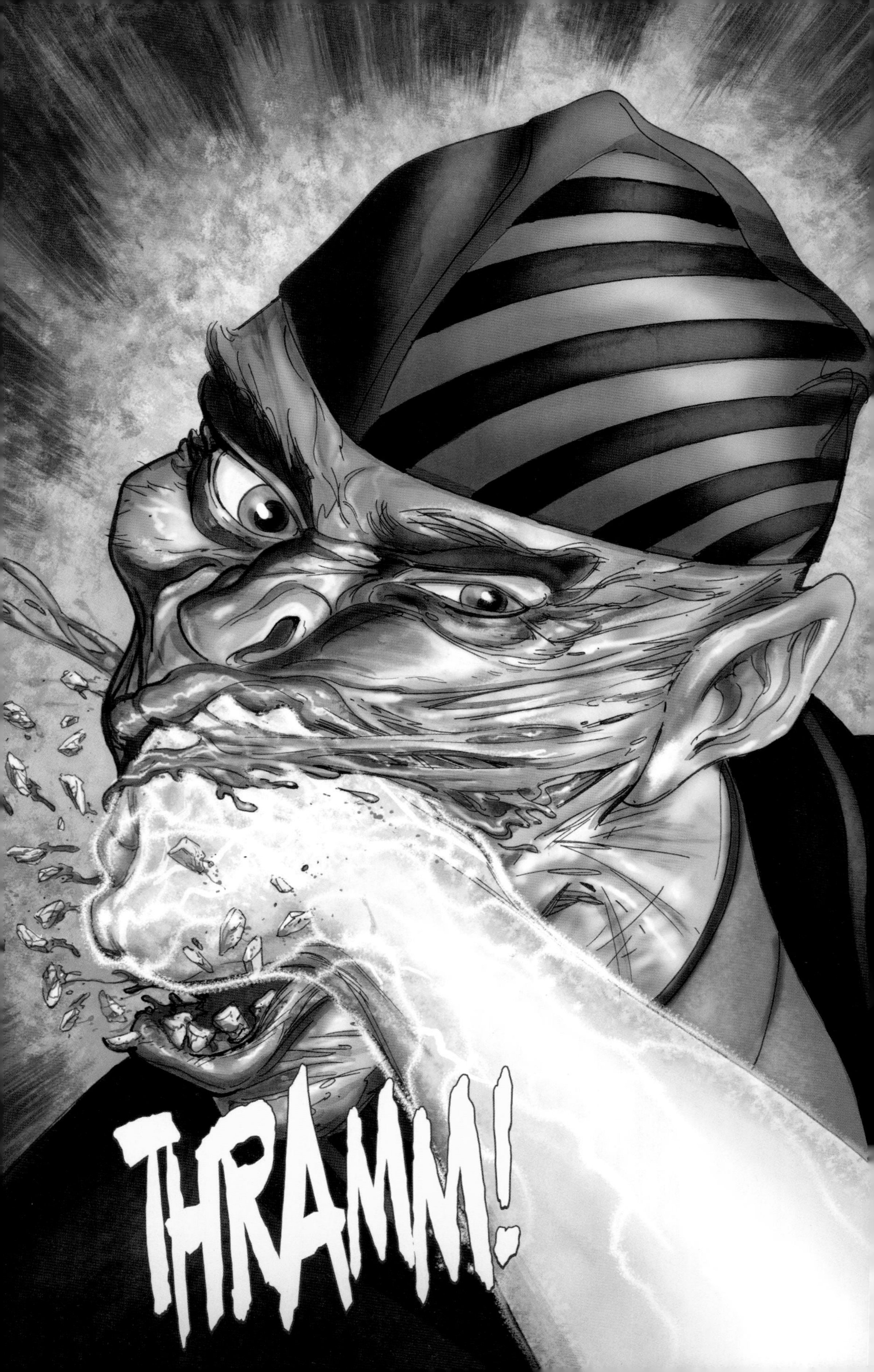
THRAMM!

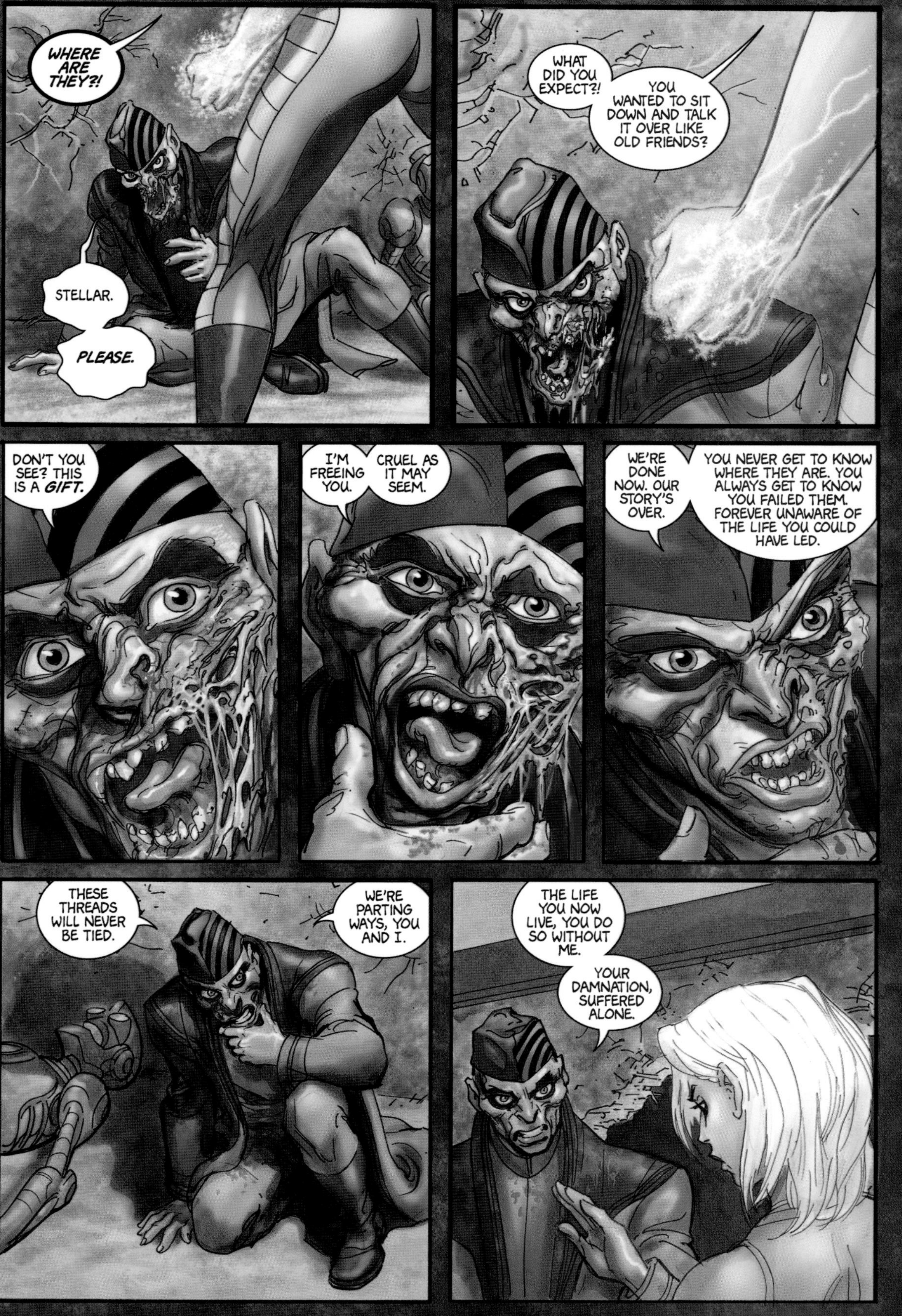
WHERE ARE THEY?!
STELLAR.
PLEASE.
WHAT DID YOU EXPECT?!
YOU WANTED TO SIT DOWN AND TALK IT OVER LIKE OLD FRIENDS?
DON'T YOU SEE? THIS IS A GIFT.
I'M FREEING YOU.
CRUEL AS IT MAY SEEM.
WE'RE DONE NOW. OUR STORY'S OVER.
YOU NEVER GET TO KNOW WHERE THEY ARE. YOU ALWAYS GET TO KNOW YOU FAILED THEM. FOREVER UNAWARE OF THE LIFE YOU COULD HAVE LED.
THESE THREADS WILL NEVER BE TIED.
WE'RE PARTING WAYS, YOU AND I.
THE LIFE YOU NOW LIVE, YOU DO SO WITHOUT ME.
YOUR DAMNATION, SUFFERED ALONE.

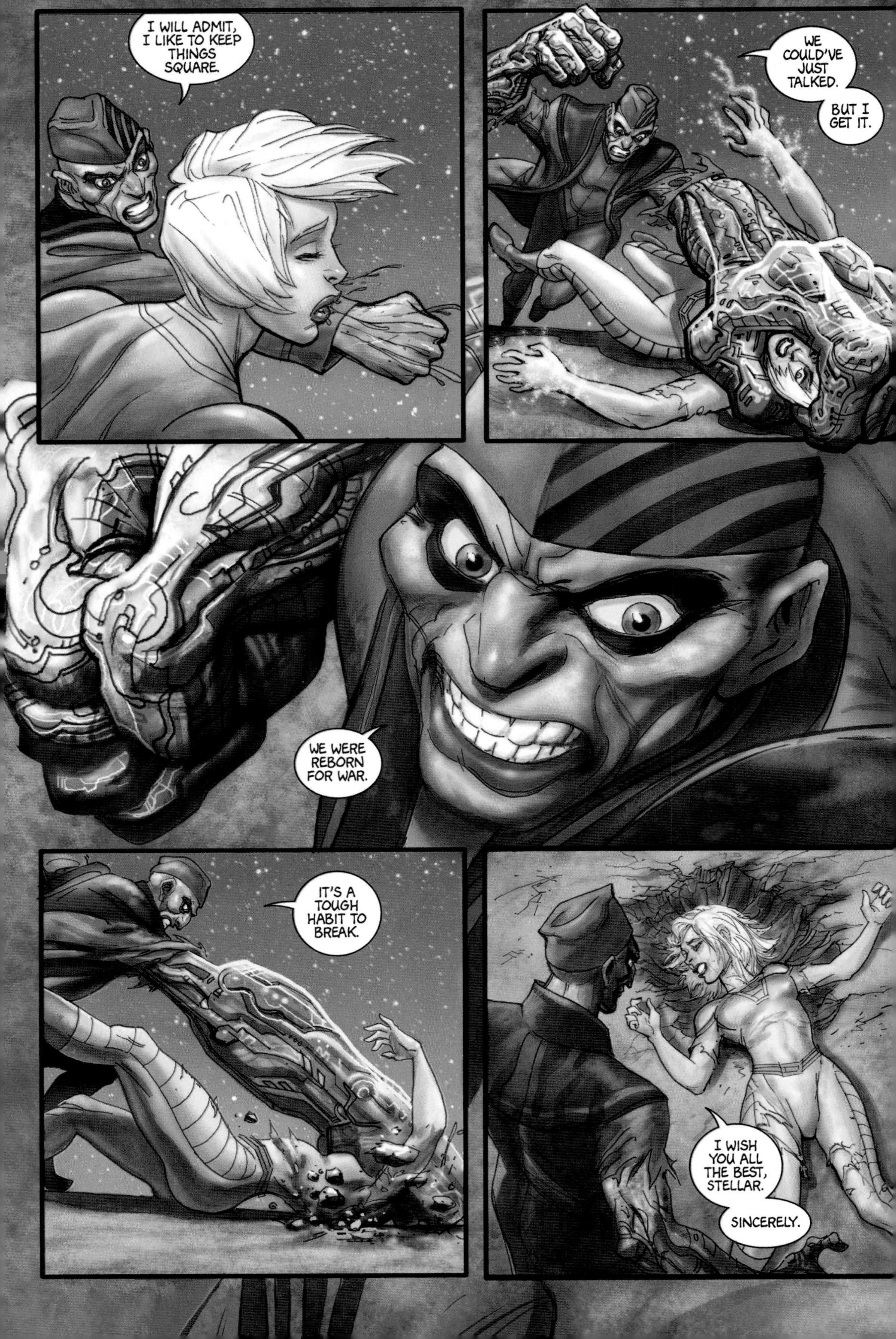
I WILL ADMIT, I LIKE TO KEEP THINGS SQUARE.
WE COULD'VE JUST TALKED.
BUT I GET IT.
WE WERE REBORN FOR WAR.
IT'S A TOUGH HABIT TO BREAK.
I WISH YOU ALL THE BEST, STELLAR.
SINCERELY.

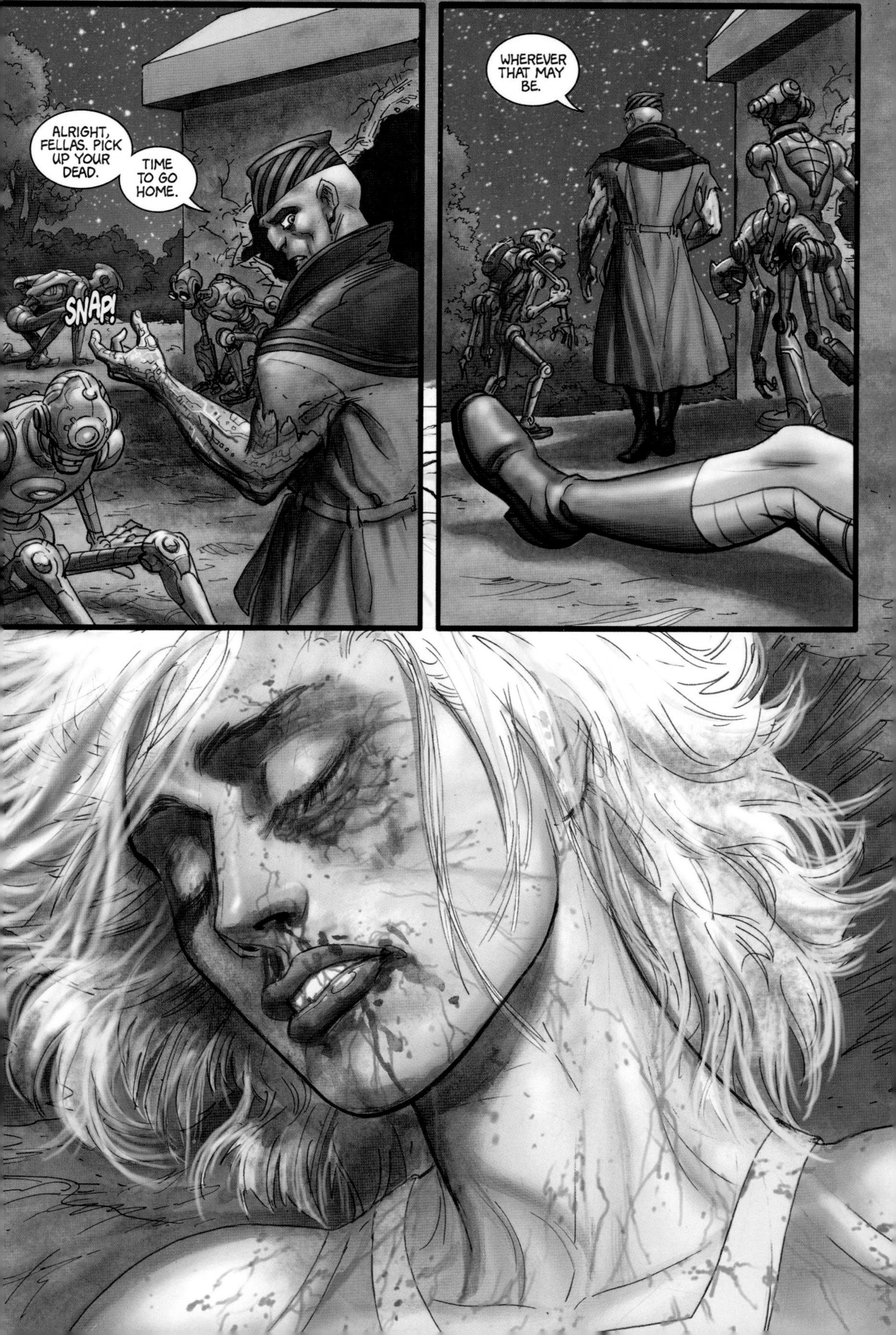
ALRIGHT, FELLAS. PICK UP YOUR DEAD.
TIME TO GO HOME.
SNAP!
WHEREVER THAT MAY BE.

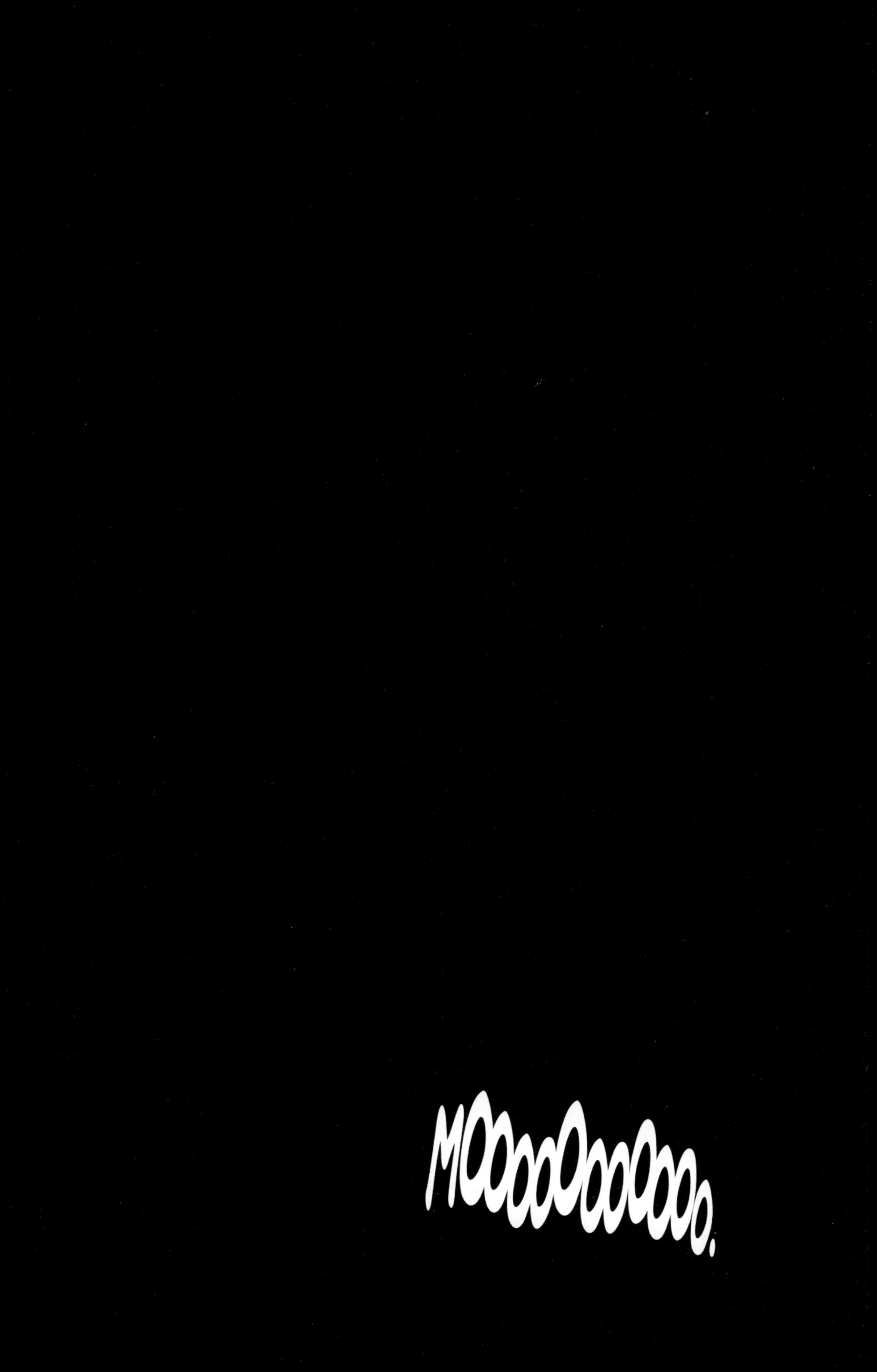
MOooOooOooo.

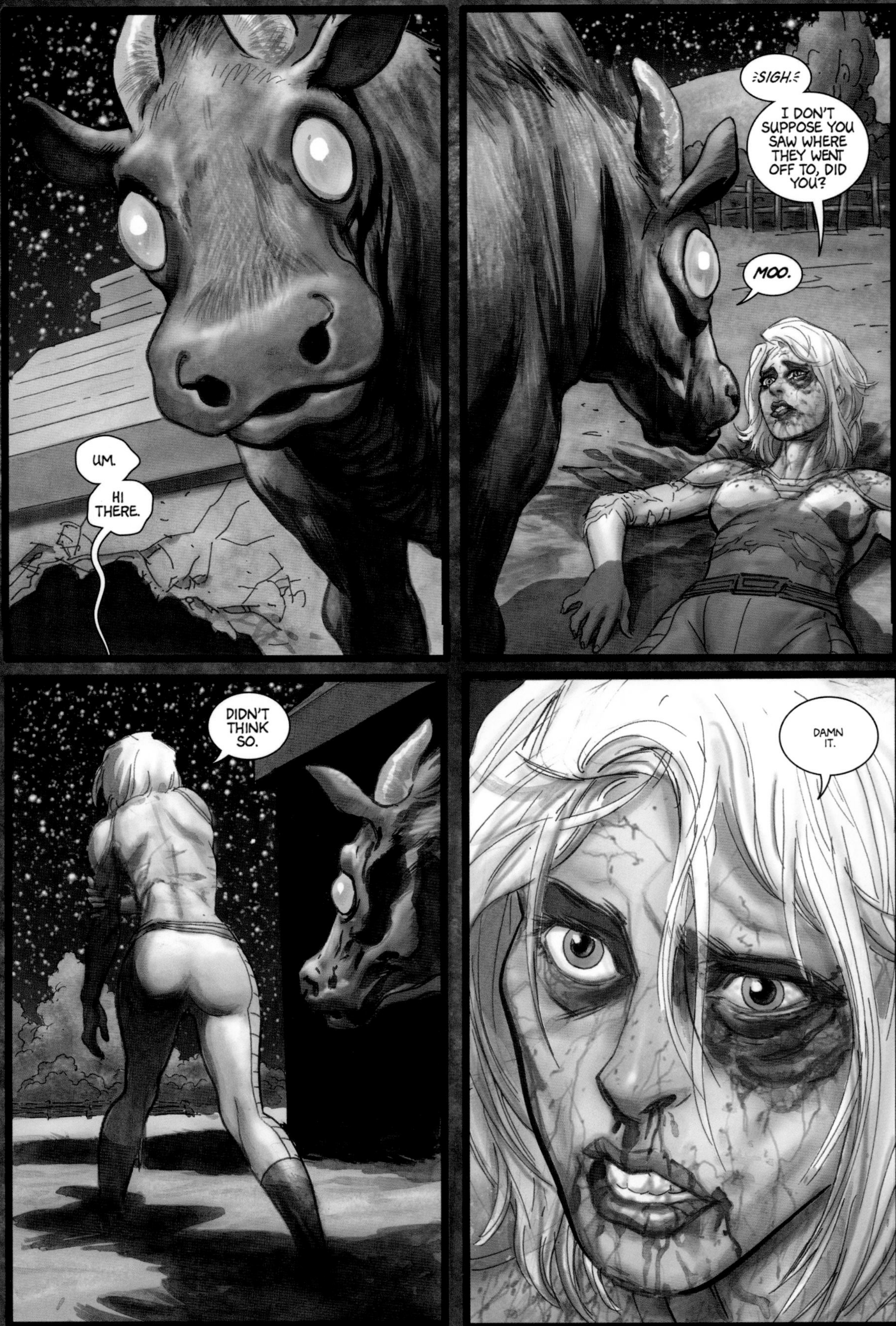
UM.
HI THERE.
SIGH.
I DON'T SUPPOSE YOU SAW WHERE THEY WENT OFF TO, DID YOU?
MOO.
DIDN'T THINK SO.
DAMN IT.

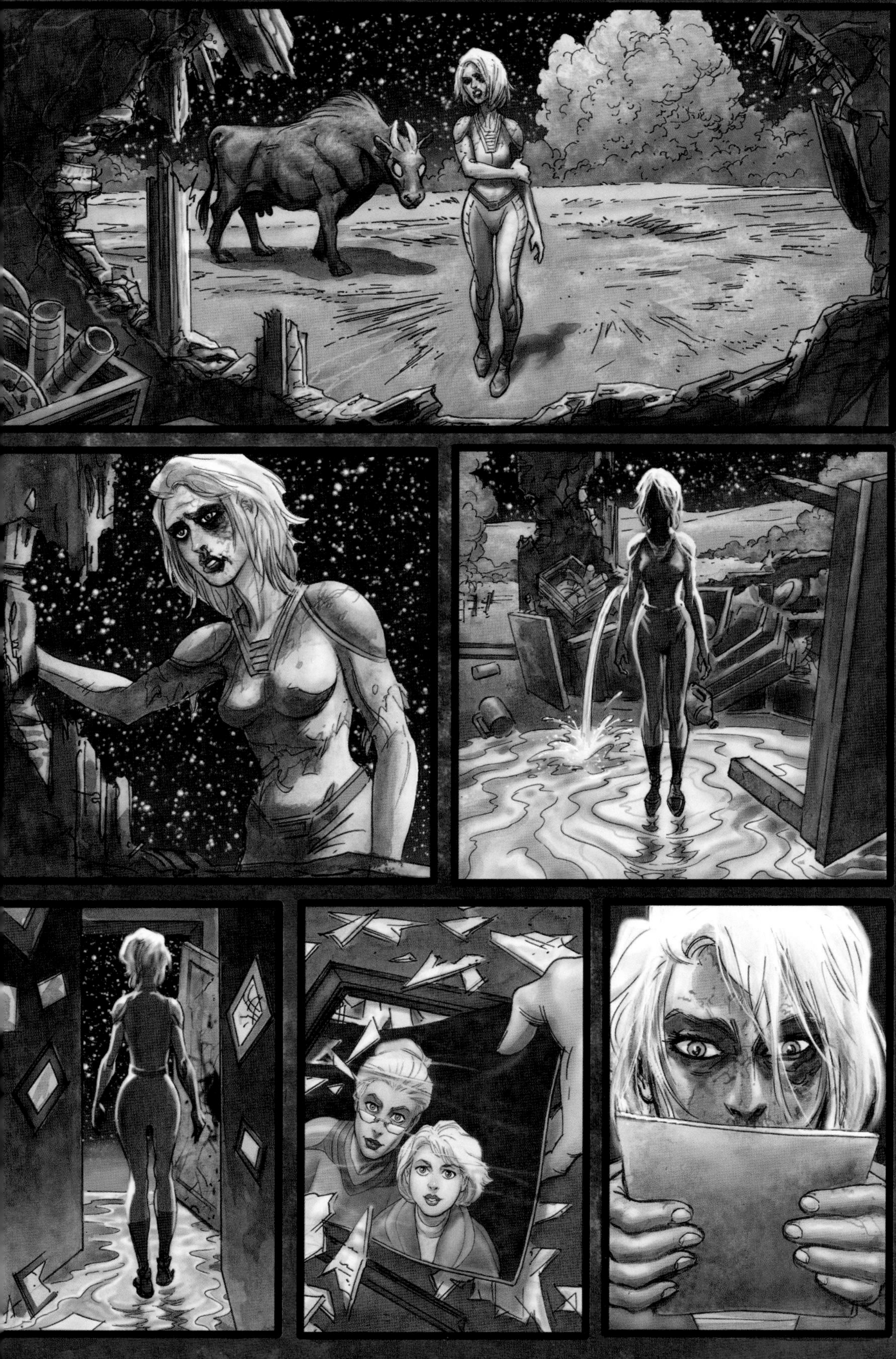

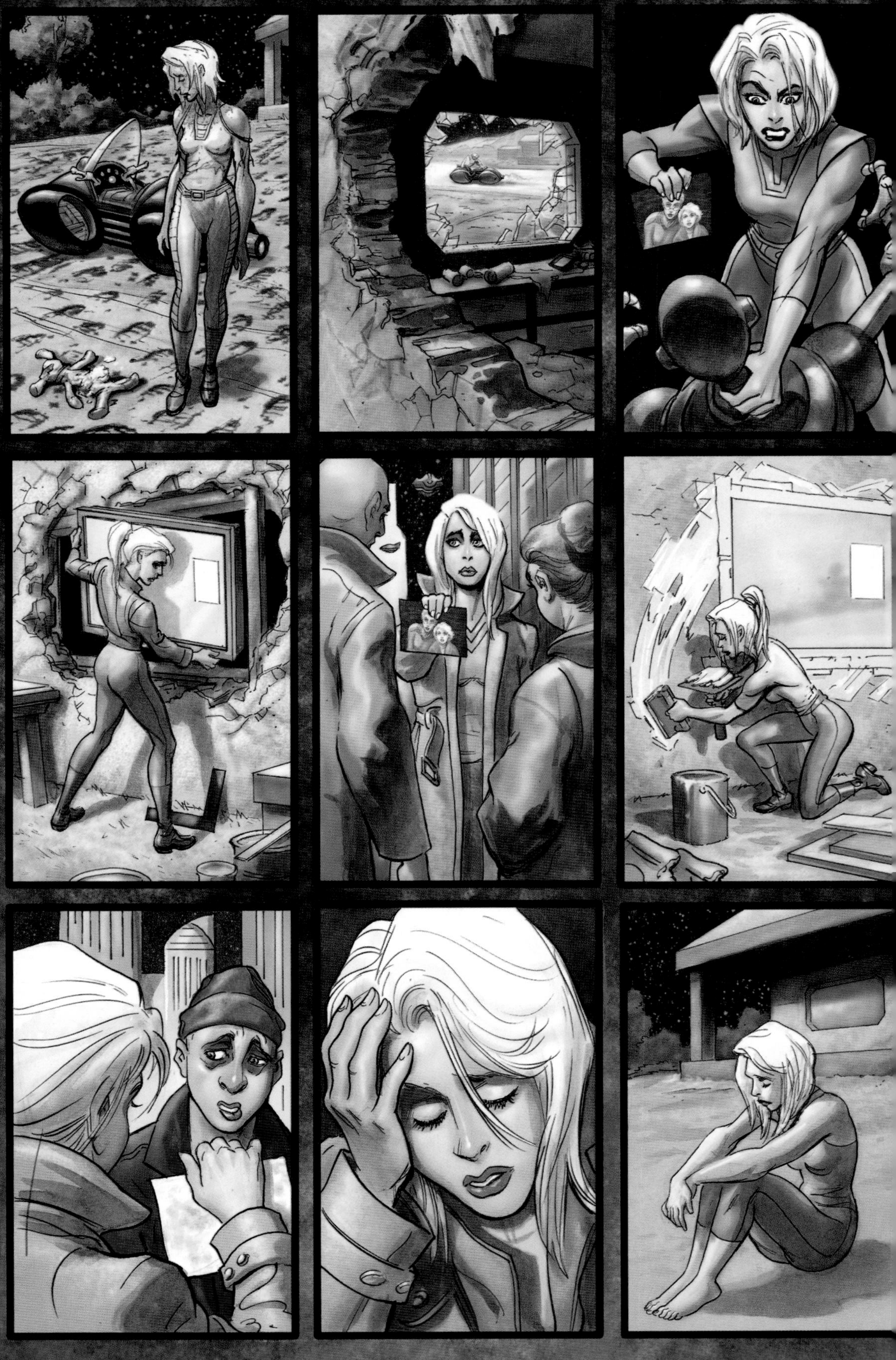

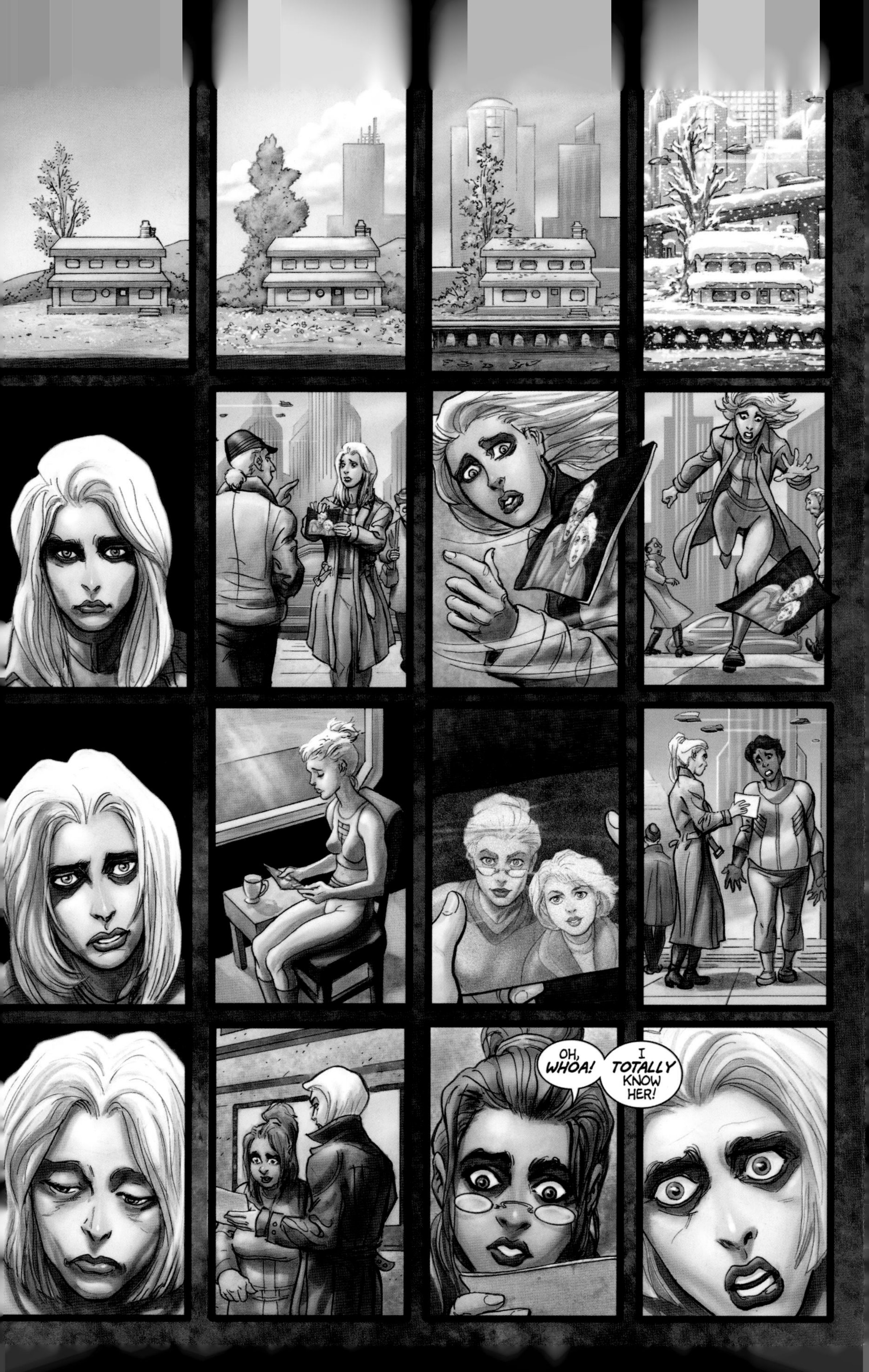
OH, WHOA!
I TOTALLY KNOW HER!

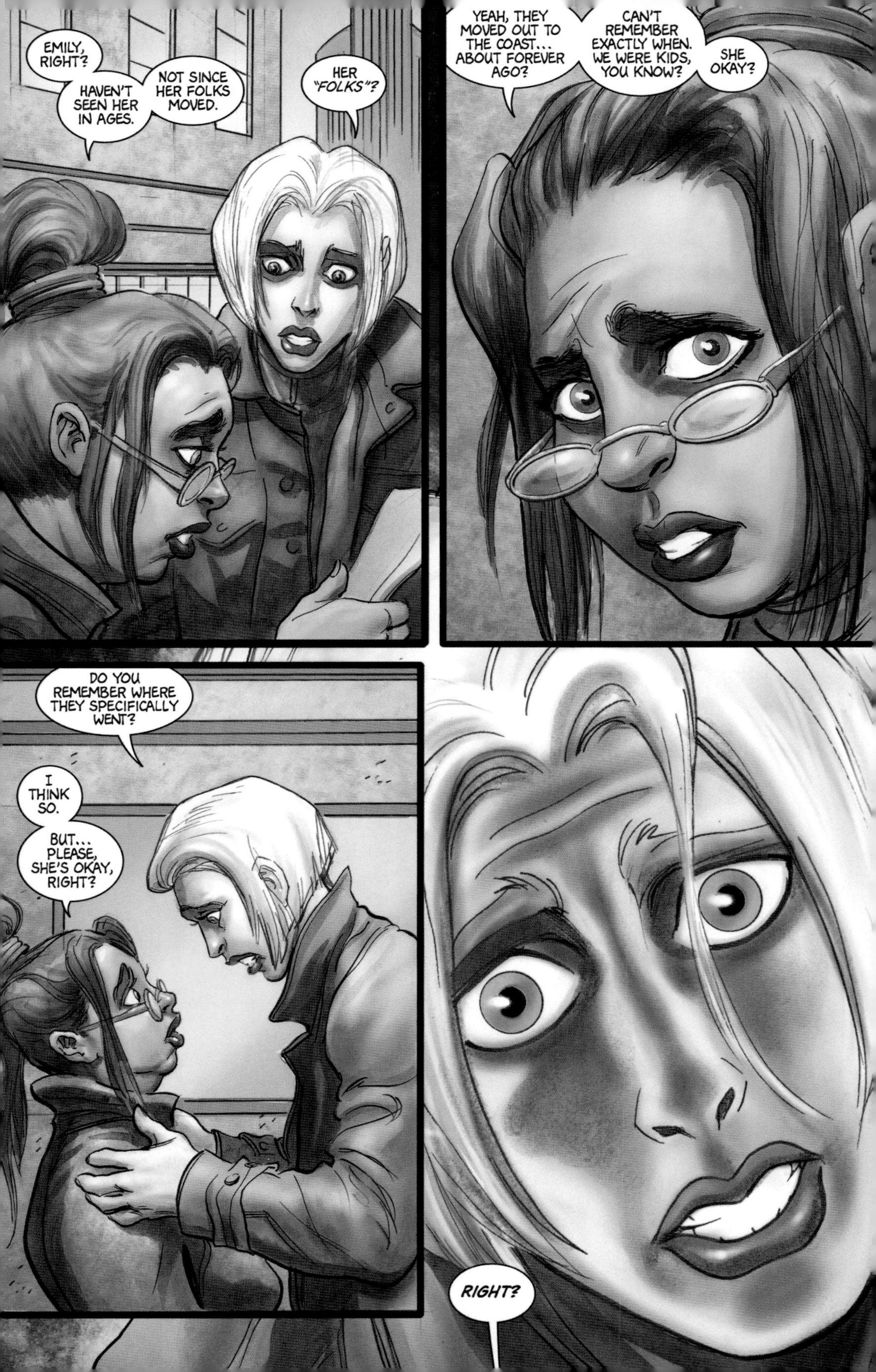
EMILY, RIGHT?
HAVEN'T SEEN HER IN AGES.
NOT SINCE HER FOLKS MOVED.
HER "FOLKS"?
YEAH, THEY MOVED OUT TO THE COAST... ABOUT FOREVER AGO?
CAN'T REMEMBER EXACTLY WHEN. WE WERE KIDS, YOU KNOW?
SHE OKAY?
DO YOU REMEMBER WHERE THEY SPECIFICALLY WENT?
I THINK SO.
BUT... PLEASE, SHE'S OKAY, RIGHT?
RIGHT?

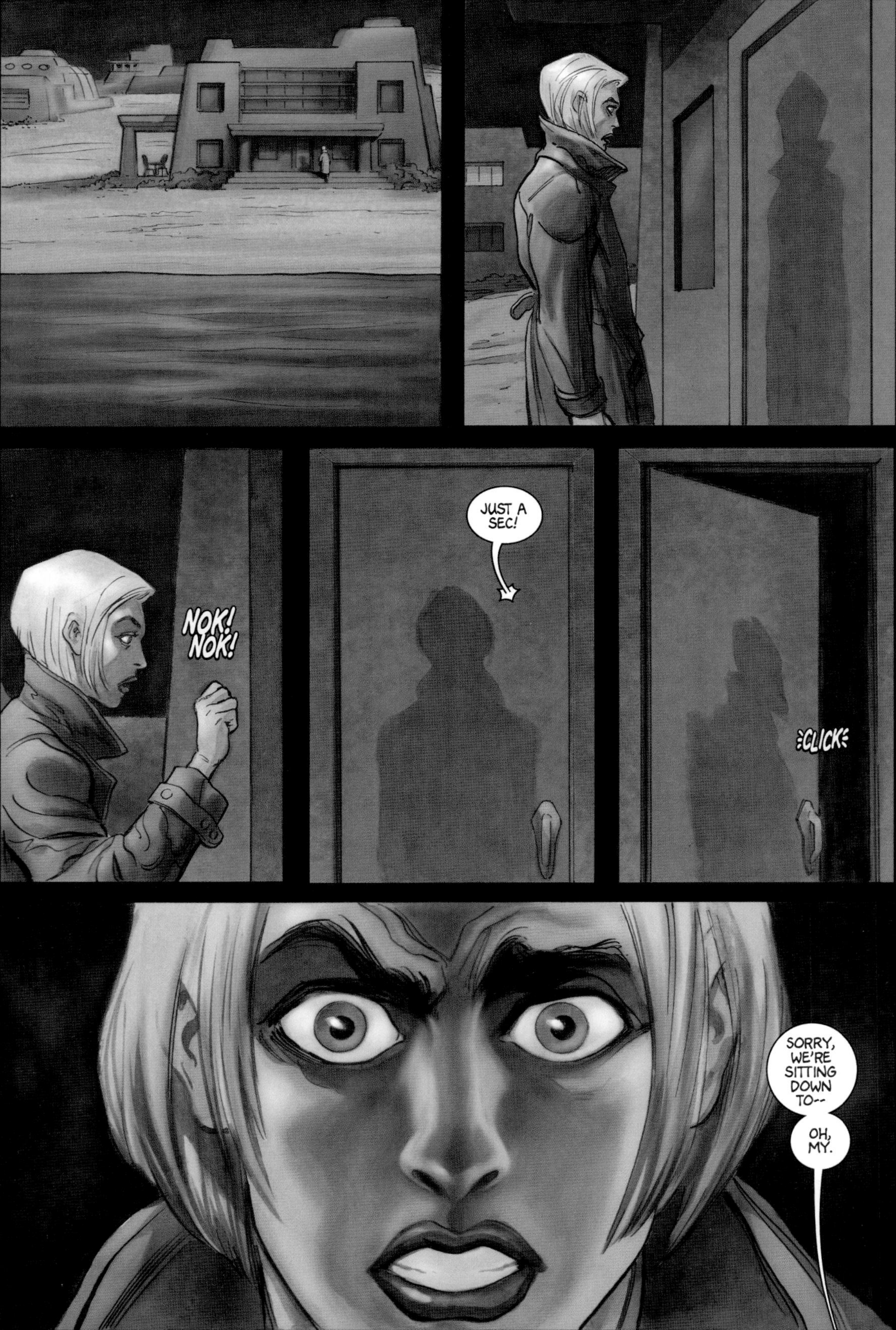
NOK! NOK!
JUST A SEC!
CLICK
SORRY, WE'RE SITTING DOWN TO--
OH, MY.

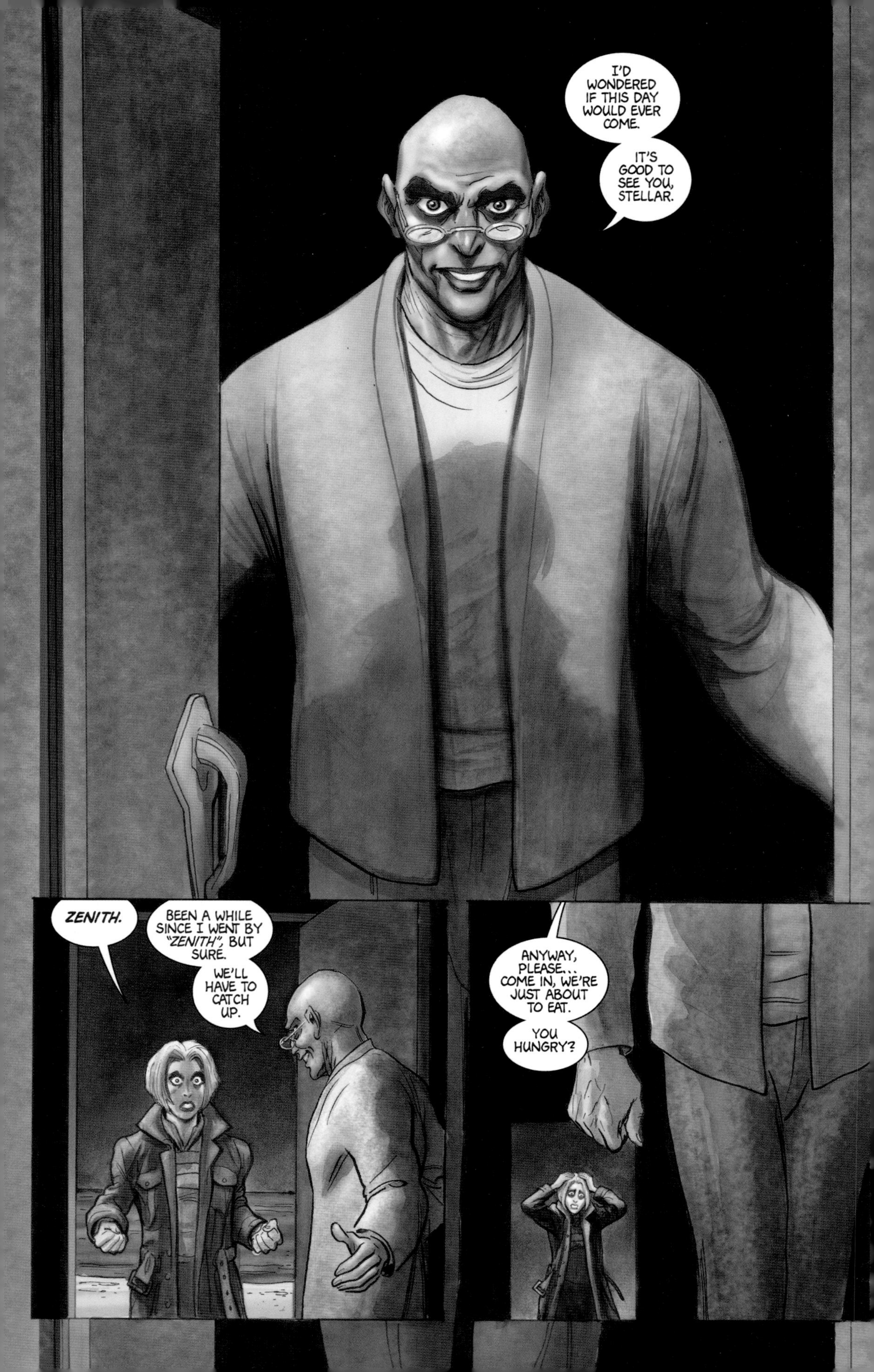
I'D WONDERED IF THIS DAY WOULD EVER COME.
IT'S GOOD TO SEE YOU, STELLAR.
ZENITH.
BEEN A WHILE SINCE I WENT BY "ZENITH", BUT SURE.
WE'LL HAVE TO CATCH UP.
ANYWAY, PLEASE... COME IN, WE'RE JUST ABOUT TO EAT.
YOU HUNGRY?

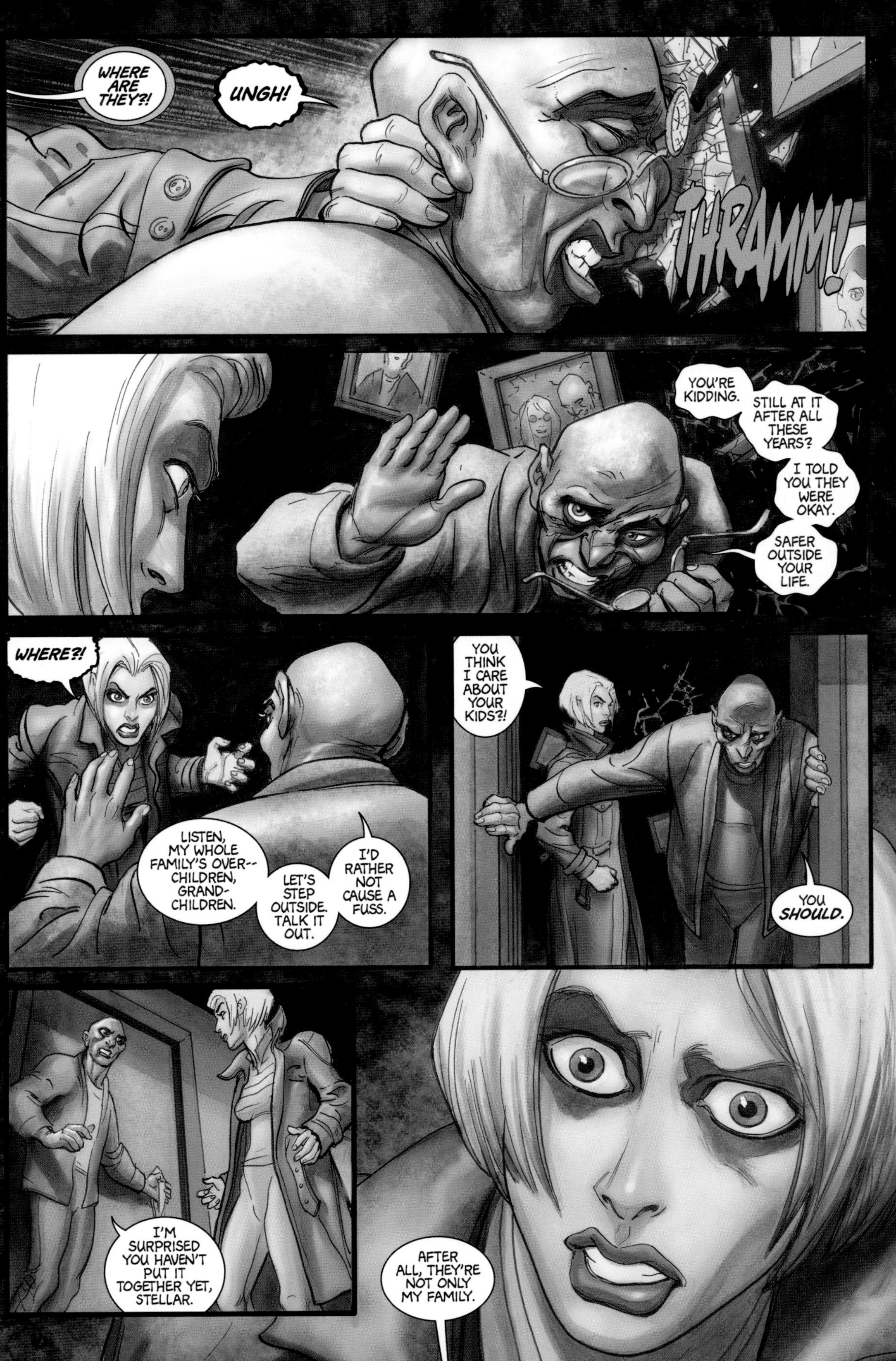
WHERE ARE THEY?!
UNGH!
THRAMM!
YOU'RE KIDDING.
STILL AT IT AFTER ALL THESE YEARS?
I TOLD YOU THEY WERE OKAY.
SAFER OUTSIDE YOUR LIFE.
WHERE?!
LISTEN, MY WHOLE FAMILY'S OVER-- CHILDREN, GRAND-CHILDREN.
LET'S STEP OUTSIDE. TALK IT OUT.
I'D RATHER NOT CAUSE A FUSS.
YOU THINK I CARE ABOUT YOUR KIDS?!
YOU SHOULD.
I'M SURPRISED YOU HAVEN'T PUT IT TOGETHER YET, STELLAR.
AFTER ALL, THEY'RE NOT ONLY MY FAMILY.

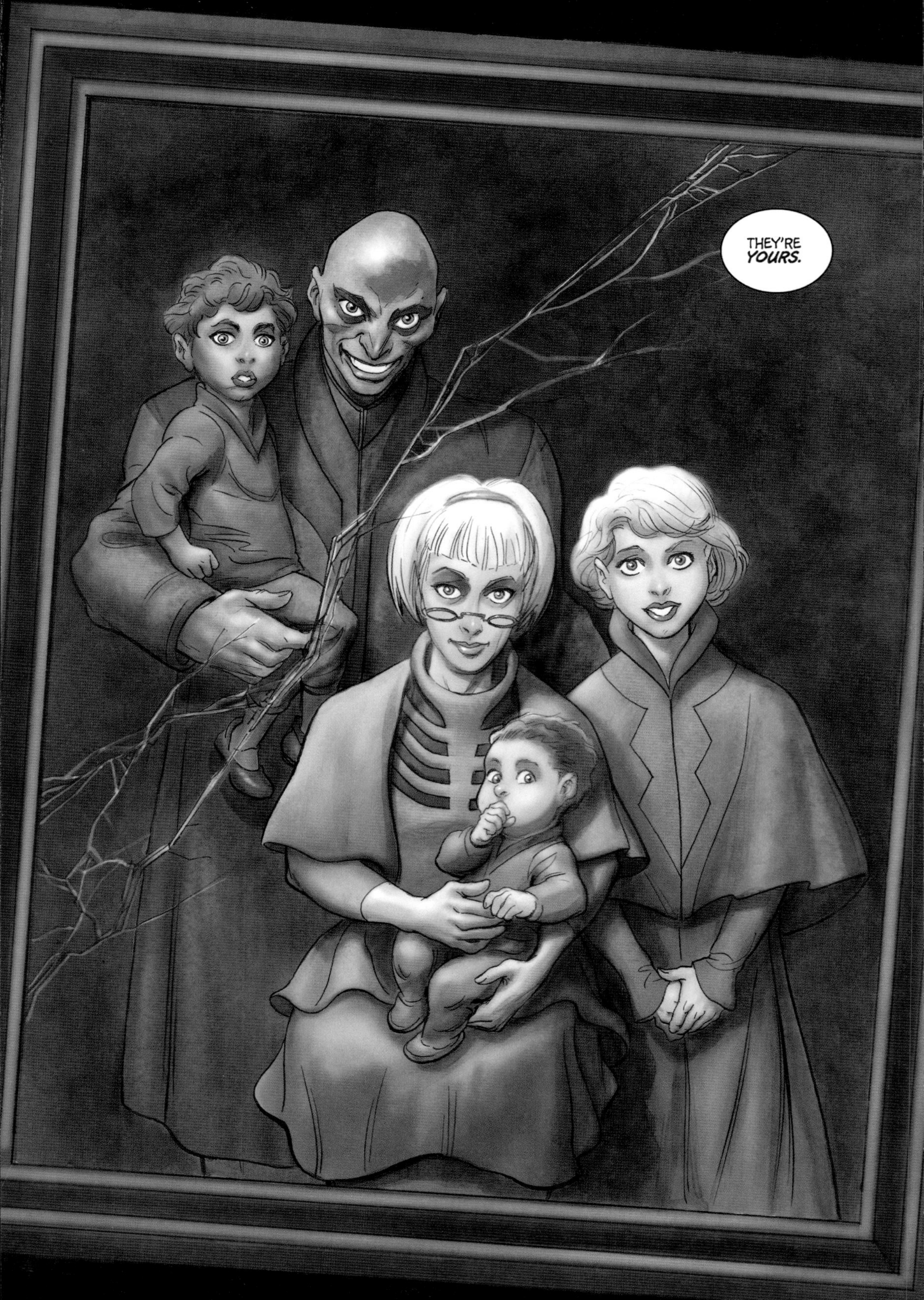
THEY'RE YOURS.

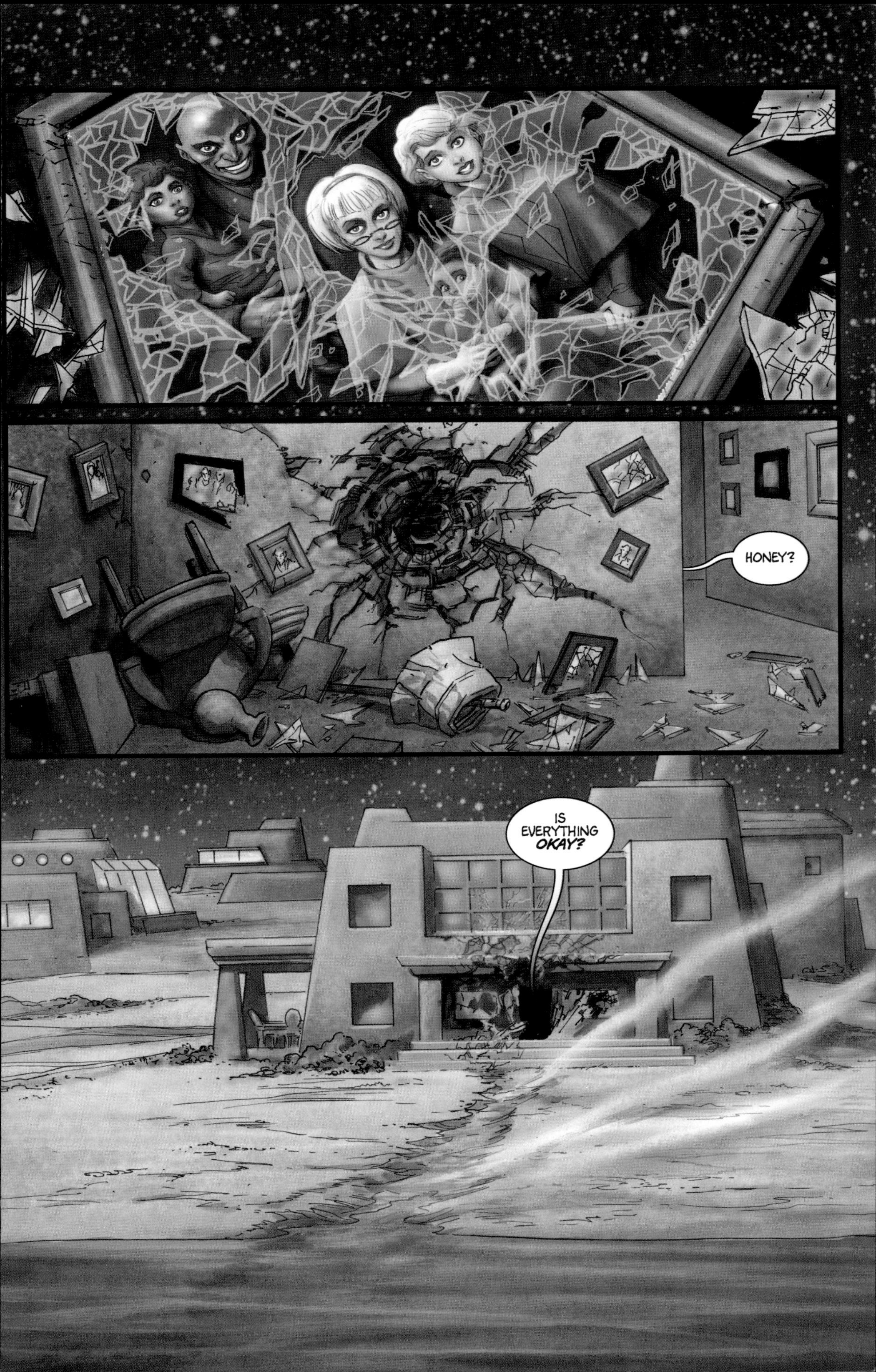
HONEY?
IS EVERYTHING OKAY?

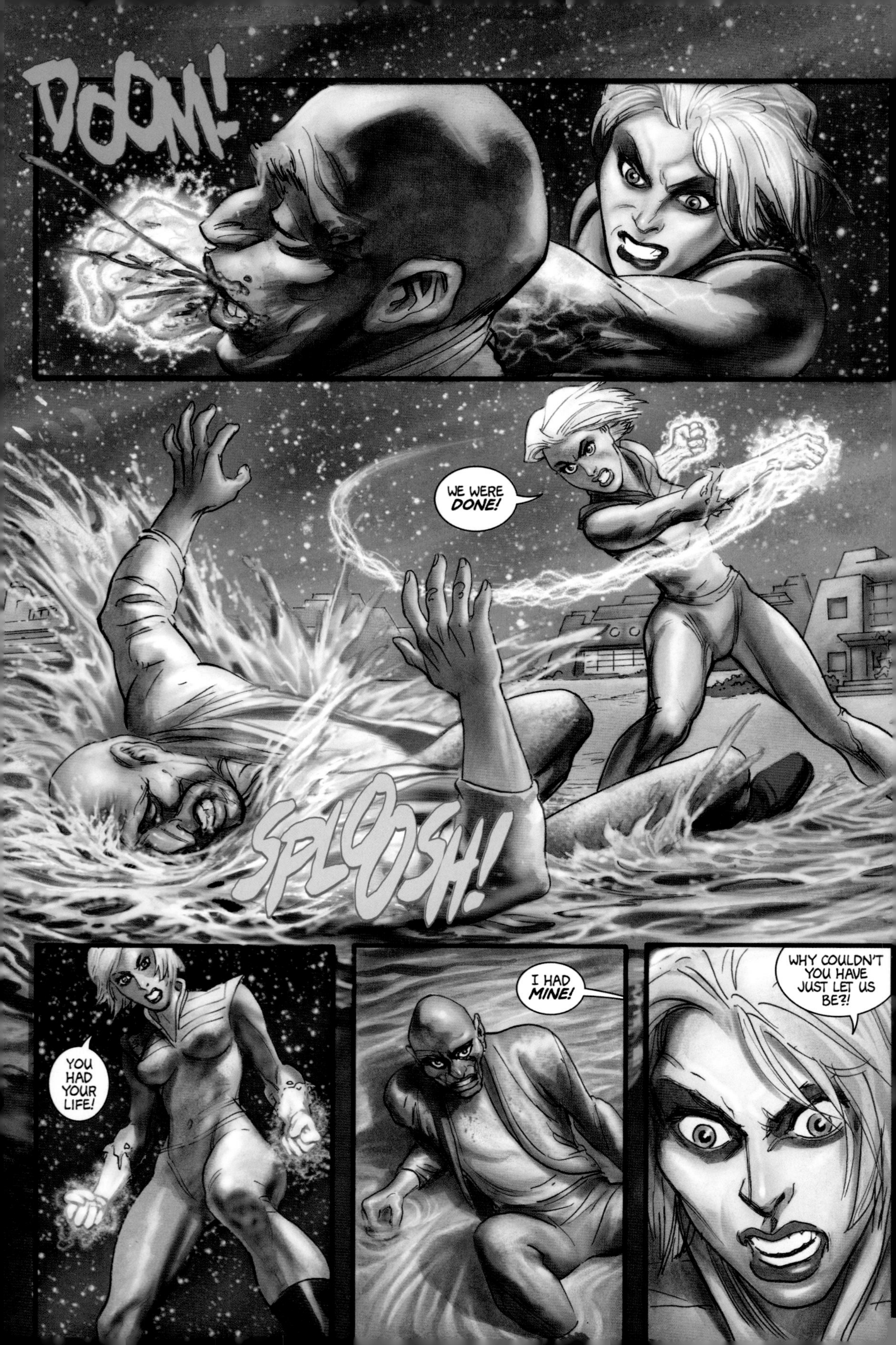
DOOM!
WE WERE DONE!
SPLOOSH!
YOU HAD YOUR LIFE!
I HAD MINE!
WHY COULDN'T YOU HAVE JUST LET US BE?!

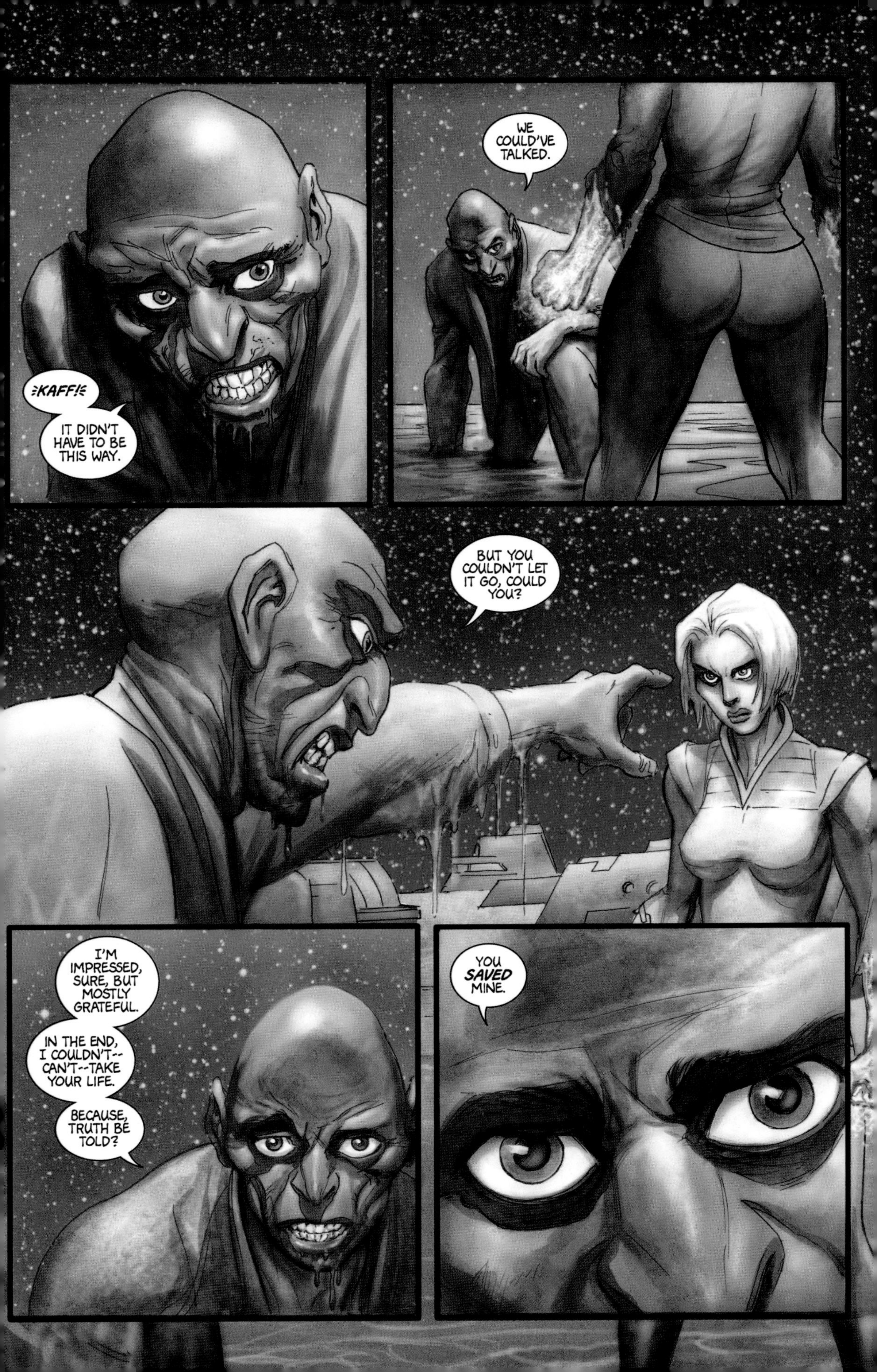

KAFF!
IT DIDN'T HAVE TO BE THIS WAY.
WE COULD'VE TALKED.
BUT YOU COULDN'T LET IT GO, COULD YOU?
I'M IMPRESSED, SURE, BUT MOSTLY GRATEFUL.
IN THE END, I COULDN'T-- CAN'T--TAKE YOUR LIFE.
BECAUSE, TRUTH BE TOLD?
YOU SAVED MINE.

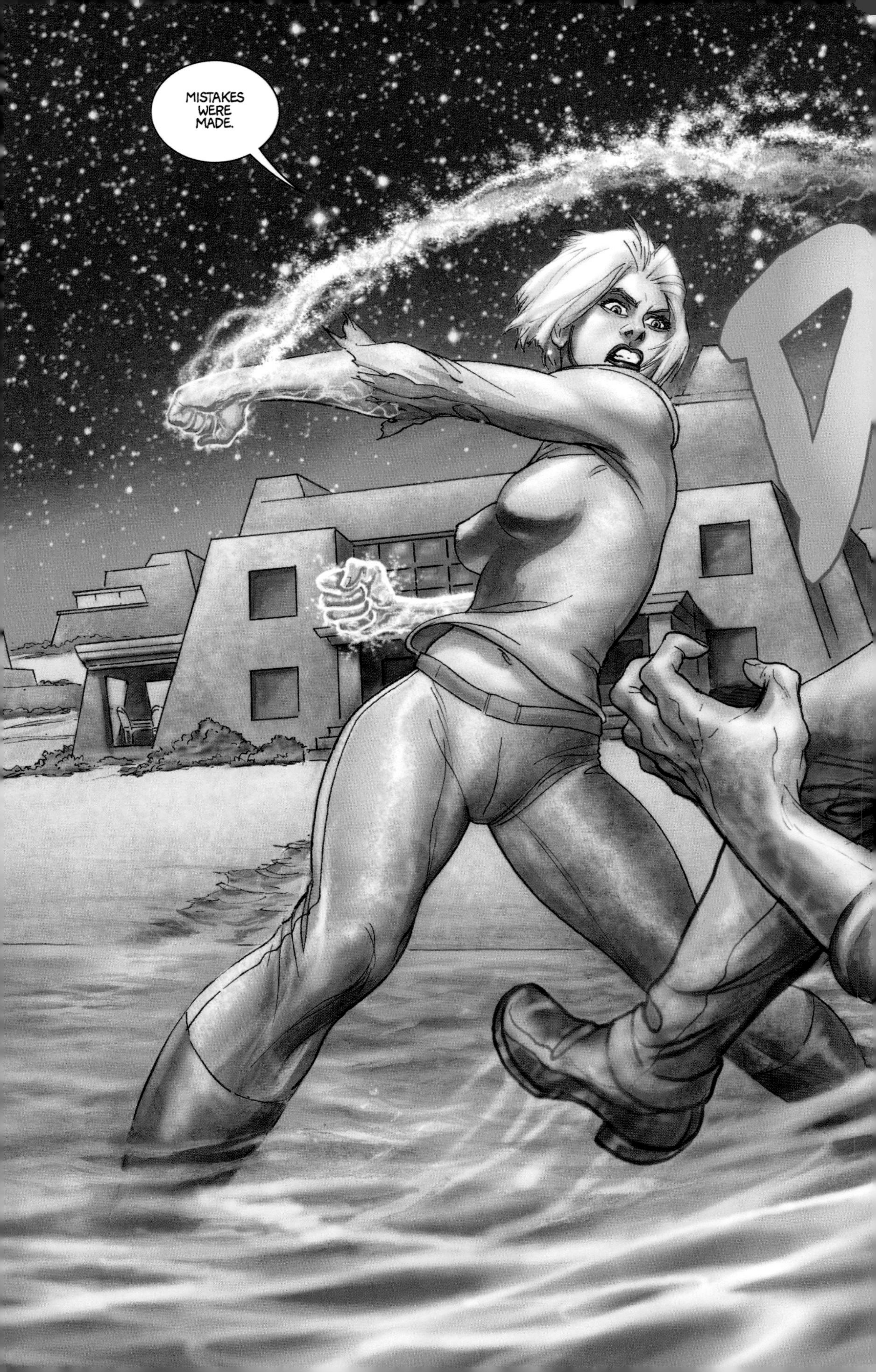
MISTAKES WERE MADE.

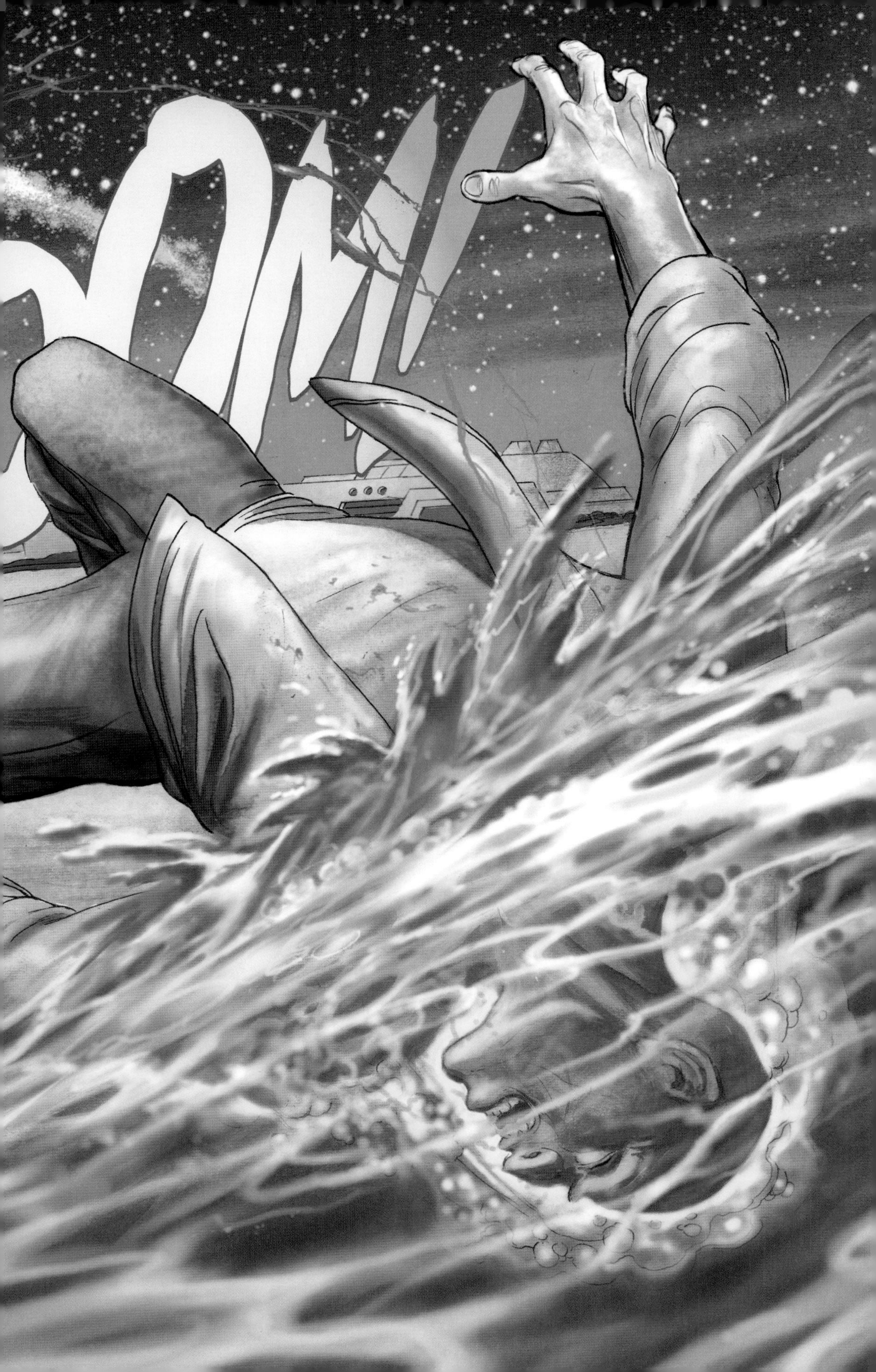
OOM!

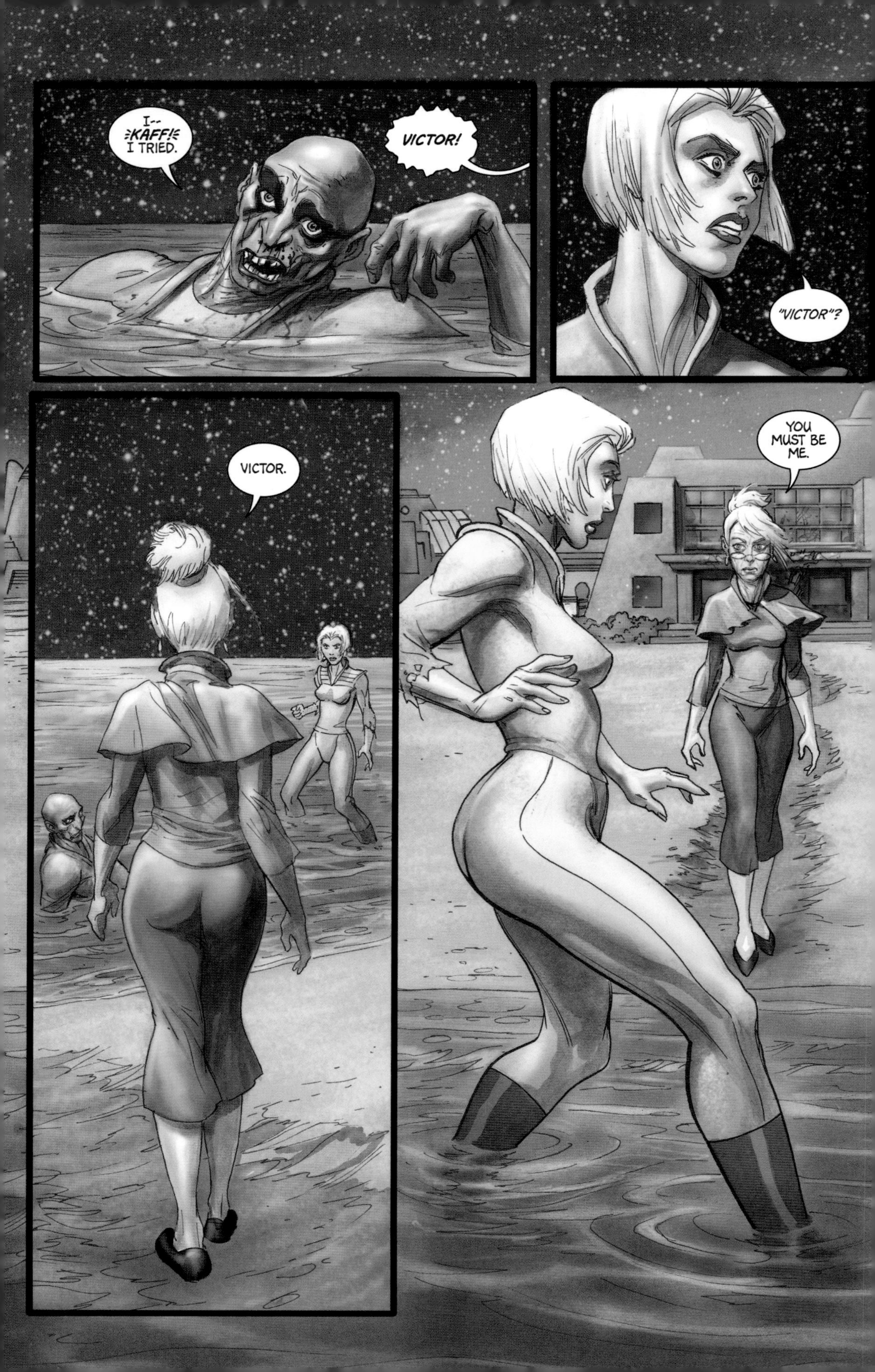
I-- KAFF! I TRIED.
VICTOR!
"VICTOR"?
VICTOR.
YOU MUST BE ME.

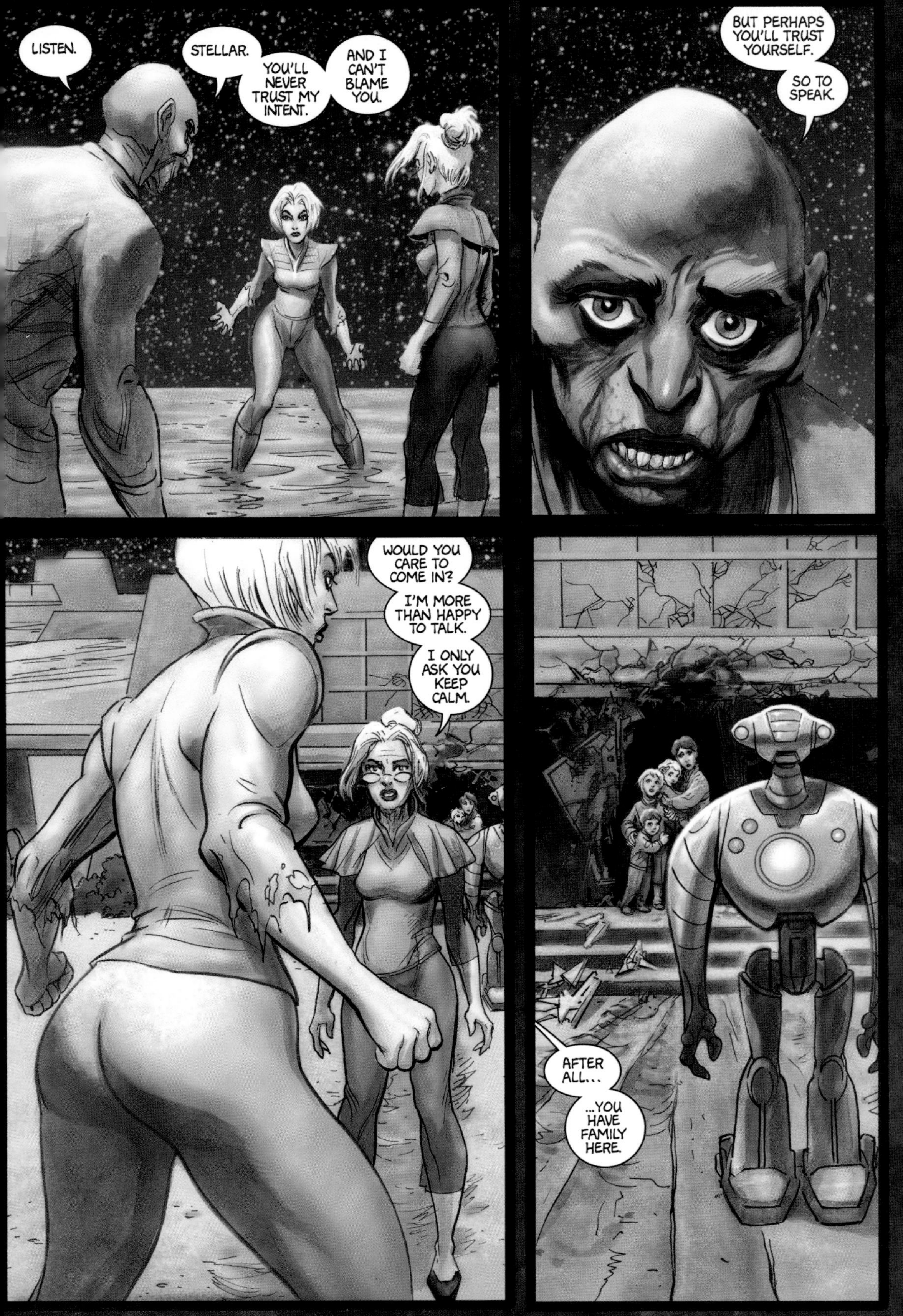
LISTEN.
STELLAR.
YOU'LL NEVER TRUST MY INTENT.
AND I CAN'T BLAME YOU.
BUT PERHAPS YOU'LL TRUST YOURSELF.
SO TO SPEAK.
WOULD YOU CARE TO COME IN?
I'M MORE THAN HAPPY TO TALK.
I ONLY ASK YOU KEEP CALM.
AFTER ALL...
...YOU HAVE FAMILY HERE.

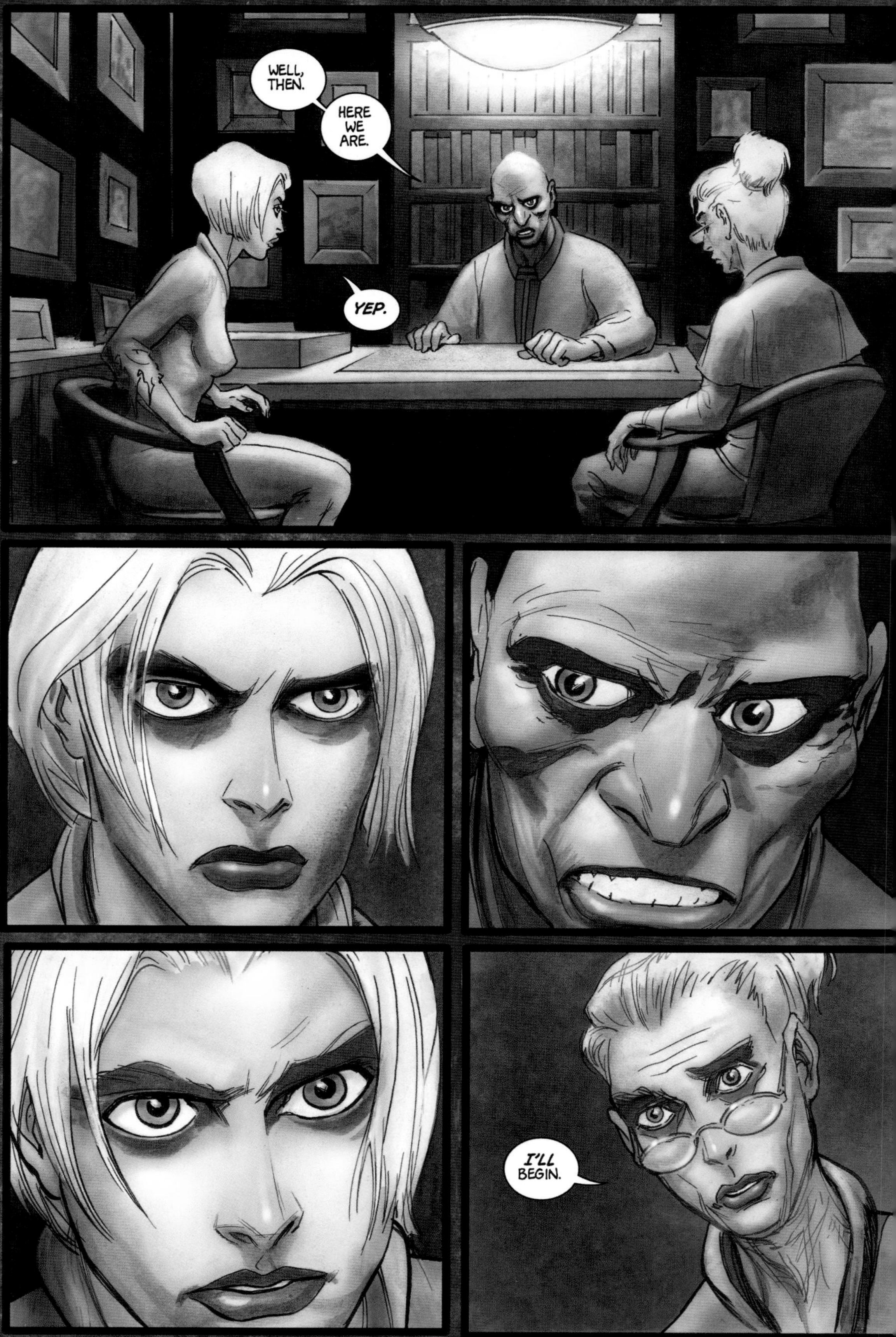
WELL, THEN.
HERE WE ARE.
YEP.
I'LL BEGIN.

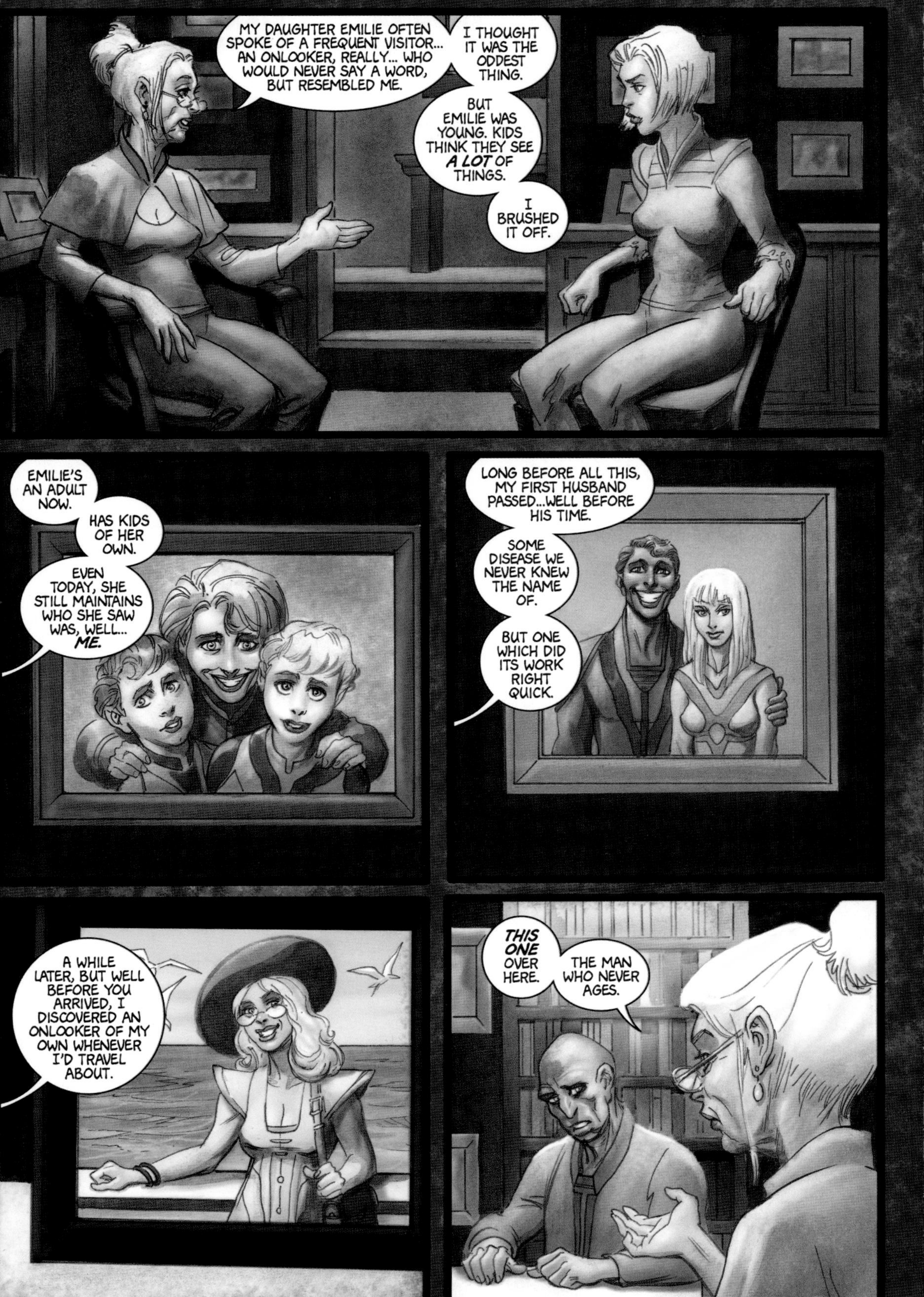
MY DAUGHTER EMILIE OFTEN SPOKE OF A FREQUENT VISITOR... AN ONLOOKER, REALLY... WHO WOULD NEVER SAY A WORD, BUT RESEMBLED ME.
I THOUGHT IT WAS THE ODDEST THING.
BUT EMILIE WAS YOUNG. KIDS THINK THEY SEE ***A LOT*** OF THINGS.
I BRUSHED IT OFF.
EMILIE'S AN ADULT NOW.
HAS KIDS OF HER OWN.
EVEN TODAY, SHE STILL MAINTAINS WHO SHE SAW WAS, WELL... ***ME.***
LONG BEFORE ALL THIS, MY FIRST HUSBAND PASSED...WELL BEFORE HIS TIME.
SOME DISEASE WE NEVER KNEW THE NAME OF.
BUT ONE WHICH DID ITS WORK RIGHT QUICK.
A WHILE LATER, BUT WELL BEFORE YOU ARRIVED, I DISCOVERED AN ONLOOKER OF MY OWN WHENEVER I'D TRAVEL ABOUT.
THIS ONE OVER HERE.
THE MAN WHO NEVER AGES.

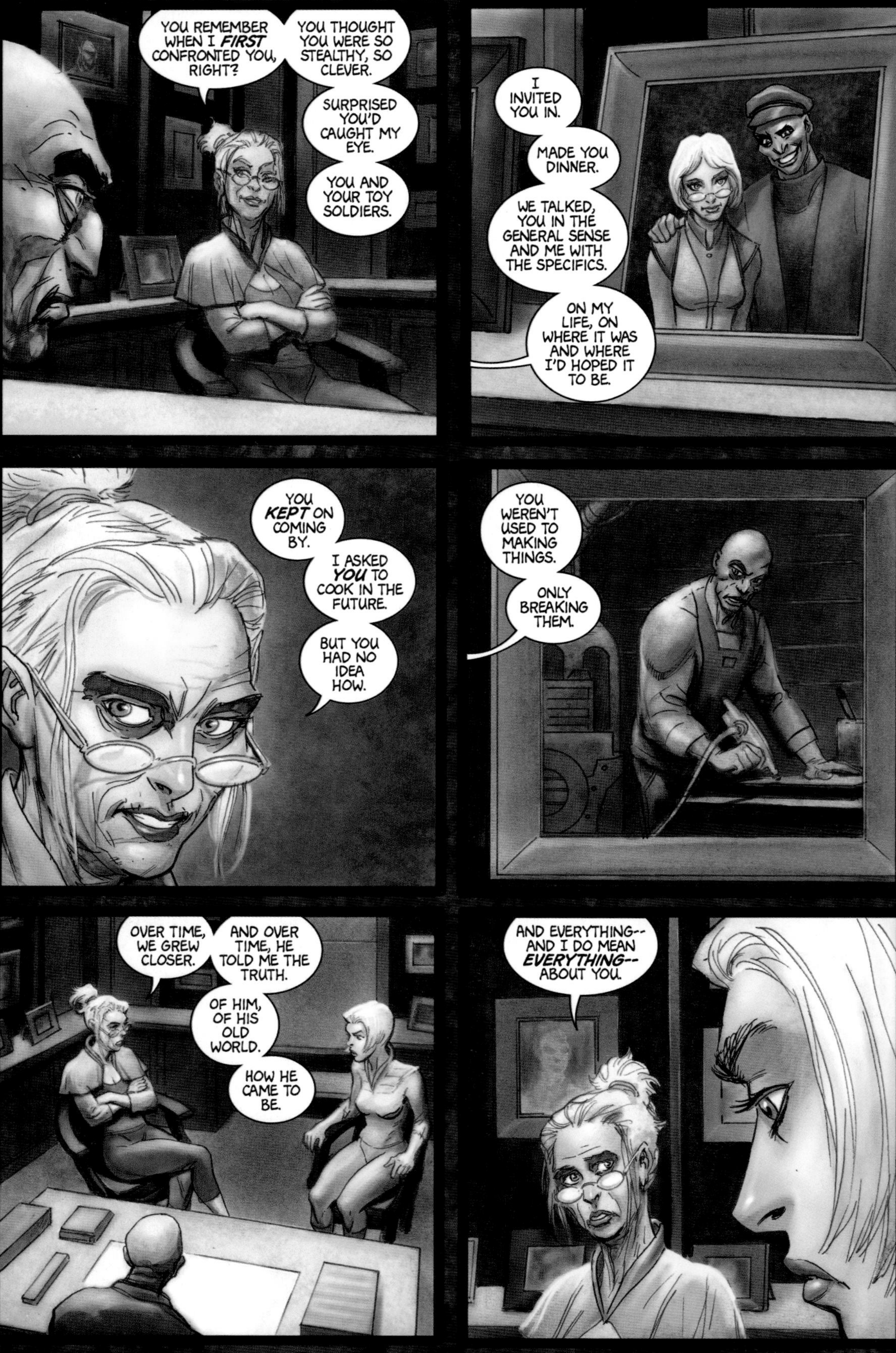
YOU REMEMBER WHEN I *FIRST* CONFRONTED YOU, RIGHT?
YOU THOUGHT YOU WERE SO STEALTHY, SO CLEVER.
SURPRISED YOU'D CAUGHT MY EYE.
YOU AND YOUR TOY SOLDIERS.
I INVITED YOU IN.
MADE YOU DINNER.
WE TALKED, YOU IN THE GENERAL SENSE AND ME WITH THE SPECIFICS.
ON MY LIFE, ON WHERE IT WAS AND WHERE I'D HOPED IT TO BE.
YOU ***KEPT*** ON COMING BY.
I ASKED ***YOU*** TO COOK IN THE FUTURE.
BUT YOU HAD NO IDEA HOW.
YOU WEREN'T USED TO MAKING THINGS.
ONLY BREAKING THEM.
OVER TIME, WE GREW CLOSER.
AND OVER TIME, HE TOLD ME THE TRUTH.
OF HIM, OF HIS OLD WORLD.
HOW HE CAME TO BE.
AND EVERYTHING-- AND I DO MEAN ***EVERYTHING***-- ABOUT YOU.

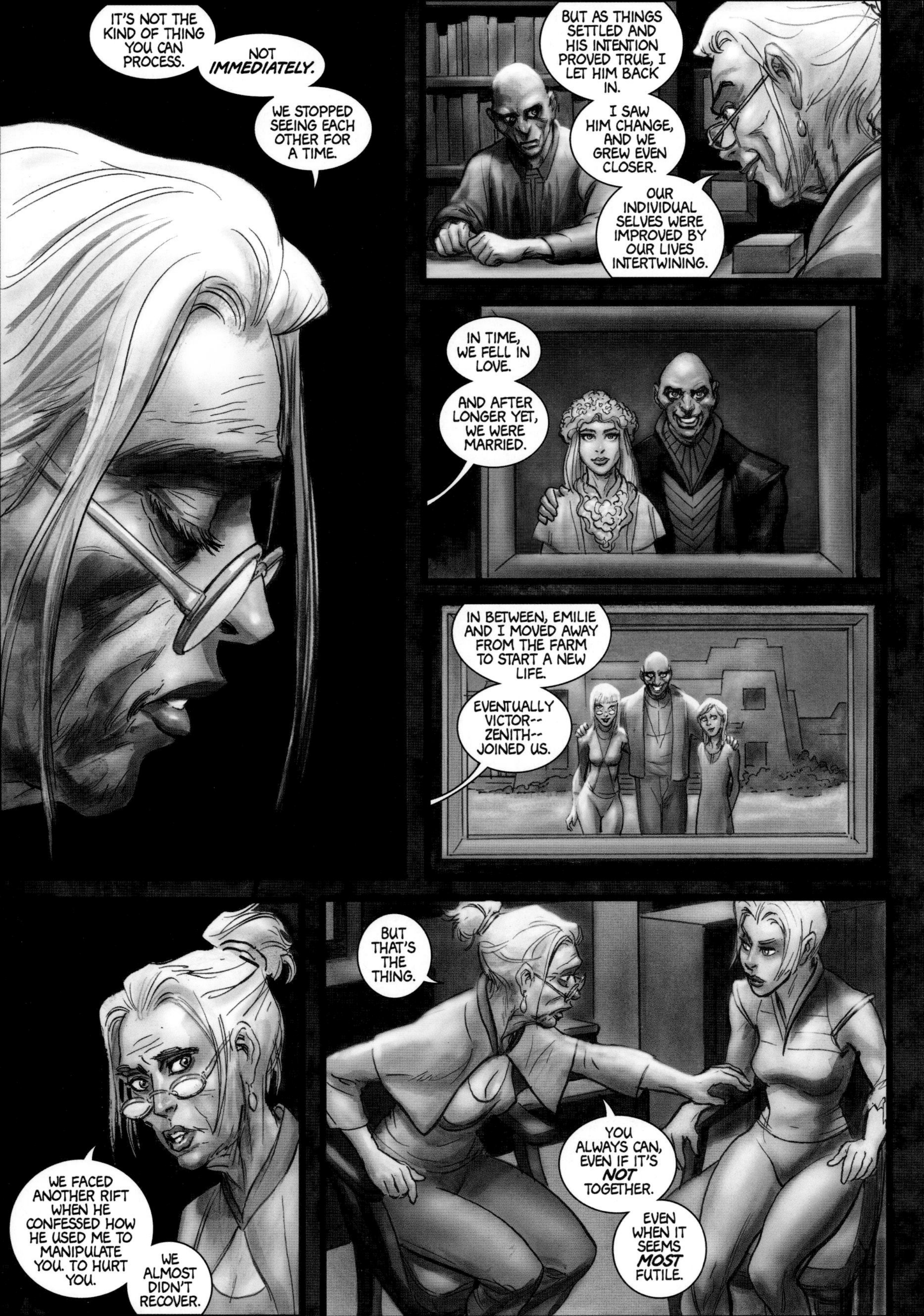
IT'S NOT THE KIND OF THING YOU CAN PROCESS.
NOT *IMMEDIATELY.*
WE STOPPED SEEING EACH OTHER FOR A TIME.
BUT AS THINGS SETTLED AND HIS INTENTION PROVED TRUE, I LET HIM BACK IN.
I SAW HIM CHANGE, AND WE GREW EVEN CLOSER.
OUR INDIVIDUAL SELVES WERE IMPROVED BY OUR LIVES INTERTWINING.
IN TIME, WE FELL IN LOVE.
AND AFTER LONGER YET, WE WERE MARRIED.
IN BETWEEN, EMILIE AND I MOVED AWAY FROM THE FARM TO START A NEW LIFE.
EVENTUALLY VICTOR-- ZENITH-- JOINED US.
WE FACED ANOTHER RIFT WHEN HE CONFESSED HOW HE USED ME TO MANIPULATE YOU. TO HURT YOU.
WE ALMOST DIDN'T RECOVER.
BUT THAT'S THE THING.
YOU ALWAYS CAN, EVEN IF IT'S ***NOT*** TOGETHER.
EVEN WHEN IT SEEMS ***MOST*** FUTILE.

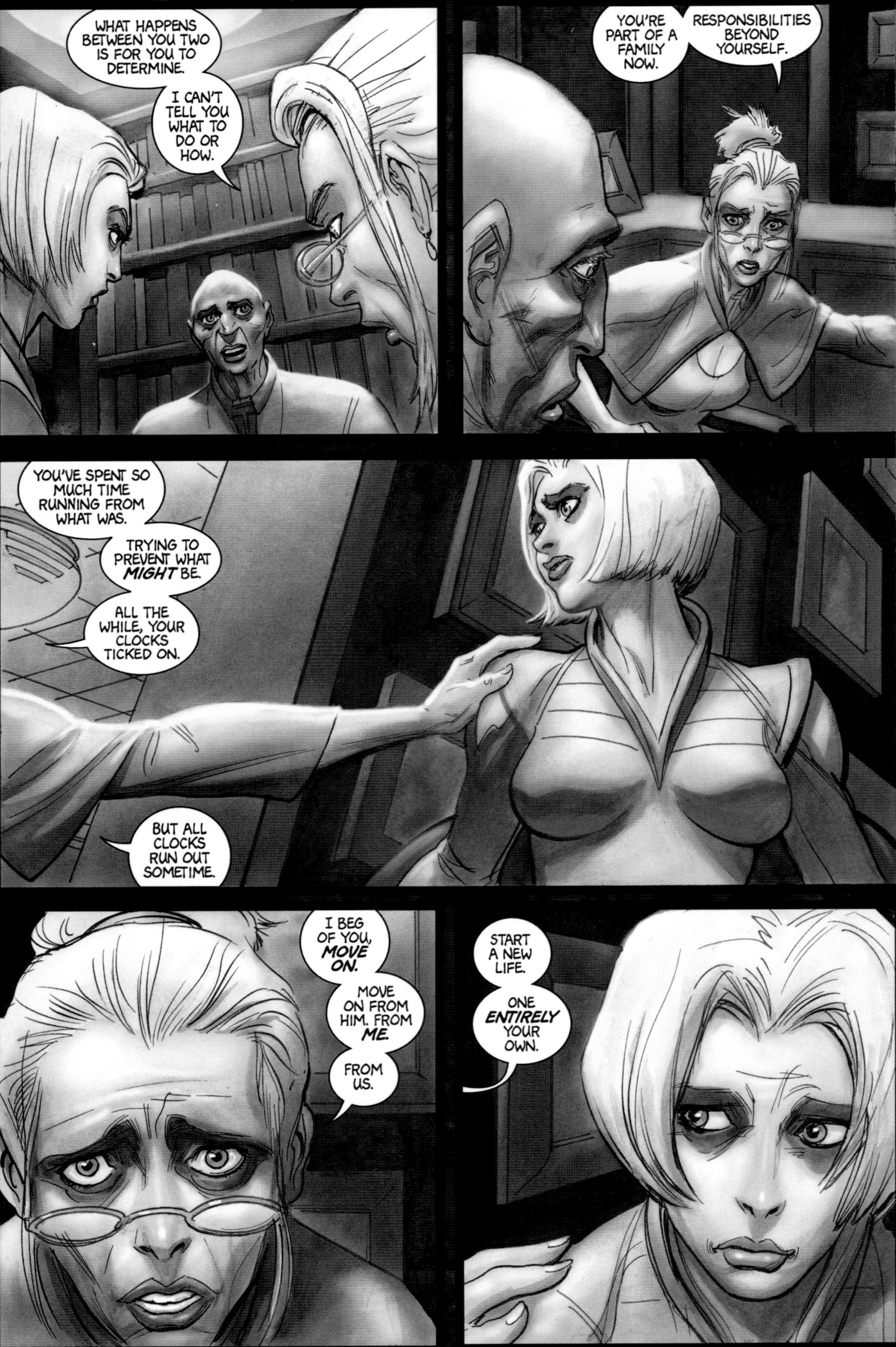
WHAT HAPPENS BETWEEN YOU TWO IS FOR YOU TO DETERMINE.
I CAN'T TELL YOU WHAT TO DO OR HOW.
YOU'RE PART OF A FAMILY NOW.
RESPONSIBILITIES BEYOND YOURSELF.
YOU'VE SPENT SO MUCH TIME RUNNING FROM WHAT WAS.
TRYING TO PREVENT WHAT *MIGHT* BE.
ALL THE WHILE, YOUR CLOCKS TICKED ON.
BUT ALL CLOCKS RUN OUT SOMETIME.
I BEG OF YOU, **MOVE ON.**
MOVE ON FROM HIM. FROM **ME.**
FROM US.
START A NEW LIFE.
ONE **ENTIRELY** YOUR OWN.

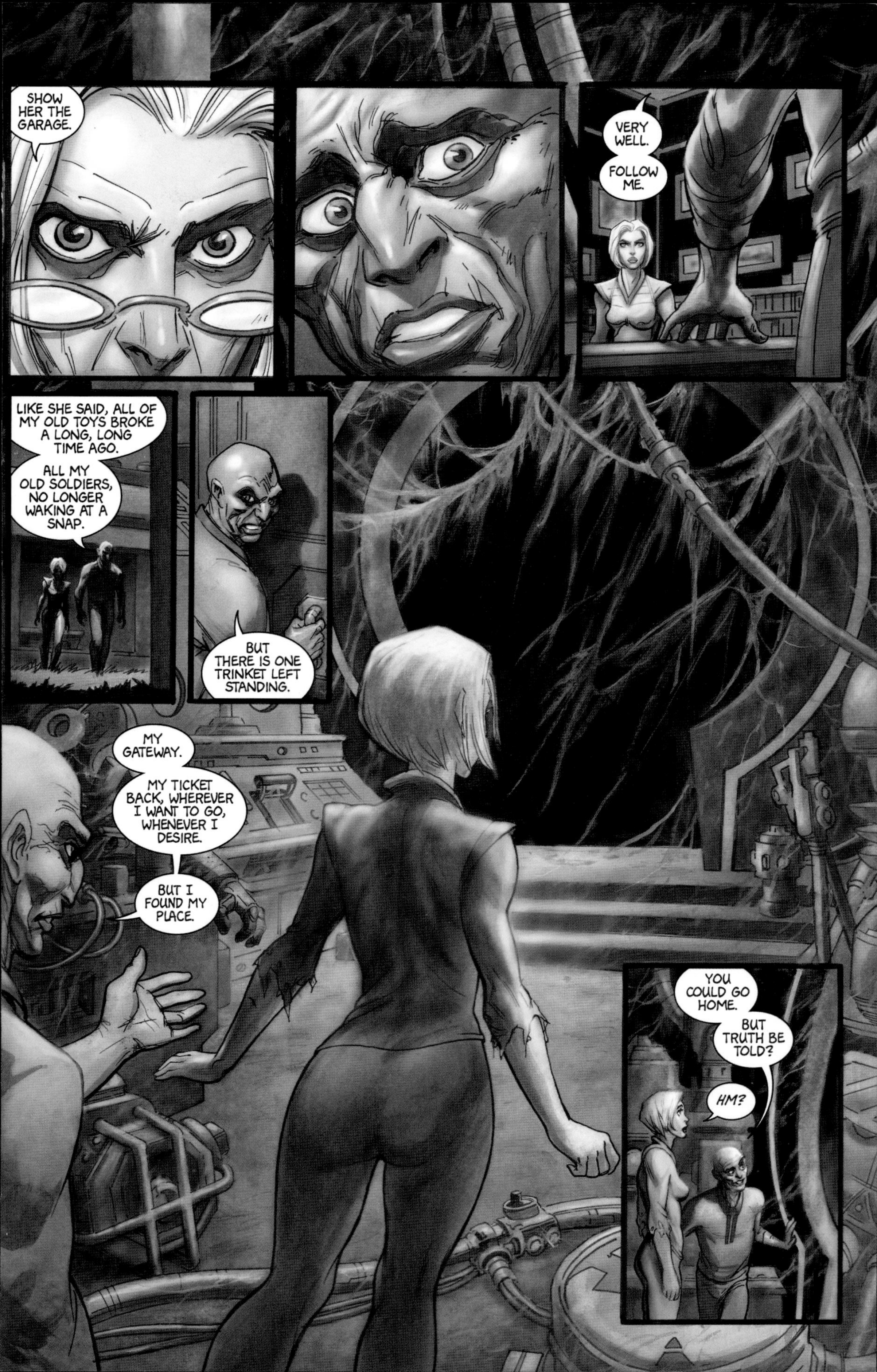

SHOW HER THE GARAGE.
VERY WELL.
FOLLOW ME.
LIKE SHE SAID, ALL OF MY OLD TOYS BROKE A LONG, LONG TIME AGO.
ALL MY OLD SOLDIERS, NO LONGER WAKING AT A SNAP.
BUT THERE IS ONE TRINKET LEFT STANDING.
MY GATEWAY.
MY TICKET BACK, WHEREVER I WANT TO GO, WHENEVER I DESIRE.
BUT I FOUND MY PLACE.
YOU COULD GO HOME.
BUT TRUTH BE TOLD?
HM?

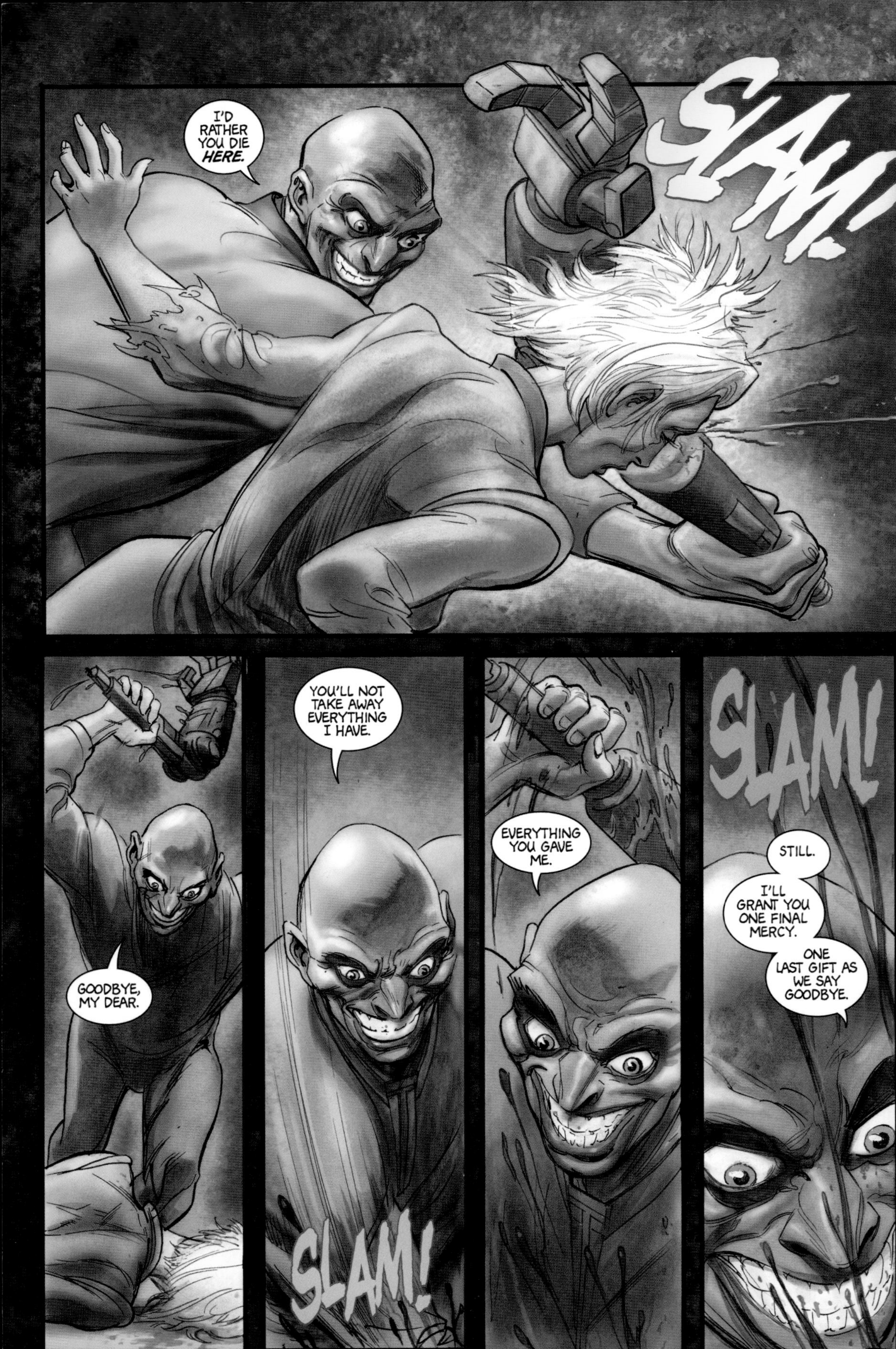
I'D RATHER YOU DIE HERE.
SLAM!
GOODBYE, MY DEAR.
YOU'LL NOT TAKE AWAY EVERYTHING I HAVE.
SLAM!
EVERYTHING YOU GAVE ME.
SLAM!
STILL.
I'LL GRANT YOU ONE FINAL MERCY.
ONE LAST GIFT AS WE SAY GOODBYE.

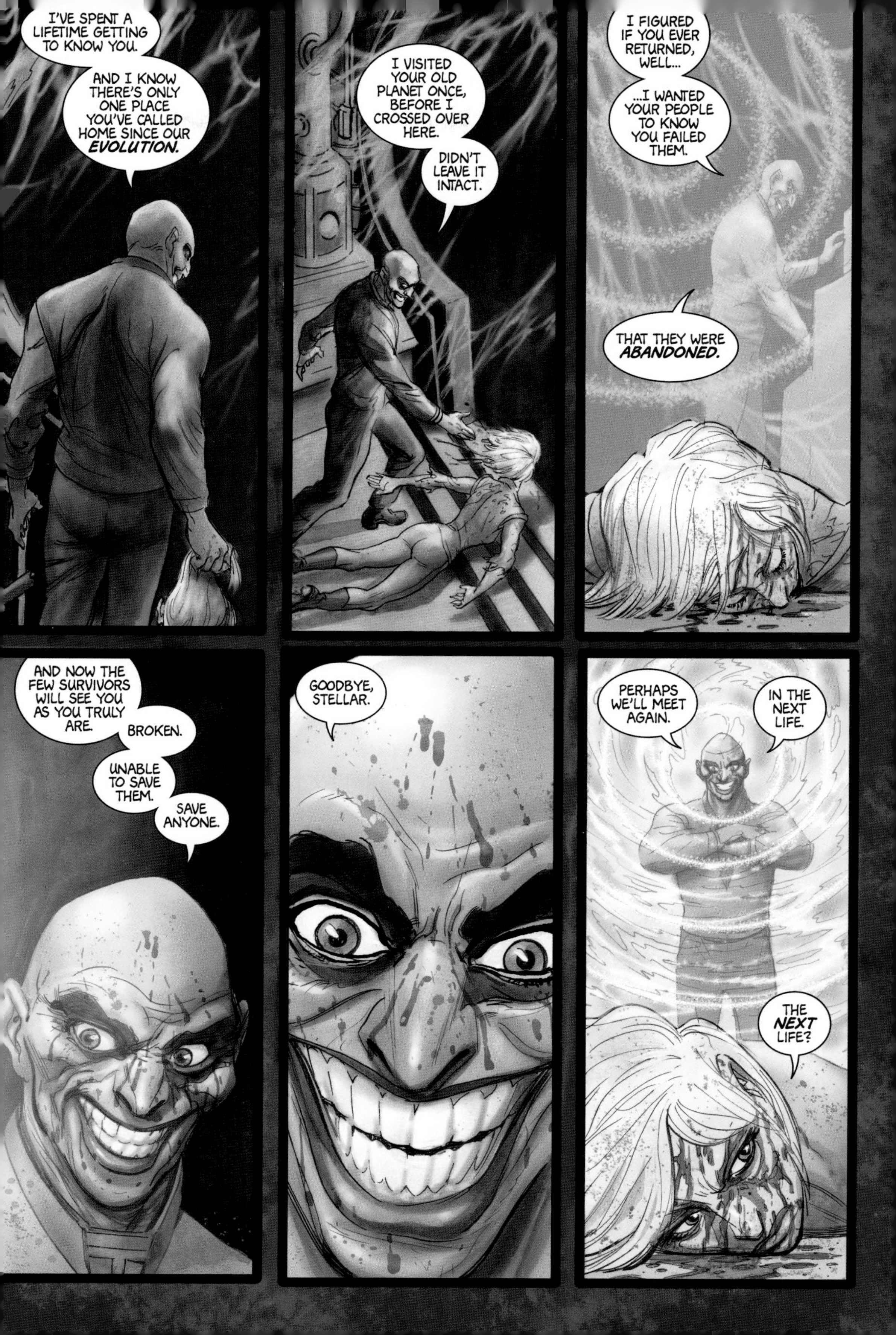
I'VE SPENT A LIFETIME GETTING TO KNOW YOU.
AND I KNOW THERE'S ONLY ONE PLACE YOU'VE CALLED HOME SINCE OUR *EVOLUTION.*
I VISITED YOUR OLD PLANET ONCE, BEFORE I CROSSED OVER HERE.
DIDN'T LEAVE IT INTACT.
I FIGURED IF YOU EVER RETURNED, WELL...
...I WANTED YOUR PEOPLE TO KNOW YOU FAILED THEM.
THAT THEY WERE *ABANDONED.*
AND NOW THE FEW SURVIVORS WILL SEE YOU AS YOU TRULY ARE.
BROKEN.
UNABLE TO SAVE THEM.
SAVE ANYONE.
GOODBYE, STELLAR.
PERHAPS WE'LL MEET AGAIN.
IN THE NEXT LIFE.
THE *NEXT* LIFE?

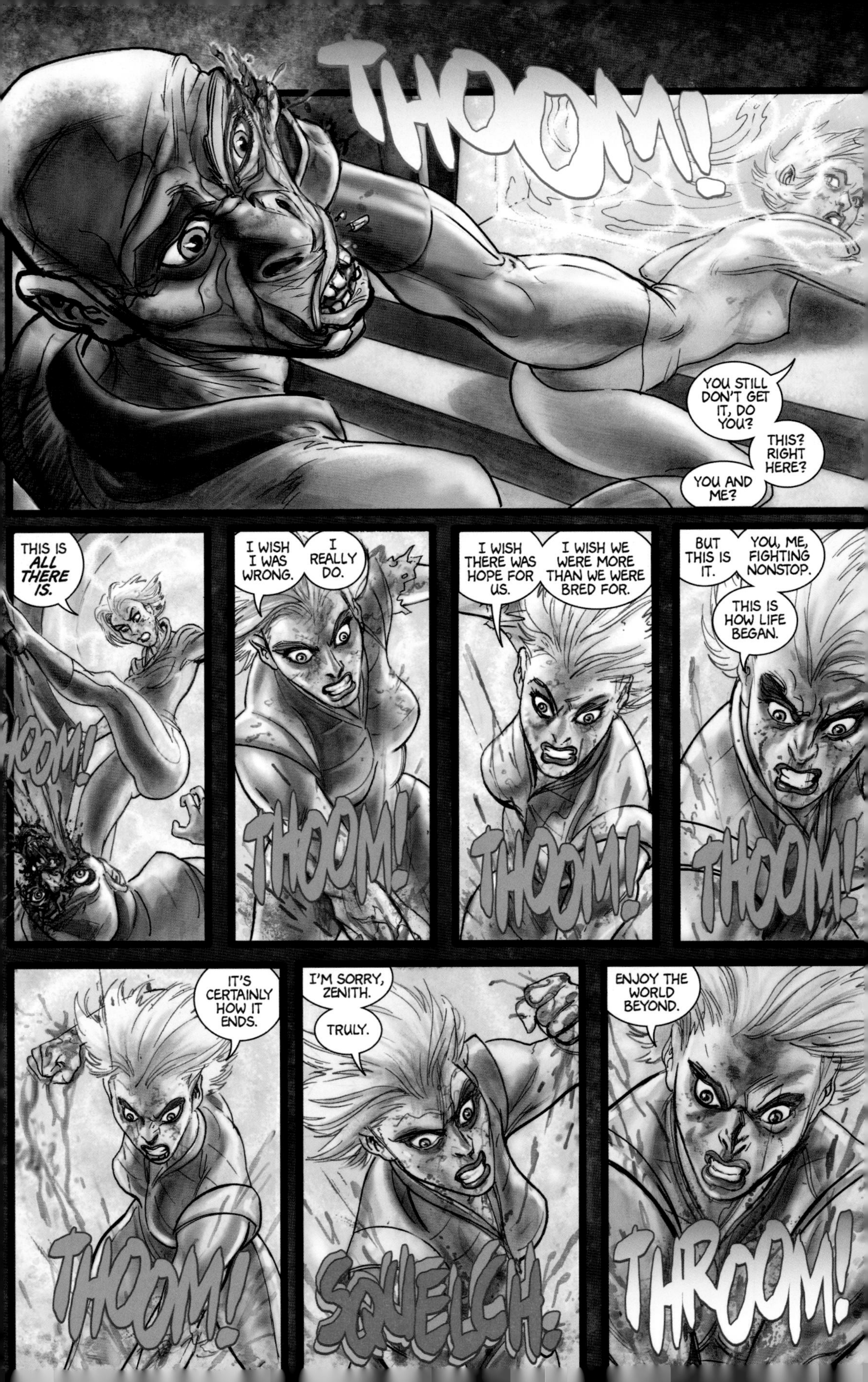
THOOM!
YOU STILL DON'T GET IT, DO YOU?
THIS? RIGHT HERE?
YOU AND ME?
THIS IS ALL THERE IS.
THOOM!
I WISH I WAS WRONG.
I REALLY DO.
THOOM!
I WISH THERE WAS HOPE FOR US.
I WISH WE WERE MORE THAN WE WERE BRED FOR.
THOOM!
BUT THIS IS IT.
YOU, ME, FIGHTING NONSTOP.
THIS IS HOW LIFE BEGAN.
THOOM!
IT'S CERTAINLY HOW IT ENDS.
THOOM!
I'M SORRY, ZENITH.
TRULY.
SQUELCH.
ENJOY THE WORLD BEYOND.
THROOM!

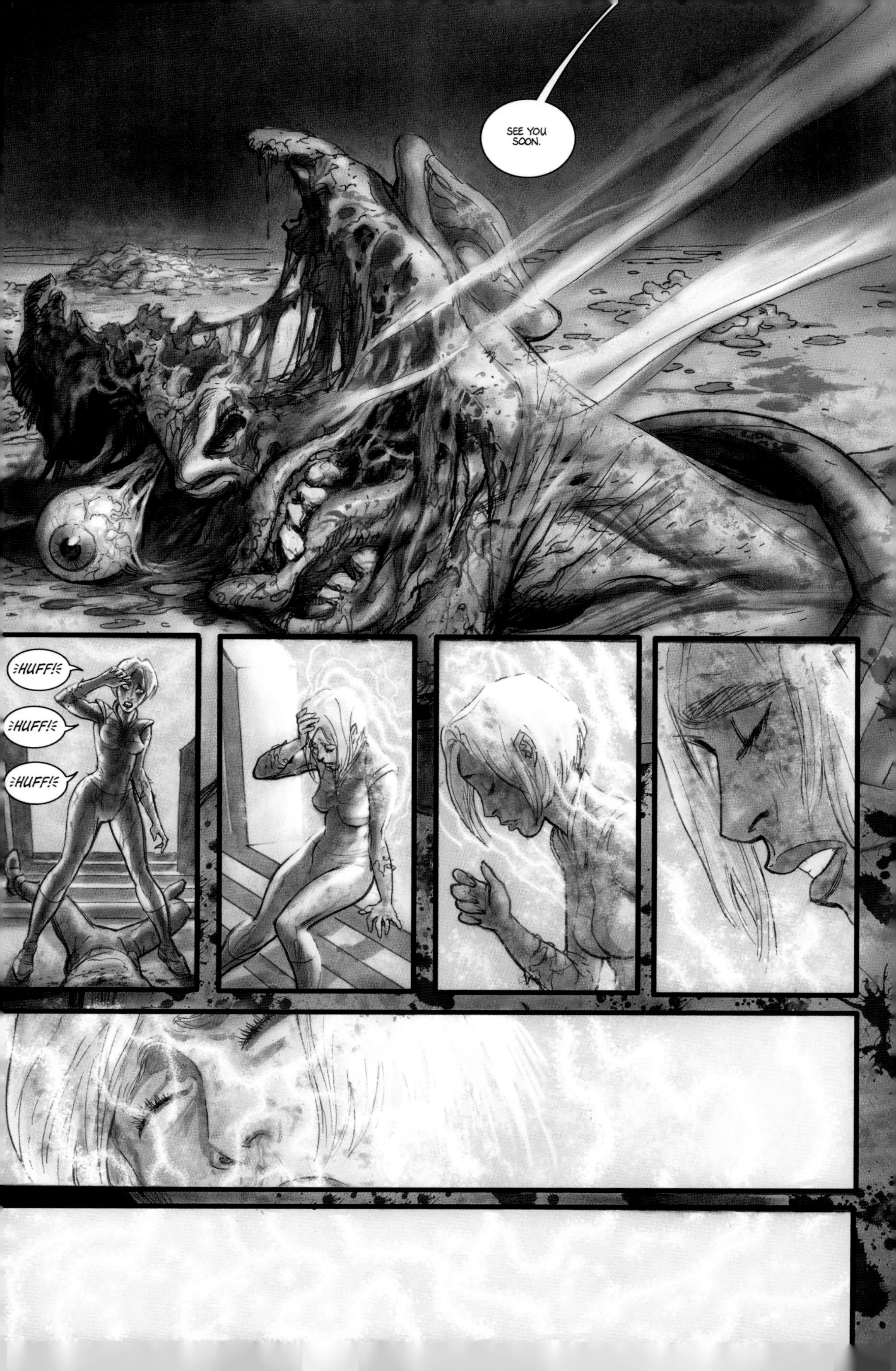
SEE YOU SOON.
HUFF!
HUFF!
HUFF!

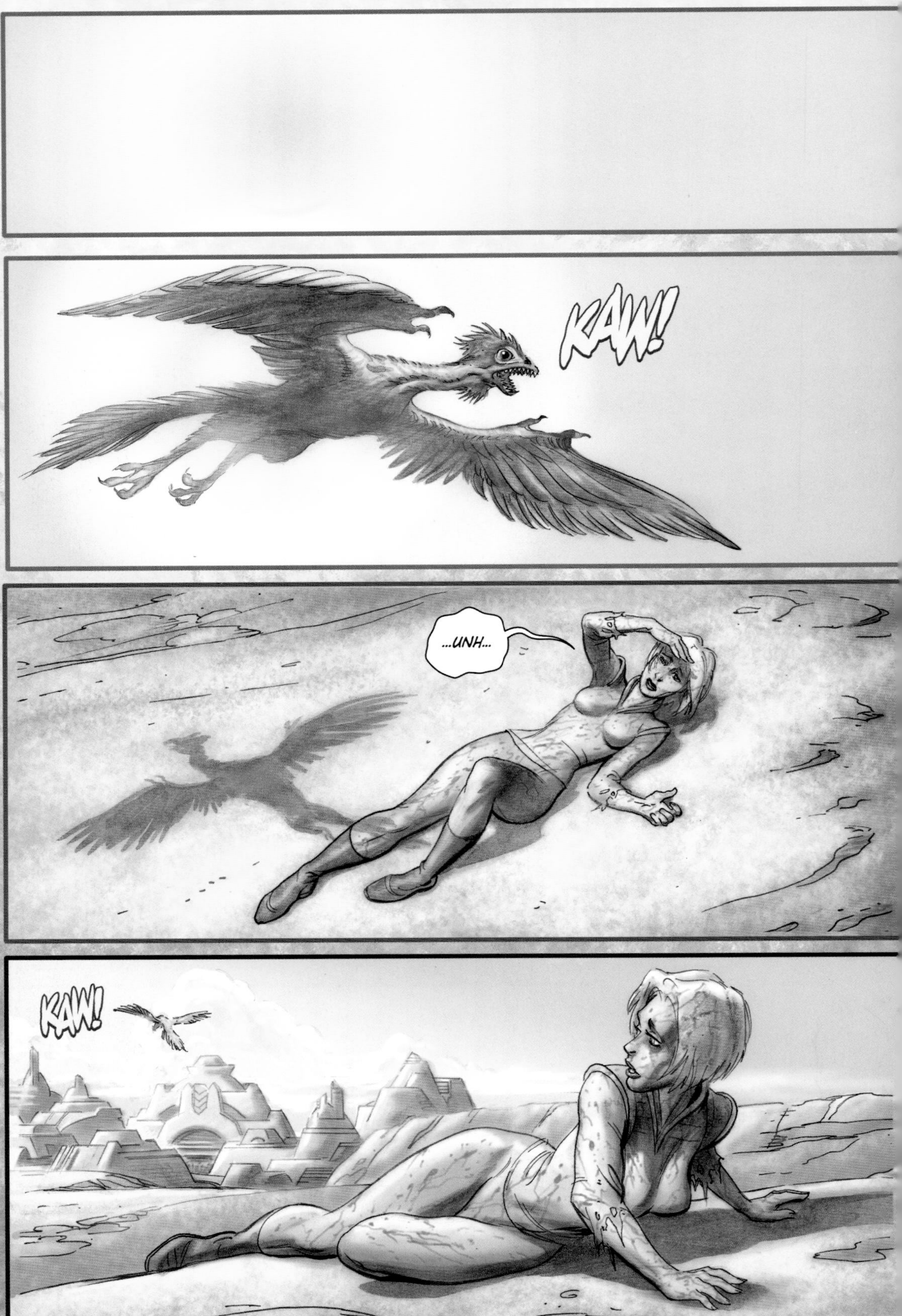
KAW!
...UNH...
KAW!

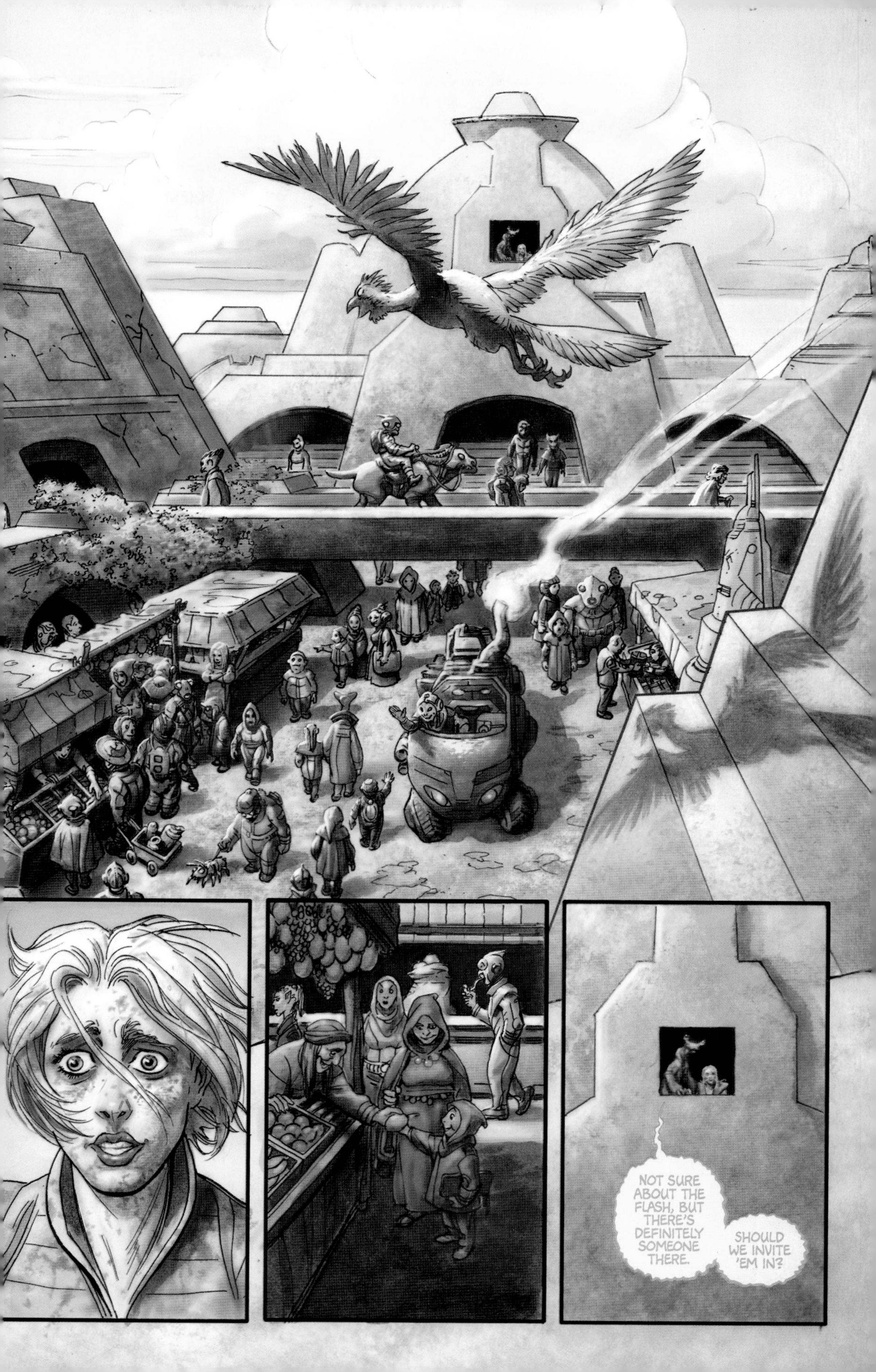
NOT SURE ABOUT THE FLASH, BUT THERE'S DEFINITELY SOMEONE THERE.
SHOULD WE INVITE 'EM IN?

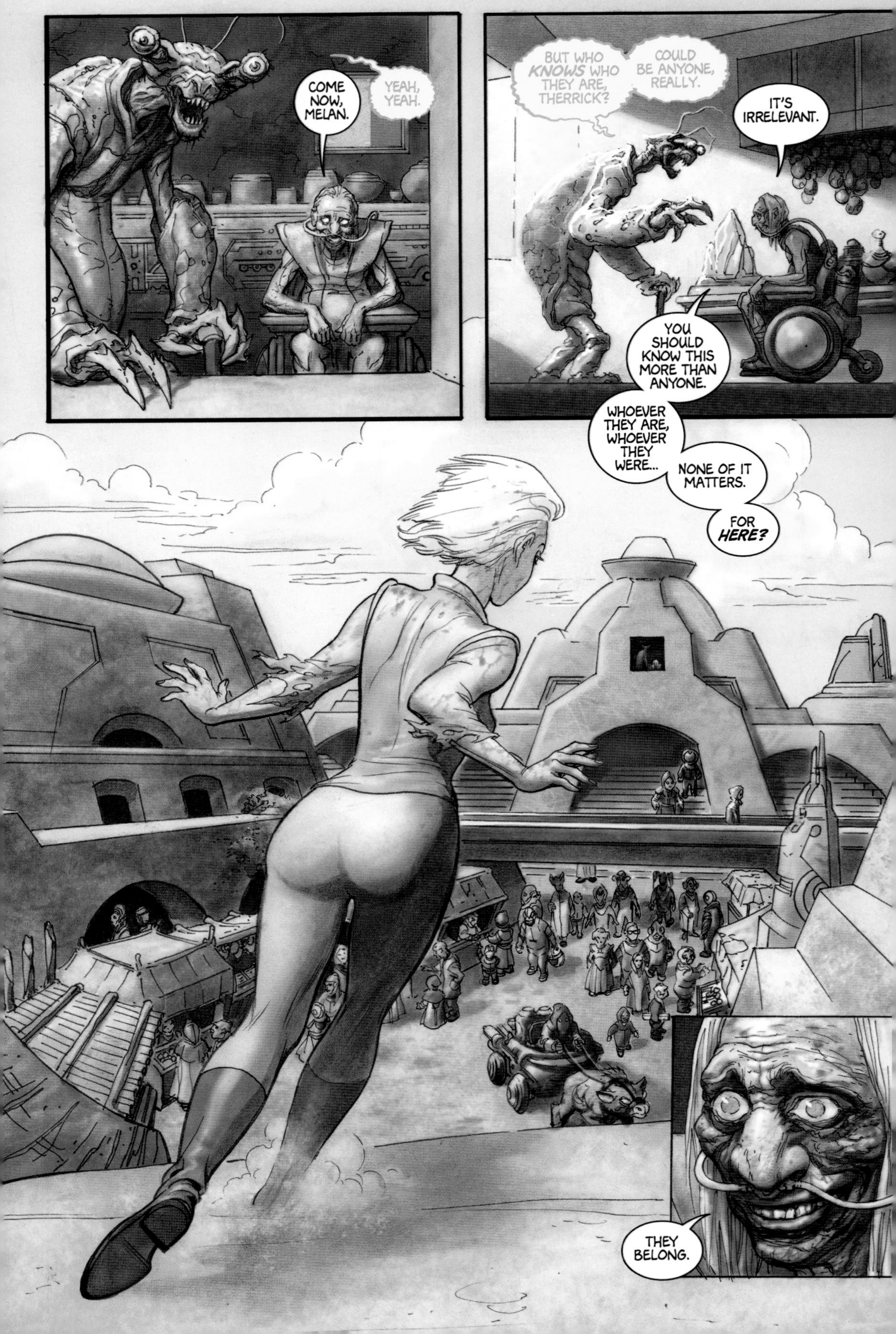
COME NOW, MELAN.
YEAH, YEAH.
BUT WHO KNOWS WHO THEY ARE, THERRICK?
COULD BE ANYONE, REALLY.
IT'S IRRELEVANT.
YOU SHOULD KNOW THIS MORE THAN ANYONE.
WHOEVER THEY ARE, WHOEVER THEY WERE...
NONE OF IT MATTERS.
FOR HERE?
THEY BELONG.

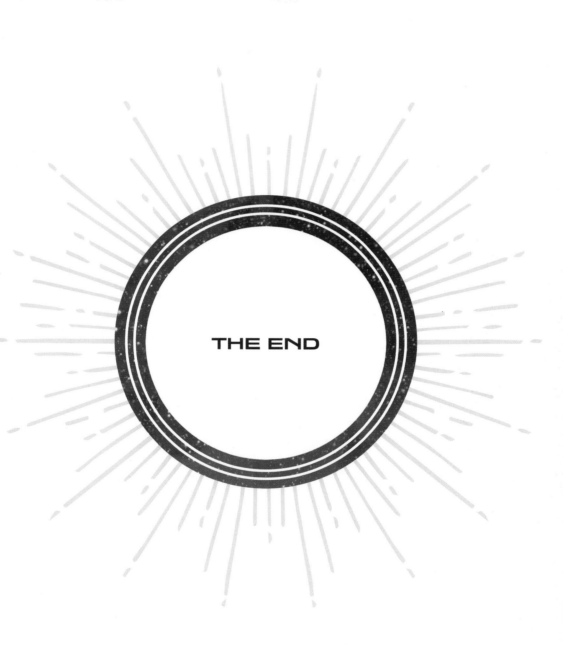

THE END

For more tales from ROBERT KIRKMAN and SKYBOUND

Daniel Warren Johnson Mike Spicer
EXTREMITY
VOLUME TWO WARRIOR

REDNECK
Donny CATES Lisandro ESTHERREN Dee CUNNIFFE
VOLUME TWO
The Eyes Upon You

VOL. 1: ARTIST TP
ISBN: 978-1-5343-0242-6
$16.99

VOL. 2: WARRIOR TP
ISBN: 978-1-5343-0506-9
$16.99

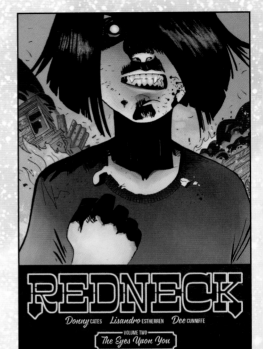

VOL. 1: DEEP IN THE HEART TP
ISBN: 978-1-5343-0331-7
$16.99

VOL. 2: THE EYES UPON YOU
ISBN: 978-1-5343-0665-3
$16.99

Gasolina

VOLUME 6: INVASION
BY KIRKMAN & AZACETA
OUTCAST

SLOTS
DAN PANOSIAN

THIEF OF THIEVES
VOLUME 6
"GOLD RUSH."

VOL. 1: BIENVENIDOS TP
ISBN: 978-1-5343-0506-9
$16.99

VOL. 2: FIESTA TP
ISBN: 978-1-5343-0864-0
$16.99

VOL. 1: A DARKNESS SURROUNDS HIM TP
ISBN: 978-1-63215-053-0
$9.99

VOL. 2: A VAST AND UNENDING RUIN TP
ISBN: 978-1-63215-448-4
$14.99

VOL. 3: THIS LITTLE LIGHT TP
ISBN: 978-1-63215-693-8
$14.99

VOL. 4: UNDER DEVIL'S WING TP
ISBN: 978-1-5343-0050-7
$14.99

VOL. 5: THE NEW PATH TP
ISBN: 978-1-5343-0249-5
$16.99

VOL. 6: INVASION TP
ISBN: 978-1-5343-0751-3
$16.99

VOLUME 1 TP
ISBN: 978-1-5343-0655-4
$16.99

VOL. 1: "I QUIT."
ISBN: 978-1-60706-592-0
$14.99

VOL. 2: "HELP ME."
ISBN: 978-1-60706-676-7
$14.99

VOL. 3: "VENICE."
ISBN: 978-1-60706-844-0
$14.99

VOL. 4: "THE HIT LIST."
ISBN: 978-1-63215-037-0
$14.99

VOL. 5: "TAKE ME."
ISBN: 978-1-63215-401-9
$14.99

VOL. 6: "GOLD RUSH."
ISBN: 978-1-53430-037-8
$14.99